Le Temps de Noël (Christmas-time), 1974 (p. 182 & 192)

JEAN PAUL LEMIEUX

"A painting is never finished . . .
. . . and neither is a book"

GUY ROBERT

GUY ROBERT

LEMIEUX

translated by John David Allan

GAGE PUBLISHING

TORONTO • VANCOUVER • CALGARY • MONTREAL

The author would like to thank Jean Paul Lemieux for his generous co-operation, and for permission to reproduce many of his paintings and published writings. The author would also like to thank all those who contributed to the illustrations for this book, especially staff of the Musée du Québec, Office du Film du Québec and Roberts Gallery of Toronto.

The majority of paintings reproduced in the text which belong to private collections do not carry the names of their owners.

On the dust jacket is a detail from *1910 Remembered*, painted by Lemieux in 1962.

The photographs for the end-papers and those appearing on pages 5, 6, 8, 16, 160, 234 and 302 were shot in Quebec City on March 26, 1975, by Robert Chiasson.

Abbreviations used for picture sources:
NGC—National Gallery of Canada, Ottawa
MQ—Musée du Québec
OFQ—Office du Film du Québec
RG—Roberts Gallery, Toronto

Canadian Cataloguing in Publication Data

Robert, Guy, 1933-

Lemieux

Bibliography: p.
ISBN 0-7715-9352-X
1. Lemieux, Jean-Paul, 1904-
2. Painters — Canada — Biography.
I. Lemieux, Jean-Paul, 1904-
ND249.L394R613   759.11   C78-001222-4

Printed and bound in Canada.

FOREWORD

"The painting points the way, not the painter.

You throw something onto a rectangle, but you never know what it's going to produce. You're guided by the painting much more than you guide it. And that can lead to something altogether different from what you had expected, from what you wanted to have happen.

A painting can drag on, it takes time, it's a slow process. But you have to take the time. Sometimes I'll even rub out my signature and start something over again on the same canvas.

As long as one is not satisfied, and one is never completely satisfied, the painting is never finished.

There's always something more to be done, always, always, always...."

JEAN PAUL LEMIEUX

(from an interview with Guy Robert held September 26, 1972 on the Ile aux Coudres)

WORD AND IMAGE

Painting at once distances and appropriates, eclipses and evokes, like writing. It both discovers and recovers, convokes and revokes, reveals and conceals. Painting exhibits and exiles. What is painted or written at once reveals and dissolves itself in the work, which always creates a screen out of its tangible substance. And on this screen appears the image. The image of ——. A re-presentation, a delegated presence, a mission. An appearance, an appearing, an a-peering.

Thus we cannot avoid setting painting and writing in both opposition and conjunction, as is clearly shown by a long Western tradition which has made their comparison the subject of much debate and discussion. It has done so under the rubric of *Ut pictura poesis* (as is painting so is poetry), from Horace[1] through the Renaissance. At issue here is the rich parade of ideas connected with the comparison between the arts, the *paragone*, which was first elevated to the rank of philosophical argument by Aristotle and turns up again and again over the centuries in the academies and salons, and more recently in the mass media. It is a set of ideas which has always had a part to play in literary aesthetics.

---

[1] *Ars poetica*, p. 361. See Rensselaer W. Lee. *Ut pictura poesis*. New York: W. W. Norton, 1967. See bibliography.

The Work of Art and the Image

Every work of art exists at the level of image and in the world of its own image, be this musical, pictorial, literary, architectural, cinematic, sculptural or choreographic. The image represents, re-presents. It is no longer exactly the thing represented, nor is it another thing altogether. As soon as it passes its point of origin and reference, it is present and soon wins an autonomous life of its own. (This is true even in so-called abstract or non-figurative art, and in most music, whose aural and affective architecture is rarely "descriptive." However this is a subject for another book entirely and has little to do with the work of Jean Paul Lemieux, whose art is strictly representational.)

The cinema, which greatly fascinated the young Lemieux and later significantly influenced his iconic syntax, provides a good example of the magic, alchemy and ethereal dynamics of the artistic image, all in spite of enormous technical constraints. Twenty-four still images are projected every second, sequentially and separately, to give the optical illusion of normal movement on the screen. The mechanical parameters of the cinematic process are concealed by parameters of a higher order — those of sequence and rhythm — which assert a grip on the imagination in a way analogous to the mechanical effects of film on the retina of the eye. Still another set of formal parameters has previously been fixed with great technical precision on the sound stages and external locations, yet in an order which usually does not correspond to the order of the finished film. The finished film itself depends on the original parameters of the scenario, the stuff of which is taken from life, real or imaginary.

Real or imaginary? Is there actually a gap or hiatus between these two realms? Are we not talking instead about experience and the imagination? And is the imaginary not part of our experience, and our experience part of the imaginary, the two together making up the real? Precisely because the image acts as a middle term, the work of art becomes a dynamic common ground for experience and the imagination: a new reality, transitory, analogical, symbolical. **10**

The image is therefore put forward as a point of transition, a bridge, a link. It comes from "elsewhere" and leads somewhere else again. It is no longer just that which gave rise to it, and it is not just that to which it gives rise in our imagination, which is the actual crucible of its creation. The image is all that and something more; it is most especially an invitation, an overture, a "breach" that cannot be filled, finished or silenced. The image speaks. A film by Ingmar Bergman or Kaneto Shindo, a little goddess from the Cyclades or a Senufo mask, Picasso's *Guernica* or Tinguely's cinematic studies for the end of the world, the palace at Fontainebleau or that of the *facteur* Cheval, the stained glass of Chartres or Duchamp's *The Bride Stripped Bare by Her Bachelors, Even*, the Songs of Maldoror or the Winged Victory of Samothrace, Beethoven's Ninth or the *Electronic Poem* by Varèse and le Corbusier—all represent systems that are partly autonomous as regards the structure of their artistic language, yet they belong to the same aesthetic universe. They give access not only to their own origins and the cosmogonies they introduce, but also to a fabulous book of alchemy, open to countless "readings."

"Paragone" and "Ekphrasis"

Let us look at the example of Velázquez's *Las Meninas*, which has been given a penetrating reading by Michel Foucault. He emphasizes that "the relation of language to painting is an infinite relation." (More precisely, this relationship concerns writing and painting and the system of relationships which can arise between two analogous languages: once again, the *paragone* and its never-ending debate.) "It is not," continues Foucault, "that words are imperfect, or that, when confronted by the visible, they prove insuperably inadequate. Neither one can be reduced to the other's terms: it is in vain that we say what we see; what we see never resides in what we say...." (Michel Foucault, *The Order of Things*, trans.)

Are painting and literature irreducible? Certainly, if taken in an absolute sense. But in the relative sense more typical of aesthetic praxis, are painting and literature not more or less complementary? The one able to add to the other and, furthermore, to all other artistic forms as well? Contemporary civilization as a whole, which is alleged to be predominantly visual, has in fact seen the publication since 1945 of more pages of text than had been written in all of history before then.

Ever since Homer first described Achilles' shield, verbal descriptions of works of art, *ekphrasis*,[2] have covered over visualized objects with a tapestry of words. These words are useful for evoking a work otherwise not demonstrable, or for calling attention to a particular portion or aspect of such a work which might go unnoticed. *Ekphrasis* may be applied, by extension, to music, theatre, film and even literature. . . . This tapestry of words thus substitutes for an aspect or fragment of the viewed object, amplifying or reducing it, nurturing or mutilating it, translating it well or badly. Although it is a representation maintaining an unstable balance between the ersatz and the magical, *ekphrasis* has in no way been rendered obsolete by the invention of photography—precisely because it does not amount to a strict transcription of one language (pictorial) into another (literary). It evokes, calls up, makes presence known, underlines not only differences but connections and correspondences between the senses as well: the process at work here is synesthesia, which goes back to Baudelaire and farther back still. And since the images shift from one sensuous domain to another (and perhaps actually *constitute* this movement, the stuff of the process whereby "scents, colors and sounds correspond"), they are therefore capable, at least on occasion, of joining in a communal celebration of the senses, caught up in a whirlwind of shared sensation

[2] See, for example, E. H. Gombrich, *Symbolic Images* (London: Phaidon, 1972) and the article by Svetlana Leontief Alpers appearing in the *Journal of the Warburg and Courtauld Institutes*, vol. 23, 1960, pp. 190-215. Vasari makes considerable use of the notion of *ekphrasis* in his *Lives*.

and enjoyment. Hence words no longer constitute a reduction or degradation of things and their images but instead make up the sign, the cryptogram, the key. A key opens the locks, which divide and enclose. As Valéry put it: "One must always give excuses for talking about painting, but there are compelling reasons for not keeping quiet on the subject. All the arts owe their existence to words. Is not the primary motivation behind any work (of art) the desire to have it talked about? Art criticism is the literary genre that condenses or amplifies, stimulates or classifies and tries to harmonize all the attitudes brought to mind by artistic phenomena. Its domain stretches from metaphysics to polemics." ("Autour de Corot," *Oeuvres*, vol. II, p. 1307)

By Way of Introduction

The two opposite poles of art criticism put forward by Valéry will be of no interest to us in our discussion of Jean Paul Lemieux's career and work. Polemics would serve no purpose in dealing with an artist who has always been known for his dry sense of humor and measured ironies, and metaphysics holds no attraction for either Lemieux or myself. But the range of criticism between these two extremes remains vast, and the Lemieux "case" is filled with intriguing possibilities.

A previous book[3] has already cleared the way to some extent, giving a description of the man himself and setting out a grid for "reading" the work. For purposes of the present book, the research was completely re-cast and developed further on several fronts — biographical, bibliographical and iconographical. Close attention was paid to Lemieux's writings, which, though richer and more numerous than one might have imagined, have remained practically

---

[3] Guy Robert. *Jean Paul Lemieux ou la poétique de la souvenance*. Quebec City: Garneau, 1968.

unknown until now. Little by little, then, as the work of nearly a year progressed, during which the author found virtually no useful documentation from the artist to help him along, the book began to take shape as a triptych: "The Artist's Life" follows Lemieux's personal and professional life from his birth in November 1904 to the fall of 1975, through nearly three-quarters of a century. There is a discussion of the principal highlights and turning points from his modest beginnings to official recognition. The different sides of his career as painter, teacher, writer and illustrator are examined in detail. Lemieux's opinions and ideas are quoted and analyzed, and provide in themselves perhaps more insight into the artist's personality than do the details of his biography. The evolution over the years of both the man and his work is illustrated by numerous photographs.

"Sequences," the second section of the book, constitutes an attempt to give a systematic reading, with the help of many illustrations, of Lemieux's post-1956 work. This period follows the emergence of the new style which has won an ever-increasing public following for the artist. In the course of this analysis the author has tried to discern a broad thematic architecture underlying the corpus of Lemieux's work.

Finally, by way of contrast to the previous section, "Convergences" is concerned with a synthetic reading of the post-1956 work. It attempts to isolate the temporal and spatial dimensions united in the "figurative reality"[4] of the work. In this way, duration

----

[4] "The artist's dialogue with his work implies the participation of the beholder. The constituents of the representational object exist not only in the consciousness and the memory of the creator but of all those who, present or removed in time and space and becoming the users of the object in question, ultimately confer upon it its only reality." (Pierre Francastel. *La réalité figurative*. p. 25)

can be re-assigned its original ritual function, that of making the pictorially delimited space the locus of a metaphorical event. Here the act of perception uncovers, through the phenomenology of the portrayal, the mirror image of itself. Hence a more enigmatic dimension is uncovered, namely imaginative fancy, which joins together the artist's work and the "reader" on a single continuum of imagination. Within this melting pot of double-faceted imagination, the functions of story-telling and representation can be united.

One picture is worth a thousand words, as the saying goes, to which one could reply that one word may be teeming with a thousand pictures of its own. But there is no point in debating the issue. It would seem preferable to let each express its "desire" for the other, pictures for words and words for pictures. Every word is part "picture" itself, an aural form when spoken, a graphic form when written. Hence the exciting possibilities of synesthesia, which will prompt us to explore some of the little-known aspects of Lemieux's work.

This book is naturally not intended to be exhaustive, in the sense that it offers final, definitive judgments. On the contrary, it puts forward one hypothesis, recognizing that many others are possible. It asks only to be judged on the extent to which it achieved its aims.

The book is heavily illustrated, by no means in a random fashion. The text and photographs have been carefully balanced and laid out in such a way as to complement each other at every stage of the analysis. Text, and texture so to speak, have been intended to "keep the relation of language to vision open" (Foucault, *The Order of Things*, p. 25) and to maintain the continuity between word and image. Both these languages are concerned with demonstrating, creating an "appearance," re-presenting. Their purpose is to make present in another way, and thus render a thing significant — to create signs, to sign.

THE ARTIST'S LIFE

Marie Joseph Jean-Paul Lemieux was born in Quebec City on November 18, 1904 and baptized as a Catholic in the Quebec City parish of Saint-Roch.[5] In astrological terms, his sun sign is therefore that of Scorpio. His ancestors Lemieux and Blouin emigrated to New France from Normandy and Poitou during the seventeenth century, and his family remained involved in commerce over the generations. His grandfather Lemieux was a general merchant, chiefly in Magog, before settling in Quebec City. His mother, Marie-Corinne Blouin, came from an old Quebec family. His father, Joseph-Flavien Lemieux, born in Sainte-Julie de Somerset, plied his trade as a textile salesman around the turn of the century, which meant that he travelled a great deal and was therefore absent for long periods of time from the family home.

Childhood in Quebec City and at Kent House

The Lemieux family spent their winters in Quebec City and their summers at Kent House, on an estate located above Montmorency Falls, downriver from Quebec City. Marguerite, Jean Paul's elder sister by ten years, Jean Paul himself and his younger brother, Henri, enjoyed a number of very pleasant vacations there up until 1915. Kent House was built in 1780 by General Haldimand, the English governor of Lower Canada, and later rented to the Duke of Kent, who gave it his name. Around 1880 the estate was acquired by a private hydro-electric firm, Quebec Power, and converted into a deluxe hotel.

---

[5] As Jean Paul Lemieux prefers to write his given names without a hyphen, we shall adopt this practice throughout the present book.

Kent House, summer 1909

Jean Paul Lemieux's earliest childhood memories go back to the annual trip that took him and his family to Kent House for the summer holidays. The journey from Quebec City to Montmorency Falls was fairly short, but it offered the excitement of travel by horse-drawn carriage in an era when the modest precursors of the streamlined machines that tear along our highways today still managed to frighten horses and children! And even at age five Jean Paul had his own version of the horseless carriage.

Another important childhood memory for Jean Paul was the tragic sinking of the Titanic the night of April 14, 1912. At the tender age of seven, he saw photographs of the ill-fated vessel in the newspapers and his imagination was soon at work, prompting him to draw scenes of undersea carnage on lengths of wrapping paper. Later he would spend hours crayoning battles which saw cowboys pitted against Indians, and other scenes in which the characters were visible inside cutaway houses. He was much inspired at the time by the American comic books which were so popular around the turn of the century: *Happy Hooligan*, *Buster Brown* and so on.

Introduction to Painting

The young Jean Paul was particularly fascinated by a large fountain situated on the grounds of Kent House. Dressed in his sailor's suit, he would while away the hours here playing with his little fleet of sailboats. More than half a century later, Lemieux would paint this fountain in the first version of a canvas titled *Eté 1914* (Summer 1914), only to paint it over in the final version (p. 288).

It was in fact at Kent House during the summer of 1914, some months before his tenth birthday, that Jean Paul met Charles Parnell, an American artist who was busy painting a series of pictures designed to brighten up the interior of the hotel's golf club. The boy was immediately intrigued by Parnell and fascinated to see how a landscape slowly took shape under the artist's brush as he worked away in the garden. Other encounters followed over the course of the summer, both out-of-doors and under the eaves of the hotel, in Parnell's studio, where other landscapes came alive with colorful flowers.

First version of *Eté 1914* (Summer, 1914), 1965

Jean Paul Lemieux and his brother Henri at Kent House, summer 1911

This was the turning point. Jean Paul asked his parents for paint brushes and a few months later, on his next birthday, they complied. They could hardly suspect that they were providing him with the tools for a long and fruitful artistic career.

During the summer of 1914 a kind of magnetic attraction drew the young Lemieux to Parnell's side almost daily, while all manner of people, faces, trees and skyscapes emerged from the artist's canvases. The drawings of the Titanic and the warfare between cowboys and Indians were now far behind him, even though such subjects continued to dominate the coloring books of other schoolboys his age. Jean Paul had already embarked on quite another adventure of the imagination and his hand now began to invent a whole series of striking pictorial visions.

Nineteen fourteen brought with it more than just Jean Paul Lemieux's discovery of painting. The next four years would be marked by the tragic events of the First World War as well as by the attendant economic crisis whose repercussions were felt as far away as Quebec, safe though Quebec was from the devastation experienced in the European theatres of war.

Life became more difficult for everyone, and the Lemieux family was no exception. Furthermore, Jean Paul's sister was seriously ill with rheumatism and the doctors recommended that she be moved to a more benign climate than that of Quebec.

California in 1916

In the fall of 1916, just as hundreds of other Quebec families were leaving for the United States in the hope of resolving their economic difficulties, Mme Lemieux set out for California with her three children. It was a long journey: interminable days and nights, an unsettling exodus towards a strange, far-off land, though a land of sunshine at least. The eleven-year-old Jean Paul's sensibilities would be profoundly affected by this journey, which was to be echoed forty, fifty, sixty years later on canvases charged with feelings of insecurity.

The Lemieux family settled in Berkeley, and Jean Paul and his brother resumed their schooling, in

Spanish church, Berkeley, California, 1917

Saint Gabriel Mission, Berkeley, California, 1917

English, with the Christian Brothers. The school was in an old rambling house which had been converted into a college. Its gardens overlooked the Berkeley campus of the University of California. Jean Paul went back to his drawing surrounded by semi-tropical flora. His sketches of Spanish missions executed in California in 1917 marked the real beginning of his portfolio.

The Lemieux family travelled a little in California, in particular to San Francisco, Los Angeles and Hollywood. The young painter-to-be retained pleasant memories of this first stay in California — the splendid beaches, San Francisco, which was to become as familiar to him as Quebec City, and the elusive attractions of Los Angeles and Hollywood. Hollywood then was in its heyday, when the earliest stars of the film world, Mary Pickford and Douglas Fairbanks, were making their first appearances before the cameras. Young Lemieux visited some of the movie studios and even watched scenes being shot for a film which starred an actress named Bessie Barisca.

Return to Quebec in 1917

In the summer of 1917, Jean Paul Lemieux returned to Quebec with his mother and brother after a one-year absence, while his sister stayed on in California and married there in 1919. This meant Jean Paul would have a pied-à-terre in California whenever he wished to make return visits. The Lemieux family settled in Montreal this time, rather than Quebec City; Jean Paul continued his studies at Mont-Saint-Louis for two years, before going on to Loyola. While he is the first to admit he was no model pupil, he has nevertheless retained a crystal-clear memory of one of his teachers — a certain Mr. Smith-Pickett — a dignified Englishman devoted to horse racing who would go through his meagre salary at the Dorval track and then actually borrow money from his more privileged pupils. Mr. Smith-Pickett found consolation for his disappointments as a gambler in the exploits of various outstanding historical figures, whose lives he would recreate for his class with great empathy — at the expense of other material on their curriculum which he deemed less important.

Jean Paul in Montreal, winter 1918

Movies, Watercolors and Montreal in 1920

It was 1920 and the silent cinema was at its
height. Montreal was one of numerous North American cities in which the movies had a large and enthusiastic following. The "Ouimetoscope" on Sainte
Catherine Street in particular gave the avid young
Lemieux much to feast his eyes on. Other halls in the
city which had once served as legitimate theatres but
were now being steadily appropriated by the cinema,
contributed to the movie feast.

It was also around this time that Lemieux began to take note of magazine illustrations by Maxfield
Parrish (1870-1966): he was fascinated by the romantic spirit of these illustrations and by certain landscapes inhabited by diaphanous young nymphs.

In 1921 Lemieux undertook to draw on a more
regular basis, for he felt the need to keep developing
his potential. During a summer holiday at Les
Eboulements, on the banks of the Saint Lawrence
River, downstream from Quebec City, he executed a
series of watercolors depicting the picturesque countryside around Charlevoix, with its rustic houses, tiny
villages and sweeping views of the river.

Schroon Lake, Roses Point, July 3, 1921

Back in Montreal he worked on his watercolor technique under the guidance of an Englishwoman whose studio he visited once a week. A spinster well on in years, she operated with a number of ironclad pedagogical principles, including one which she never tired of repeating: "When the mountains are far away, they must be blue, because they are far away."

This was not how the apprentice watercolorist saw things, not least because his perception of blues was somewhat abnormal owing to a degree of color-blindness. However, not wishing to challenge the authority of his venerable teacher, he quietly painted his mountains with the color labelled "blue" on the tray. It was from this very instructor that the young Lemieux learned to appreciate the pitfalls of teaching fine art. When, some fifteen years later, he took up a career as a teacher of painting and drawing himself, he would refrain whenever possible from any unto-ward interference with his students' visual and picto-rial learning, preferring to let them paint according to their own vision ... especially when it came to the choice of colors for distant mountain peaks!

———

Half a century later Lemieux talked fondly of the Montreal he knew in the early 1920s: "It was a rather English city, with lots of trees, where people kept pretty much to themselves. There were a few automobiles in the streets, which hardly went any faster than the horse-drawn carriages. The Victorian buildings on Sherbrooke Street, which was very quiet and dignified, gave it a British air. And close by there was the mountain with its vast park, Mount Royal." Still in his teens, Lemieux was embarking on his romantic period. And for all that it was still so close, he was smitten with nostalgia for his childhood, in particular for the times spent at Kent House and Montmorency Falls. The latter, would indeed become the subject of his first oil painting in 1923.

Learning to Paint: 1926-1929

By the beginning of 1926 Jean Paul Lemieux had turned twenty-one and needed to begin thinking in more concrete terms about his future. In the spring he entered the Montreal studio of painter Marc-Aurèle de Foy Suzor-Côté, in the rue Sainte-Famille.

Chutes Montmorency (Montmorency Falls), 1923, 20 x 15 cm, OFQ

Les Eboulements, summer 1922

Despite the master's great success in painting at the time, he was at pains to warn the easy-going Lemieux about the pitfalls of an artistic career. A few months later, Lemieux left Suzor-Côté's studio and in September 1926 enrolled for classes at Montreal's Ecole des beaux-arts, which had been founded in 1922 and opened in 1923. The Ecole was first run by a French artist, Emmanuel Fougerat, then from 1925 to 1946 by a French Algerian, Charles Maillard, who received from the Quebec government not only a generous salary, but also a two-month annual excursion back to the cultural headwaters of Paris. The Ecole thus encouraged slavish reproduction of all that was most conservative in the output of the Paris academies. However, those who had long been clamoring for an Ecole des beaux-arts in Montreal, artists such as Edmond Dyonnet, Clarence Gagnon and Suzor-Côté, had had something else in mind altogether. What they wanted was free studios of the sort organized by the Art Students' League of New York. In the place of some such dynamic formula, Montreal found itself saddled with a scaled-down but none the less faithful copy of the most hopeless sort of Paris academicism, which did much to arrest the development of the plastic arts in Quebec at the time. It would take a long struggle and a series of violent confrontations in 1944-45 between Maillard and painter and teacher Alfred Pellan before the Ecole had this artistic yoke lifted.[6]

Lemieux, in any case, patiently pursued his apprenticeship at the Ecole for three years, under Maillard's directorship and worked especially closely with two teachers, Maurice "Monsieur" Félix and Henri Charpentier. But it was a third teacher, Edwin Holgate, who exercised the greatest influence on him, and in 1931 he would come across Holgate again, much to his delight and benefit.

Despite the close friendships he had developed at the Ecole with Jean Palardy and Jori Smith, Jean-Charles Faucher, Goodridge Roberts, Louis Muhlstock, Ernest Newman and Paul-Emile Borduas, Jean Paul Lemieux had had enough of academic instruction by the spring of 1929. He therefore said goodbye to the idea of copying dusty old plaster replicas of classical works of art, as well as to the frustrating experience of trying to study modern art through the unsatisfactory medium of poor-quality monochrome reproductions. Lemieux intended to go to Europe and see for himself the works of Gauguin, Van Gogh, Renoir, Matisse, as well as those of older artists who held some fascination for him — Piero della Francesca, Joachim Patinier, El Greco.

Early Illustrations

Between 1926 and 1928 the young Lemieux sketched an ever-larger number of life drawings, landscapes and still lifes. In 1927 he executed five illustrations for Robert Choquette's novel *La pension Leblanc,* having agreed with the author that his drawings should emphasize the rustic aspects of life in the Quebec countryside. However, the resultant illustrations played down the anecdotal side in favor of a solidity of composition which balanced off massive black shapes against a counterpoint of finely hatched surfaces.

Île aux Coudres, 1926

---

[6] For more details, see G. Robert, *Pellan*, pp. 40-46, and G. Robert, *L'Art au Québec depuis 1940*, p. 19 and pp. 64-65.

Drawing of children, 1926, 25 x 35 cm

Illustrations for *La pension Leblanc*, 1927

25

Illustrations for *Le Manoir hanté*, 1928

In 1928, Lemieux made ten illustrations for *Le Manoir hanté*, by Régis Roy. These illustrations were executed in the manner of woodcuts, or linoleum engravings, and utilized massive black shapes carved out with a bold and sure hand, relieved by black hatching on a white background, or vice versa. Once again, anecdotal effects are reduced to a minimum for the sake of a particular graphic conception.

The illustrations for these two books, which were signed "Paul Lemieux" rather than "Jean Paul Lemieux," were executed by a young man who was now obsessed with the idea of getting to Europe.

The Trip to Europe: 1929

In June 1929, Jean Paul Lemieux, accompanied by his mother, finally embarked for Europe. He was twenty-five years old. Travelling on the same ship, as it turned out, was one of his teachers from the Ecole

26

des beaux-arts, "Monsieur" Félix. Their journey took them first to London, where Jean Paul was very impressed by the Egyptian section of the British Museum. Later in the summer they were in Biarritz and made a rapid swing through Spain. They then went back to France, first to Brittany where Jean Paul sketched farmers out in the fields, then Chartres, where he paused long enough to make a quick drawing before settling in Paris for a few months. Mother and son took lodgings in Montparnasse, where the young painter frequented la Coupole, the celebrated artists' café. It was there he encountered fellow countryman Clarence Gagnon, a fifty-year-old artist with a considerable reputation in Canada. Gagnon invited Lemieux up to his studio and Lemieux took advantage of this opportunity to examine the older artist's work closely. One of his projects was the illustration of a deluxe edition of Louis Hémon's famous *Maria Chapdelaine,* published by les Editions Mornay, an edition which has since become much sought after by bibliophiles.

The young Lemieux, with two book illustration credits to his name, had plans for earning his living as an illustrator on his return to Montreal. In Paris, meanwhile, he spent some time in the Académie Colarossi, in the studios of the Grande Chaumière, one of the most reputed "ateliers libres" ("free schools") of the period, and in the studio of Professor Sète, where he familiarized himself with the styles of illustration which had come into fashion in magazines such as Vogue and Harper's Bazaar.

Yet the charms of Versailles and its gardens, of Paris and her museums, had begun to wear on Lemieux whose impatient temperament was not well suited to the life of the interminable tourist. He was suddenly homesick and anxious to return to Quebec.

By a curious coincidence, three Quebec painters, each of whom would later become famous, all happened to be living in Paris at the same time. Alfred Pellan was domiciled there almost continuously from 1926 to 1940, as was Paul-Emile Borduas from November 1928 to June 1930, although he was in the provinces from June to December 1929. And of course Lemieux himself was in Paris for the greater part of 1929. Borduas and Pellan did not know each other at the time and it was in fact Lemieux who first introduced them in Quebec City in 1940. Borduas and

Paimpol landscape, Brittany, 1929, 10 x 15 cm

Lemieux had met some years earlier at the Ecole des beaux-arts in Montreal, but were fated not to meet in Paris the year of Lemieux's stay. While they shared a great nostalgia for Quebec, Pellan, on the other hand, threw himself into the bohemian life of Paris enthusiastically and became associated with the Surrealists.[7]

Paris at the time seemed decadent to Lemieux. He was deeply convinced in any case that he would never be able to undertake the great projects of which he dreamed, outside the land of his birth — the land for which he felt such a bittersweet nostalgia.

Nevertheless, Paris in 1929 was lively enough and this was in large measure thanks to the surrealist wing of the artistic avant-garde. Two key books by André Breton had just appeared in the bookstores, *Nadja* and *Le Surréalisme et la Peinture*. The first Surrealist Manifesto was reprinted with a new preface and the second was being drafted. So was a pamphlet entitled *Un Cadavre,* which attacked Breton for his sectarianism and his proclivity for excommunicating opponents from the artistic domain over which he professed to reign as spiritual leader. In the same year the paintings of Max Ernst, as well as of an exhibitionistic young Catalan, cropped up at different locations in Paris. Dali's notorious short film *Un Chien andalou*, made in conjunction with Luis Buñuel, opened on October 1 at Studio 28 and shocked the Paris public.

Lemieux seemed unmoved by the contemporary surrealist uproar, as did, somewhat surprisingly, his future colleague Paul-Emile Borduas. While Lemieux would always keep his distance from both the personalities and aesthetics of Surrealism — distrustful as he was of a kind of painting he judged to be unduly subject to somewhat far-fetched literary imperatives — Borduas, for his part, was in fifteen years to become one of Surrealism's most ardent apologists in Montreal.[8]

---

[7] For more details, see G. Robert, *Pellan*, pp. 30-32, and G. Robert, *Borduas*, pp. 21-23.

[8] See G. Robert, *Borduas*, pp. 22-23, 141-148 and passim.

Studio JANS

After returning to Montreal in December 1929, Lemieux pooled his resources with two old friends and classmates from the Ecole des beaux-arts, Jean Palardy and Jori Smith, in order to set up a commercial art firm which they called JANS and for which they found studio space in Beaver Hall Square. The firm lasted only six months, just long enough for a few of their friends and fellow artists to get into the habit of stopping by in the late afternoon to have a beer, a coffee or some tea. JANS shut down at the beginning of the summer of 1930, for lack of both steady customers and enthusiasm for commercial work on the part of the three young artists, who would all go on to find more fulfilling outlets for their talents. Jean Palardy, in conjunction with his wife Jori Smith, herself a gifted painter, later became a leading specialist in the field of Quebec handicrafts. His years of patient research were crowned by the publication in 1936 of a masterful study entitled *Les Meubles anciens du Canada français* (French-Canadian Antique Furniture). Lemieux too would retain his attachment to the traditional art forms of Quebec and become a leading crusader for their preservation. In the meantime he pursued his career as a teacher of painting from 1934 to 1965, while his reputation as a painter grew and he became established as an imposing figure on the Canadian art scene.

Le petit page de Frontenac, 1930

During the spring of 1930, Lemieux was busy designing a number of bookplates and making twelve illustrations for *Le petit page de Frontenac*. This was a tale set in the time of French colonial rule and was written by an author then popular with children, "Maxine" (the pen name of Marie-Caroline Alexandra Bouchette Taschereau-Fortier). Lemieux's passion for traditional Quebec and especially for the architecture of the French régime, is evident in several of the drawings for the book, which was first published by the Librarie d'Action canadienne-française as part of a series designed for use as school prizes. The book was republished by les Editions Beauchemin, which had given it a seventh printing by 1952, while eliminating the next-to-last illustration and resetting the text in order to shorten it by about ten pages. The graphic merits of these illustrations fell considerably short of those achieved by

29

Wildcat Canyon, California, 1930, 28 x 25 cm

Chez les Sauvages, 1931

Lemieux in both *La pension Leblanc* and *Le Manoir hanté,* or for that matter in a later project, *Chez les Sauvages.* Here the imperatives of content clearly took over from the artist's preoccupation with form, probably because of certain specifications imposed by the client, who wished to spare his school-age readership any excesses of artistic license.

A Trip to the United States and Return to the Ecole in 1931

After the JANS team disbanded, Lemieux was forced to reorganize his life. He needed a breathing space and in the fall of 1930 went to spend a few months in California with his sister who had lived there ever since 1916. He painted some of the finest landscapes of his early career in California. One in particular, entitled *Wildcat Canyon*, was vigorously composed and married simplicity of design to rich texture.

Lemieux made the most of his return trip from California in early 1931. He stopped to visit museums and art galleries in Chicago, New York and Boston, and took a close look at the realist school of contemporary American painting. He was interested in the implicit or explicit social commentary contained in the works of Edward Hopper, Thomas Hart Benton, Grant Wood and Marsden Hartley. Before long, echoes of the realist school would turn up in Lemieux's own canvases.

Illustrations drawn from engravings dating back to 1796,
for *Chez les Sauvages*, 1931

Congé (Holiday), 1932, 15 x 15 cm

Lemieux next made a dozen illustrations for *Chez les Sauvages*, a book written by a Marist brother, Ernest-Beatrix. It was published jointly in Montreal in May 1931 by the Librairie d'Action canadienne-française and les Editions Albert Lévesque, with a cover by Alyne Gauthier. Lemieux's drawings were more faithful to the spirit of the text than they were inventive, though four of them show a bold handling of the background which was divided obliquely into two solid sections of white and black.

Also during 1931 he contributed four drawings to a book of science-fiction written by Emmanuel Desrosiers and entitled *La Fin de la Terre*. These images were the distant and somewhat clumsy harbingers of a series of drawings Lemieux would execute forty years later, inspired by his premonition of a nuclear holocaust which was to reduce North America to one great radioactive ruin in the year 2082.

In the fall of 1931, Lemieux returned to the Ecole des beaux-arts, where he painted still lifes, a few portraits and landscapes, all with little enthusiasm. Until that point he had worked predominantly with watercolors and gouache, but now was more intrigued by painting in oils — particularly because of the possibilities of nuance offered by oils. He began working on scenes of typical, everyday Quebec life and painted a number of family groups.

En famille (At Home), 1931, 18 x 18 cm

La partie de cartes (The Card Party), 1932, 23 x 28 cm

Les Eboulements, 1935 (p. 39)

Lemieux was approaching thirty and had made up his mind to terminate his studies at the Ecole des beaux-arts, even if his aesthetic appetite had not had its fill of varied and stimulating fare. He began to frequent the studio of Edwin Holgate whom he had known since his early days at the Ecole in 1926. Lemieux admired Holgate's abilities as both teacher and artist, though Holgate's painting had little direct influence on Lemieux's own work.

Lemieux studied the rudiments of woodcut technique and painted life models at Holgate's Burnside Street studio in Montreal. Another visitor to the Holgate studio was the young poet Hector de Saint-Denys Garneau. They had become acquainted a few years earlier at the Ecole des beaux-arts and would often have coffee together in the late evening. With the 1937 publication of *Regards et jeux dans l'espace*, Garneau's reputation as a writer would come to the fore, thereby pushing his drawings, watercolors and paintings into the background, despite the great significance they seemed to hold for Garneau.

The landscapes of the Group of Seven held much fascination for Lemieux at the time, above all because they rejected the tired aesthetic of academy painting which held sway over the Montreal art scene throughout this period. Their strong colors and bold compositions were a breath of fresh air and ushered in, as Lemieux himself later put it, "a climate of freedom which had not existed before." This was the inspiration for a number of canvases, such as *Soleil d'après midi* (Afternoon Sun) of 1933.

Soleil d'après midi (Afternoon Sun), 1933, 76 x 86 cm, MQ

1910 Remembered (detail), 1962 (p. 200)

Teaching: A New Career Begins

Jean Paul Lemieux finally received his diploma from the Ecole des beaux-arts in the spring of 1934, and at the opening of the academic year 1934-35 began his career as an art teacher, giving drawing and decorative art classes. At the age of thirty he saw the economic wisdom of a teaching career, as it would allow him to earn his living, stay in intimate contact with the art scene, paint for himself over the long holidays and avoid perilous commercial ventures such as JANS.

In 1934 Lemieux collaborated with a friend from the Ecole, René Chicoine, on the illustration of a little text for children called *L'Epopée canadienne* (The Canadian Epic), written by Jean Bruchési, a future cultural administrator and ambassador. The illustrations reflected the narrative vein popular at the time in school texts and were of no aesthetic interest.

After a year of teaching at the Ecole des beaux-arts, Lemieux moved to the Ecole du meuble (Montreal Technical School), where he taught drawing and painting from September 1935 to June 1937. The Ecole du meuble had been in existence since 1930 and soon became one of the principal crucibles for Quebec's artistic revival, under the careful but inspiring direction of Jean-Marie Gauvreau, who shared Lemieux's enthusiasm for the traditional arts and handicrafts of Quebec.[9]

The Ecole du meuble offered an excellent artistic climate in which to work, even though Lemieux's studio was located right next to the automotive shop, from which undoubtedly emanated enough noise to drown out any goings-on in the studio. Whatever its physical drawbacks, academic freedom at the Ecole du meuble was incomparably greater than at the Ecole des beaux-arts, which remained paralyzed by its backward-looking principles until 1945. It was at the Ecole du meuble that architect Marcel Parizeau introduced Lemieux to several of the leading lights at the Paris School, who up to that point had left him somewhat indifferent. Lemieux's attention was also

Teaching staff of the Montreal Technical School in 1935: Léo Fontaine, Jean-Marie Gauvreau, Alphonse Saint-Jacques, Alberic Gagnon and Jean Paul Lemieux (*Technique*, Montreal, November 1935, p. 447)

---

[9] See Gauvreau's article "1930-35" in *Technique* (Montreal), vol. 10, no. 9, November 1935, pp. 447-455.

drawn to the young Quebec painter, Alfred Pellan, who had lived in Paris for ten years. A number of his drawings and paintings later inspired Lemieux to write an article which was published in 1938.

Charlevoix and Traditional Art

During the summer holidays from 1932 to 1935, Lemieux took up residence in the Charlevoix region with his friends and former JANS associates, Jean Palardy and Jori Smith. There he worked on drawings, watercolors and oil paintings, which evolved slowly from a lyrical and sensuous interpre-

Ile aux Coudres, 1932, 30 x 40 cm, OFQ

Village, 1934, 61 x 76 cm (Willistead Art Gallery, Windsor)

Linoleum engraving, 1933, 13 x 15 cm

De dos (Back View), 1932, 15 x 10 cm

Madeleine, 1935, 76 x 56 cm

tation of nature towards a more geometric and Cézannian approach to the landscape and houses. A 1933 lino-engraving of a Charlevoix village recalled some of Lemieux's recent work in the medium at Holgate's studio. A 1934 painting entitled *Maison aux Eboulements* (House in Les Eboulements) earned Lemieux the Brymner Prize, awarded in an open competition to Quebec artists under thirty-five years of age. The competition was organized by a cultural institution dating back to 1860, which until 1948 had been called the Art Association of Montreal. In 1948 it changed its name to the Musée des beaux-arts de Montréal (Montreal Museum of Fine Arts). This success encouraged Lemieux to participate regularly over the next twenty years in the annual exhibitions of the Royal Canadian Academy.

The summer vacations spent in Charlevoix brought Lemieux into close contact with the popular art of the region. Along with the director of Montreal's Ecole du meuble, Jean-Marie Gauvreau, and friends like Jean Palardy, Jules Bazin and painters Paul-Emile Borduas and Stanley Cosgrove, Lemieux took part in research projects on the traditional and popular art forms of Quebec. Under the guidance of Marius Barbeau and Gérard Morisset, they catalogued many fine examples of antique furniture, pottery, silverware and tools which turned up in village after village, in the shadow of Quebec's many old parish churches.

Early Writings

In November 1935, Lemieux published an article, written in English, in a bilingual Montreal magazine called *Technique*. The article, "A New Modern Setting in Montreal," described in detail a new "Beauty Salon" which had just opened on the fifth floor of Morgan's department store. Lemieux had warm words of praise for the man who designed the salon, Omer Parent. Parent was a graduate of the Quebec City Ecole des beaux-arts and had gone to Paris on a scholarship with Pellan in 1926. He returned before his colleague in 1928 and took up a position the following year at Morgan's. Parent would later teach at the Quebec City Ecole des beaux-arts from 1936 to 1970, then found the Ecole des arts visuels at Laval University, all the while pursuing his own work as a painter.

In 1935 Lemieux began to court Madeleine Desrosiers, a graduate, like himself, of Montreal's Ecole des beaux-arts. Soon he was painting her portrait. The woman who in two years' time was to become his wife would reappear frequently in Lemieux's work, in a variety of situations and moods.

"A Young Painter with Promise"

During the summer of 1935, Lemieux painted some of his finest landscapes of that period, in and around the Charlevoix region. A watercolor entitled *Les Eboulements* shows what pleasure the artist took in simply letting his brush flow lightly over the paper, before giving lively definition to one corner of the village and to the landscape sweeping away towards the river. An oil painting entitled *Paysage en Charlevoix* (Landscape in Charlevoix County) gives even greater play to the texture and picturesque quality of the region. And in a small oil painting on wood entitled *Baie Saint-Paul*, Lemieux outlines a dramatic relationship between sky, rugged coast and river with great analytic simplicity.

Over the summer of 1936, Lemieux did a series of landscapes in another part of Quebec, Estrie. This was accompanied by a change in his treatment, for he now showed a more sensuous attachment to plant life and the soil. On the one hand, he was finding inspiration in the aesthetics of the Group of Seven; on the other, he was exploring ideas broached by Goodridge Roberts which would lay the groundwork for his own reputation as painter over the next thirty years.

In a review published in the newspaper *Le Canada* on May 4, 1937, Henri Girard had this to say about Lemieux's participation in an exhibition of work by former students of Montreal's Ecole des beaux-arts, held at the Scott Gallery on Drummund Street:

"L'Assemblée [The Assembly] and *Maisons à Magog* [Houses at Magog] have put Jean Paul Lemieux in the front ranks of young French-Canadian painters. In the first of these, Lemieux has achieved in the language of the painter what Robert Choquette achieved in his *Curé de Village*: a unique expression of the French-Canadian man. I see in it a new way of representing our rural folk as they really are, with a touch of irony and a large measure of affection. This is not caricature, but rather a light-hearted way of looking at reality. Some may feel that the composition lacks unity, that the focus of interest is a little unsettled. I would have

Les Eboulements, 1935, 25 x 35 cm (color p. 33)

Baie Saint-Paul, 1935, 14 x 18 cm, OFQ

Charlevoix, (Charlevoix County) 1935, 63 x 84 cm, OFQ

Cantons de l'Est (Eastern Townships), 1936, 56 x 76 cm, MQ

to agree. Yet this picture marks such an important development in the realist approach to the study of French-Canadian life that it would be peevish to pick a quarrel over some shortcoming that the painter himself will doubtless overcome in another work of similar inspiration. The painting entitled *Maisons à Magog* is executed in an altogether different style. Jean Paul Lemieux here shows great talent for interpretation and execution. It is indeed the work of an artist who has mastered his tools and who knows how to give memorable expression to his taste and culture.''

Commenting on the same exhibition, which brought together work by Stanley Cosgrove, Armand Filion, Jean-Charles Faucher, René Chicoine, Madeleine Desrosiers and other former students of Montreal's Ecole des beaux-arts, the reviewer for *La Presse* newspaper wrote on May 8 that Lemieux had a delightful ability to mix the humorous with the rustic, and to delineate with great perception some of the most colorful characters of traditional Quebec society. The reviewers were agreed in their praise for Lemieux's subtlety and solidity as an artist—especially in regard to *Maisons à Magog* — and drew flattering comparisons with Utrillo, Dufy and the Impressionists.

Exhibition of May 1937: at the far left and right, *L'Assemblée* (The Assembly) and *Maisons à Magog* (Houses at Magog)

Marriage, and Return to Quebec City in 1937

On June 12, 1937, Jean Paul Lemieux and Madeleine Desrosiers were married in the Montreal parish of Saint-Louis de France. They subsequently left Montreal for Lemieux's native Quebec City, where he had been hired to teach painting and drawing at the Ecole des beaux-arts. In early October, 1937, he thus began a career that was to last twenty-eight years, until his retirement from teaching at the Ecole in 1965. Lemieux was chosen for this post over Paul-Emile Borduas, who subsequently replaced Lemieux at the Ecole du meuble in Montreal. Borduas later did much to create a climate at the Ecole du meuble conducive to the flowering of artists such as Jean-Paul Riopelle, Jean-Paul Mousseau and Marcel Barbeau — something that might have seemed more likely to occur at Montreal's Ecole des beaux-arts had it not been suffering so badly from the academic paralysis we have already described.

Lemieux withdrew from that battle once and for all. Very early in his teaching career in Quebec City he undertook to open a drawing class for children. This he did in the spirit of a significant new development centred in Montreal, in which Borduas and Brother Jérôme Paradis played key roles.[10]

Newly married and securely employed, Lemieux found himself pleased to rediscover his hometown at the age of thirty-three, and eager to move on several fronts at once: teaching painting at the Ecole des beaux-arts and drawing to children; painting and exhibiting his own work; publishing a number of articles, and even giving a few lectures.

An Address on Gauguin

On the successive Thursday afternoons of March 31 and April 7, 1938, Lemieux delivered a two-part address to students and visitors at the Ecole des beaux-arts on the life and work of Paul Gauguin. Lemieux had been fascinated by Gauguin's tortured career for some years. He discussed the misfortunes and exalted adventures of the painter's life, showing

Tête (Head), 1937, 36 x 25 cm

---

[10] For more details, see G. Robert, *Jérôme, un frère jazzé*, and G. Robert, *Borduas*, in the index under "pédagogie et enseignement," p. 332.

himself to be entirely in sympathy with the quest for an authentic primitive life unspoiled by industrial civilization. In the late nineteenth century such a civilization could still be found in Tahiti, if one penetrated to the interior of the island, into the region of Mataiea. It was probably there in 1893 that Gauguin painted the enigmatic *L'Esprit des Morts veille*, which became in Lemieux's eyes one of the great achievements of world art.

The talk ended with the projection of reproductions of Gauguin's works, at which point Lemieux took the time to comment on one of the great questions that has haunted him all his life: the place of man in the universe. This was a problem that the "strange genius of Gauguin" had confronted so well in the famous painting entitled *D'où venons-nous? Que sommes-nous? Où allons-nous?* (Where do we come from? What are we? Where are we going?) — Lemieux had experienced the singular power of this impressive work in the Boston Museum a year or two earlier. He felt great admiration for Gauguin, who had died under the most miserable circumstances in the Marquesas Islands and yet had once said: "Barbary has restored me to youth." Lemieux, who tried to impart some of his fascination with Gauguin's strange destiny to his audience, would also try to apply some of Gauguin's artistic ideas in his own work.

A Series of Articles for *Le Jour*: "Pellan"

The four articles published by Lemieux in the Montreal newspaper *Le Jour* in 1938 brought a breath of fresh air and an unaccustomed sense of humor to the meagre annals of pre-1940 Quebec art criticism. Intelligently and perceptively written by a thoughtful painter and teacher, the articles in question were supported by a penetrating analysis of the artistic climate in Quebec — which in many ways was a depressing one at the time. Lemieux refused to yield to the prevailing spirit of parochialism; instead, he swept out the cobwebs, invited discussion, provoked debate, opened windows on the outside world, underlined the importance of certain new talents who were being denied recognition and suggested improvements.

The first of these four articles appeared on May 4, 1938 and was entitled "Notes sur quelques toiles de

Pellan" (Notes on a few canvases of Pellan's). It opened with the exclamatory remark—"What a name Pellan has already made for himself!" Lemieux was here being more prophetic than matter-of-fact since Pellan had left Quebec in 1926, at the age of twenty-two, right after graduating from Quebec City's Ecole des beaux-arts, and did not return to his native province until he was driven from France by the Nazi invasion in 1940. Lemieux was therefore quick to add that while Pellan was busy carving out a niche for himself in Europe, he was practically unknown in his native country. The article concentrated its critical remarks on a number of Pellan's works then on exhibit at the Ecole des beaux-arts in Quebec City. The author proved a skilful critic, capable of putting his finger on the prominent artistic sources that inspired Pellan (chiefly Picasso and Braque), yet without reducing the young artist's accomplishments to a catalogue of outside influences. More importantly, Lemieux proved able in these paragraphs to tackle the broader questions, such as the need for Quebec artists ("Canadian" artists, he wrote) to break out of the "narrow confines" of their own folklore. It was important that they expose themselves to developments in the world around them and not be content to rest on the laurels garnered for their initial successes at home.

Lemieux found in Pellan's work a "subtle handling of color," a "real understanding of how to balance form," and "unusual rhythm which manages to satisfy both senses and intellect at once...." "He is never satisfied once he has achieved an objective, but is always determined to go further, forever further, in pursuit of his ultimate goal...." "He is a tireless seeker" with a "prodigious talent" which "must be represented in his native land" — specifically in the collections of the Musée du Québec. Thanks in part to Lemieux's enthusiastic support, Pellan would two years later win pride of place in the art museum of his hometown with a full-scale exhibition of his work. This exhibition became one of the prime detonators in the series of cultural explosions that finally shook Quebec's artistic world from its lethargy during the forties.

"Survey of Contemporary Painting"

The second in this series of articles appeared in *Le Jour* on June 18, 1938. Entitled "Survey of Contemporary Painting," it sketched the evolution of "modern" painting from Delacroix to abstract art, taking in the Impressionists, Cézanne and Seurat, Gauguin and Van Gogh, the Fauves and the Cubists, the Dadaists and the Surrealists. The first and last two paragraphs give a clear statement of the aesthetic ideas and opinions that would shape Lemieux's long dual career as painter and teacher. They were ideas which the present author found echoed nearly forty years later in the course of interviews held with the painter in 1974 and 1975. This is how they were expressed in the 1938 article:

"Painting is the illusory appearance of an object, a scene or a person on a surface."

"The painter's eye is a sentient mirror which reflects the changing image of the world and objects in it and interprets them on canvas through a personality and a set of sensibilities."

"The real work of art is the image of a civilization and a synthesis of those ideas which distinguish it from others; if an artist's work says nothing about his epoch, it can only be mediocre."

"The real artist is the one who expresses what he sees, who reveals all that he is and all that he feels; he is not content to copy, rather he interprets in accordance with the emotion that stirs him."

"Surrealism is a morbid and unhealthy art form, typical of our troubled times, a far-fetched search for the images of the subconscious."

"Abstract art is Cubism gone wrong, which combines colors and forms for their own sake, without regard for the subject being treated; the product of a decadent society."

"Too often present-day painting puts one in mind of the darker side of humanity and illustrates the driven, anxious quality of our era and the grim future that lies in store." (We should recall that these prophetic lines were written in 1938, on the eve of the Second World War.)

"A troubled era cannot produce untroubled art; contemporary painting is in transition; it is tortured, unsettled, looking for new formulas, like humanity itself; it cannot retrace its steps; it is the reflection of a society which is crumbling away and from which a new world, a new Renaissance, will spring."

The second article written for *Le Jour*, from which the preceding extracts are taken, was joined to the third in the series to form the text of a lecture given at the Ecole des beaux-arts on November 30, 1939. It was then published as a unit in the Quebec City paper *L'Evénement-Journal* on December 1, 1939.

"Painting in French Canada"

The third article appeared in *Le Jour* on July 16, 1938. It was entitled "Painting in French Canada" and proved to be the most stimulating of the four articles. Taking as his point of departure the low esteem in which many outsiders held Quebec art, Lemieux described his subject in terms which verged on ridicule, but which were, sad to say, for the most part fair and accurate. What could a cultivated visitor expect to see in Quebec in 1938? Public buildings which were nothing more than "poor imitations of the classical and the Gothic or else ludicrous copies of Renaissance styles"; churches which featured "an atrocious mixture of all sorts of styles" and might drive away the visitor "disgusted with all their Italian frescoes and assembly-line statues"; a provincial art museum, in Quebec City, filled with "stuffed animals; a few old bits of sculpture in the stairwells, relics of a time when we had better taste; a huge cardboard windmill; a long line-up of landscapes, rustic scenes and portraits with sanguinolent backgrounds." A visitor sizing up French-Canadian art in 1938 would therefore be forced to come to the conclusion put forward by Lemieux: "They are a very quaint people, but they don't know the first thing about Art."

Lemieux continued his article with the following remarks: "There are undoubtedly some remarkable painters, some remarkable artists to be found in our province. A few could even be described as having a good deal of talent, but can we boast a Diego Rivera, an Orozco, a Benton, a Grant Wood, to name only a few of the leading Mexican and American painters?" There was of course Suzor-Côté and Clarence Gagnon, but "their painting sacrifices all to the subject being treated" (i.e. picturesque landscapes); "they cannot bring themselves to attempt a more radical interpretation, a more searching inquiry into the real essence of things; they are content to remain at the surface, without going any further; Marc-Aurèle Fortin is one exception to the rule, with virtues found almost nowhere else among French-Canadian painters of the naturalist school: boldness, spontaneity, a fresh new vision and deep sensibilities tinged with a certain restlessness."

What were the reasons for this pathetic "artistic backwardness" in Quebec around 1938? Lemieux first of all ruled out the superficial suggestion that Quebec was still young and had a weak economy, since similar circumstances had not prevented a real artistic blossoming in Mexico and elsewhere. The reasons cited by the author were many and were to be found "in our educational system, in our apathy towards all matters of the mind, in our mistrust of all those who think differently from us, in our automatic respect for anything produced abroad, in the backward mentality of our smug and self-satisfied leaders; all these factors have held us back, thrown up obstacles in our path, discouraged many who might have attempted something really worthwhile, and wiped out all intellectual and artistic progress."

This description constitutes one of the most lucid analyses of the cultural situation in Quebec at the time, and singles out Jean Paul Lemieux as an observer with a unique point of view at a time when neither the leaders nor the populace of the province showed anything but indifference to the problems involved. For all that Lemieux was perceptive, he was not necessarily pessimistic or despairing, because, as he put it, "all is not lost yet." There were a few young artists who were making a vigorous attempt to "move our pictorial art to a higher plane," and Lemieux stressed the importance of encouraging the accessibility of this art. He had some words of wisdom as to how young artists should be treated: "We must neither expect them to produce only masterpieces, nor treat as masterpieces everything they produce; we must find a happy medium, for too much praise is as bad as too little."

The author then spoke out against the amateurism which had helped reinforce a "triumph of bad taste." He also had harsh words for the "misappropriation of the landscape"; "the reason a lot of landscapes get painted is undoubtedly that they sell well." Making reference to the American initiative in commissioning murals from painters (the Federal Art Project of 1933-43), Lemieux put the following question: "Why can't we do the same thing here? In addition to providing work for our artists, it would give a little color to the interiors of our public buildings, which are usually drab and uninteresting. We should not overlook the boost such a scheme could give to the advancement of Art, nor the great educational value it might have for the public."

Lemieux wound up this third article by pointing to the need for a "struggle against the Italian monopolization" of religious art, and cited some verse in praise of French culture, which for the Québécois would come to play a messianic role in an America likely destined to become the "new artistic centre of the world."

"Notes on Drawing"

The last article of the series appeared in *Le Jour* on October 1, 1938 and was titled "Notes on Drawing." Here Lemieux the teacher undertook to plead a case for the art of drawing, in a tone that had something of the sermon about it, basing his argument on quotations from Il Tintoretto, Ingres and Gauguin.

"It is unfortunate that our painters, especially our younger painters, consider themselves capable of dispensing with drawing; and that they believe color to be capable of making up for any shortcoming in perspective or anatomy, which they take to be a mere matter of luck and not, as they should, a matter of substantial analysis and study of form, something requiring a consummate mastery of the art of drawing."

These remarks on drawing, first published in the fall of 1938, would be republished in the magazine *Regards* in March 1942.

The Exhibition of November 1938

During the summer of 1938, Lemieux and his wife Madeleine resided in Port-au-Persil, a little village on the north shore of the Saint Lawrence River between La Malbaie and the mouth of the majestic Saguenay River. The couple were both busy painting landscapes in the area, particularly the sweeping panorama of Saint-Siméon, at that point where the Saint Lawrence, though still technically a river, begins to widen and fill with the high tide as if in anticipation of becoming a real gulf.

From November 15 to 22, 1938, Quebec City art-lovers were treated to a joint exhibition of the works of Jean Paul Lemieux and his wife Madeleine Desrosiers, at the Galerie Morency, 54 rue Couillard. It comprised 67 oil paintings, watercolors, and gouaches completed in the preceding four or five years. The exhibition was well publicized in the local press, announcements appearing in *Le Soleil*, *L'Evénement-Journal* and *L'Action catholique*.

On November 12, *L'Action catholique* invited its readers to visit the exhibition: "Madeleine Desrosiers, a medal winner at Montreal's Ecole des beaux-arts, has on display a number of paintings which cannot fail to please the visitor with their novel treatment and choice of subject-matter, nor to satisfy the discerning eye of the connoisseur who appreciates conscientious work. All Quebec City's art-lovers and connoisseurs will find delight in these delicious two-dimensional poems. — Jean Paul Lemieux's work is more personal than ever, in a different key, without any attempt to grab attention with calculated effects. His art is spontaneous and new, very new." The article ends with a quotation from an article published by Henri Girard in *Le Canada* on May 4, 1937, concerning Lemieux's two paintings, *L'Assemblée* and *Maisons de Magog*.

———

The November 1938 exhibition prompted a significant article from the pen of Gérard Morisset, a personality well known in Quebec's artistic community at the time. Morisset, a notary devoted to the cause of traditional art, was an honorary attaché of the national museums of France and director of drawing instruction for the province of Quebec. On November 14, Morisset published a review in *Le Soleil* in which he referred to "the sparkling good taste, the delicacy of line and softness of contour, and the healthy, tempered vivacity" of Madeleine Desrosiers' works. As for Jean Paul Lemieux, a close friend of Morisset's, the reviewer praised his "good-natured realism, part of a healthy outlook on life completely devoid of morose thoughts of any kind." He went on to add that the painter paid no heed to what was in or out of fashion as far as painting was concerned, and instead developed a style all his own, beyond the confines of any academy, old or new, with a manner he described as "slightly tart, sometimes heavy, but always enjoyable."

"Reflections on Art," 1938

The year 1938 came to a close for Lemieux with publication on December 17 of his article "Reflections on Art" in the supplement to *L'Evénement-Journal*.

Noting first of all that "educating the ears has always been easier than educating the eyes," Lemieux stressed that there was a greater need to promote familiarity with painting than with music, because in day-to-day life more people were exposed to music than to good painting. The author also deplored the lack in Quebec City of exhibition space offering proper lighting, security and floor layouts suitable for displaying works of art.

This article was a natural extension of the series which appeared in Montreal's *Le Jour* earlier in the year, and in it Lemieux returned to a theme he had discussed in the June 1938 article: "We are living in a time of confusion and the effects have been felt in all the arts; eras of tranquility engender tranquil art, troubled times produce troubled art." The painter closed by striking a humanist note which was a heartfelt one for him: "As long as there are men on this earth, they will try to give to the objects and sounds which surround them form, balance and harmony, and thus carry on the civilizing task of Art in the world."

Talks on William Blake and on Contemporary Painting

On March 30, 1939, as part of the "Thursdays" program of the Ecole des beaux-arts, Lemieux gave a talk on the life and work of the English engraver, poet and painter William Blake (1757-1827). Sketching in a background of life in London around the turn of the nineteenth century, Lemieux pointed out the contrast between the unhappy fate of Blake the man, and the far-reaching vision of Blake the artist, which transformed the circumstances of his life and made it

Les beaux jours (Fine Days), 1938, 63 x 51 cm

enormously rich. Lemieux was particularly fascinated by the strange symbolism which haunted Blake's work and gave it its esoteric flavor, a quality at once bewitching and unpredictable. A solitary figure whose visions frightened or scandalized his contemporaries, when they were not altogether blind to his creative revelations, Blake pursued his disturbing inspiration in the face of all opposition to its furthest limits, to the dizzying threshold of the ultimate secrets of the universe, where everything becomes lucid in the unfathomable mystery of being.

———

At the fifth Salon of Beaux-arts graduates, held at the Art Association of Montreal in April 1939, fifteen artists shared the galleries; but three dominated the exhibition, according to *La Presse* reviewer Reynald in his article of April 19—Stanley Cosgrove, Jean Paul Lemieux and Jean-Charles Faucher. Lemieux was described by the writer as the "most thoughtful" painter of the group, who "has nothing of the satirist about him, yet sets one to thinking simply with the ardent melancholy of his images," which were typically Canadian "in the best sense of the term." A picture such as *Les beaux jours* (Fine Days) (1938) illustrates this point nicely. Its air of nostalgia is pointed up by the attitude of the young woman who is seen somewhat ambiguously both from the rear and in profile, her eyes lowered or half-closed, looking out over a Charlevoix landscape whose past glory as a vacation paradise has faded forever.

On November 23, 1939, an exhibition of paintings by Stanley Cosgrove at the Ecole des beaux-arts was the occasion for two talks, one by Paul Rainville on the Norwegian composer Grieg, the other by Jean Paul Lemieux on the evolution of painting in France and Quebec over the preceding few generations. Lemieux's lengthy address comprised two of the four articles published in *Le Jour* the previous year (the second, "Survey of Contemporary Painting," published June 18 and the third, "Painting in French Canada," published July 16); the whole text was republished in Quebec City's *L'Evénement-Journal* on December 1, 1939.

A Visit to the Lemieux Studio in 1940

As part of a series of articles on visits to artists' studios, Guy Roberge published an interview with

Dans le temps (Through Time), 1967 (p. 202)

Un âge va, un âge vient . . . (One Generation Comes, Another Goes), 1972 (p. 201)

Jean Paul Lemieux and his wife in *L'Evénement-Journal*, on February 10, 1940. Since September 1939, the couple had been living in an old stone house at 636 avenue Royale in Beauport, on the cliffs of Courville — very near Kent House, where Lemieux had spent his summer vacations as a child.

"They live a calm and reflective existence, away from any distractions, in a house of simple and elegant design. From their window they overlook the river, the Ile d'Orléans and the Laurentians. And on the other side of the mountains lies Charlevoix, their favorite region because it is the most picturesque in the province."

Guy Roberge teased Lemieux about how lucky a painter like himself was to have the lovely Montmorency Falls next to his house. He was scarcely surprised to hear Lemieux reply: "I'm the sworn enemy of Montmorency Falls, as I am of the Rocher Percé and sunsets," which prompted his wife to exclaim, "Not to mention moonlight!" Lemieux detested sentimentality and the preciosity of style that usually went along with it. Although he would later paint some remarkable landscapes bathed in the light of the setting sun — or even in moonlight — he was always careful to set a particular poetic mood using a *sfumato* which is virtually unique in Canadian painting. "Suggest rather than describe," as Gauguin advised.

Let us return for a moment to the two painters in 1940, as Guy Roberge saw them in their home. The couple had already laid there the foundations of a fine collection of Quebec antiques, through which prowled their cat Ferblantine and their dog Toto.

Commenting briefly on his one-year stay in Paris some ten years earlier, Lemieux pointed out that he had gained much from his tour of the art museums and that a careful examination of the most important collections and exhibitions was worth more than any number of art teachers. This elicited a quiet protest from the author of the article:

"'Is this not heresy coming from a professor of the beaux-arts? . . . '

'This is the former student talking,' Lemieux replied, 'grateful for having got off lightly.'"

Lemieux remarked during the same interview that his favorite painters were still the Impressionists and Post-Impressionists, especially Degas and Renoir, but that Quebec painting could not help but feel a certain influence from American painting. Indeed, for some years Lemieux had taken an active interest in the work of the American realist school known as the "American Scene."

Roberge singled out a number of canvases which were to be seen in the Lemieux studio at the time — *Enterrement à la campagne* (Country Burial), *Séance de la commission scolaire* (Meeting of the School Board), *Après-midi en famille* (Afternoon at Home) — all of which related to the American Scene movement. There was also *Maison de mineur dans un village abandonné* (Miner's House in an Abandoned Village), which gave an uncompromising view of one aspect of the misery of life in Quebec. It belonged in a series of paintings dealing with "the life of the colonists and was realistic enough to give even a politician of social realism pause for thought".... Roberge, alluding to *30 Arpents* (Thirty Acres), the novel of social realism by Ringuet, protested that "in Quebec, the established critics will not countenance realism in painting, especially if the reality is cruel or idiotic, any more than it countenances realism in literature."

Article on Pellan, 1940

Fron 1940 on, Jean Paul and Madeleine Lemieux spent their summers on the north shore of the Saint Lawrence River in the region of Charlevoix, where year after year they were drawn to picturesque villages like Les Eboulements and Port-au-Persil. Lemieux patiently painted the landscapes and inhabitants of this area between Petite Rivière and the mouth of the Saguenay.

In June 1940, on the occasion of a major exhibition of works by Alfred Pellan at the Musée de Québec, Lemieux introduced Pellan to Paul-Emile Borduas. The two artists, who had never met before, were soon to develop a fierce rivalry in Montreal, a subject which the present author has treated in his studies on the two painters in question.

zied ac
Beaucl
Pony. l
heavyv
being p
Rumill
Pages i
ing pe.
Paris je
French
stir the
notion

the art
down (
of real
wards l
had go
century
elsewh
painter
Society
stimula
from B(
Those
Quebec
spring (
1943. I
father A
Le Divo
exhibiti
His tall
history
ture as
Fernand
contribu
around
visiting
come h(
realism,
and left
Arcane

The Qu

H
ergies b
effacing
had his

Lemieux later devoted one of his most important articles to Pellan's work. It was published on November 8, 1940, in the Quebec City newspaper *Le Temps*. From the very opening of the article, the reader is aware just how pleased the author is to be dealing once again, after the article of May 4, 1938, with a talented colleague, born like Lemieux in Quebec City and only a year and a half his junior. Lemieux's enthusiasm carried him beyond the work of Pellan himself, and encompassed the examples of Matisse and Picasso, Van Gogh and Cézanne, Goya and Vermeer, Bonnard and Braque. The author broadened the scope of his article considerably, to include a kind of statement of his personal aesthetic, his conception of art. Here are some of the principal points of the article:

Art is "a long slow evolution."

An artist's work unfolds in a "gradual evolution, of which each canvas is a stage."

"Art is like a labyrinth: one must search long and hard before finding the tunnel that leads to the light."

"Outside influences have a large part to play in the work of every painter; no one can escape the great works of art of the past; no one can claim to create something which is not at least tinged with some preceding thought or vision."

"There is nothing new under the sun, only transformation, a metamorphosis of what has already been done."

"The past is itself the result of a long evolution lost in time."

If he studies "avidly and intelligently," the artist will discover "forms which lie dormant in him, of whose presence he is unaware."

The painter "uses his subject and does not let his subject use him"; "the subject is only a means and not an end in itself."

The artist "tries to express visions which stream out of his subconscious as incoherently as dreams, the ceaseless movement of life and the objects of the world."

"Art knows no borders; the real artist paints for the joy of painting and the whole world is his domain."

polemics, in the evolution of the cultural and artistic situation in Quebec. In Quebec City the prevailing cultural climate remained calmer than in Montreal, where there had always been a certain taste for noisy demonstrations. Unsuited by temperament for public debate or collective action, Lemieux waged war in his own manner: publishing articles, lecturing, giving art lessons to children as well as teaching his own students. His work, and his personal life, rested on a set of principles to which he gave firm allegiance: the need for independence of mind; a clear preference for acting on an individual rather than collective basis; a profound respect for the indigenous artistic heritage; the need to improve the lot of the Quebec artist; a great curiosity for what was going on in the art world elsewhere; and, lying beneath all this, perpetual good humor and a light-hearted way of looking at the world around him.

Lemieux was perfectly in sympathy with the cultural stance taken by Father Couturier in his 1941 address at the University of Montreal. Lemieux himself had already written and argued that art was a vital social force which must be allowed to live according to its own destiny, on its own terms, in pursuit of its own goals; that preserving artistic traditions did not mean clinging to a certain number of tired, worn-out clichés; and that progressive painting has over the centuries always had to fight in order to safeguard or reclaim its freedom of action—to get out from under the constant threat posed on the one hand by the academies from inside the art world, and on the other by an unsympathetic public whose tastes are shaped by these same academies. Lemieux had also written that the artist must not resort to a slavish imitation of the appearance of things, but must on the contrary invent new visual, indeed *visionary*, architectures. This, he claimed, had been the case over the past century with all the leading movements in painting— Impressionism, Pointillism, Symbolism, Fauvism, Expressionism, Cubism, Surrealism, Constructivism and Abstract Art. Moreover, every artist must have the courage to pursue his own discoveries to their logical conclusion, in all honesty, and be true to himself and his own most profound intuitions while at the same time accommodating himself to the spirit of his times. And all this without falling into the traps of fashion and the covert neo-academicism of the avant-garde.

The "Indépendants" of 1941

On January 18, 1941, the Quebec City newspaper *Le Soleil* published a critique, written by Lemieux, of the exhibition of engravings being held at the Ecole des beaux-arts. In it the author deplored "the lack of imagination among most of the participants in their choice of subject-matter" and remarked that a "showy concern for virtuosity" stifles the artistic imagination. He went on to say that the chosen themes were "conventional" to the point of being boring to the visitor, who could, however, still salvage his time by studying the different engraving processes there represented.

In the spring of 1941, the artistic community of Quebec was shaken by another assault, this time from more daring sources. The exhibition of the "Indépendants," presented in Quebec City at the end of April and in Montreal at the end of May, was a watershed for the year 1941 in much the same way the Pellan retrospective was a watershed event in the same two cities for 1940, and Borduas' gouaches exhibition at Montreal's l'Ermitage was a high point of the 1942 season. The 1941 exhibition, however, was different from the other two, which were one-man shows, in that it brought together the work of eleven painters, all with very distinct concerns but all fired by the same enthusiasm, the same desire to rejuvenate and revivify the activities of painting. The names of Jean Paul Lemieux and Jacques de Tonnancour did not figure among the eleven in question; for the moment these two artists were making a more significant contribution through their writing than through their painting.

The exhibition of the "Indépendants" performed a function which was to be vital for the evolution of the artistic climate in Quebec: that of challenging the academic teaching practices prevalent in most of the schools and studios. The director of Montreal's Ecole des beaux-arts, Charles Maillard, was imprudent enough to get involved in the public debate which had begun in the newspapers, and he attracted some stinging verbal assaults for his trouble. With the support of a number of European personalities who were in Quebec at the time, such as Alain Couturier, who wrote the preface for the "Indépendants" catalogue, the most committed young artists took up the fight against the reigning academic philosophy— a fight which would continue unabated until 1948, and which finally drew the attention of a wider public to the artistic discoveries and adventures of these young Québécois artists.

In his own quiet way, Lemieux had become aware over the years of the great need in art for fresh ideas. He realized it would be very unhealthy for Quebec's artistic community to shut itself away in a kind of closed economy, since this would tend to precipitate internal struggles and pointless navel-gazing. He was therefore quick to accept an invitation to write a column on artistic activities in Quebec City for the English-Canadian magazine *Maritime Art*, published at Acadia University in Wolfville, Nova Scotia since October 1940. Lemieux's column appeared regularly, in English, under the title "Coast to Coast in Art," from October 1942 to July 1943, i.e., in the magazine's last five issues. It ceased publication only to give way in October 1943 to a new magazine called *Canadian Art*. This magazine was published first in Ottawa, then in Toronto, changing its name in January 1967 (number 104) to *Arts Canada*. Lemieux's contributions, still in English, continued in *Canadian Art* from October 1943 (number 1) to June 1944 (number 5), giving the readership an account of the principal exhibitions mounted in Quebec City. His reviews were mixed. While he praised the merits of artists such as Pellan, Clarence Gagnon, Mary Bouchard, Simone Hudon, Madeleine Laliberté, Benoît East, Jean Soucy, Holgate and Marc-Aurèle Fortin, as well as the virtues of antique Quebec furniture, he also found distasteful elements. Lemieux deplored the banality of a series of works by René Richard, warned against the perils of abstract art and attacked artists of the "I-have-to-be-modern-at-all-costs" mentality—who usually succeeded only in underlining their own lack of sincerity. It was in fact his deeply felt need for an aesthetic sincerity and authenticity that prompted Lemieux to make remarks such as the following: "Modern art seems to have given birth to innumerable eyesores" (*Maritime Art*, July-August 1943, p. 159). "The machine age with its deadly uniformity is spreading and crushing all that gave Quebec its unique character among the cities of America." (*Canadian Art*, February-March 1944, p. 121)

The Cultural Situation in Quebec in 1941

In November 1941, Lemieux published some "Notes on Art in Quebec City" in *Regards*, an ephem-

Sugaring-off party and exhibition, around 1940
(Photos Madeleine Laliberté)

eral cultural magazine published in Quebec City by André Giroux who would later make a name for himself as a novelist. Lemieux's article looked beyond the geographical boundary set by the title and offered a lucid description of the cultural situation across the province of Quebec. As in other articles by Lemieux, the interest is heightened here by the author's keen sense of humor. In order to let the reader judge for himself Lemieux's talents as a writer and his particular bent of mind—which combines a keen eye for the problems close to home with an ability to see well beyond the confines of his own community—the text of this article is here given in full.

"Not so long ago, there were few of us outside a very small élite whose knowledge of painting was not limited to the insipid efforts of Bouguereau's followers and the sentimentalities of the Barbizon school. Landscapes had to be utterly picturesque, and were unthinkable without the usual herd of cows and the inevitable cottage in a grove of trees, everything being finely wrought. Portraits had to be exact likenesses, nudes as fleshy as possible. There was the anecdotal painting which moved old spinsters to tears and the mythological painting which gave gentlemen past their prime something to feast their eyes on. That was all fine, the system worked well. It was the kind of art that had the support of the majority. People weren't so much after a celebration of color as a good story. They expected the painter's work to be strictly photographic. Painting was simply the faithful reproduction of the beautiful things we find around us. The artist's task was to copy nature in as slavish a way as possible. He had to please everyone, which meant putting aside any vestige of personality or individuality if he wanted to make a living from his art. How much talent must have been wasted in trying to satisfy an ignorant clientèle whose own bad taste managed to stifle any other vision of the world but its own!

"A number of misconceptions about artists also used to be current in various quarters. Among those for whom art amounts to a collection of frames adorning the livingroom walls or to the statuette supporting a lamp at the foot of the stairs, it was said — and still is — that painting is a nice pastime for adolescent girls....Small wonder, with the convents having had a monopoly on the teaching of art for so long, that this art form came to be looked on as an exclusively feminine preserve. And yet history shows that the number of successful women painters has always been very small. Another equally absurd misconception which has been difficult to shake off is that of the artist as Bohemian. People of good intentions, having been exposed to *La Vie de Bohème*, novel and opera alike, got the idea into their heads that painters were eccentric creatures with long hair, who lived with their models in tiny garrets and wound up dying of consumption in impoverished circumstances. That would make poor Murger the one to blame for all the fathers who have ever refused to let their sons take up painting as a career! Fortunately, these rather far-fetched ideas are tending more and more to disappear from the collection of preconceptions we carry around with us, and are making room for a more enlightened approach to art and artists. Nowadays there is an appreciable minority which realizes that painting is a difficult art and demands complete commitment on the part of the painter, that it involves a continuous series of challenges, setbacks and renewed efforts, all directed towards a final goal which justifies the hard work and the sacrifices.

"People are now taking a greater and greater interest in painting around Quebec City. They want basic information, they want to understand what is going on in this field. Only a few years ago exhibitions were rare and lectures on this subject far between. An artistic education had to come from books and from reproductions which were often very bad. Our local painters exhibited, but without much encouragement. The situation was, in a word, deplorable. Then Quebec City's Ecole des beaux-arts inaugurated a series of exhibitions open to the public which had as their purpose to encourage appreciation of and interest in the plastic arts. This series introduced a considerable number of people to good painting for the very first time. The lectures which were given as part of the same program also had their own beneficial effects.

"Looking at the list of painters who exhibited at the Ecole, we find Cosgrove, Marguerite Scott, Simone Hudon, Sylvia Daoust, Albinson, Biéler, Roberts, Madeleine Laliberté and Jean Soucy, all of whom show a very personal vision and technique. We might also mention the magnificent exhibition of Polish art held in May 1939 which, unfortunately, had very few visitors. Then we had the pleasure of seeing the red-chalk drawings of Aristide Maillol and Charles Despiau, two masters of contemporary sculpture. A point to note about this exhibition: it was mounted behind closed doors and restricted to a privileged audience. Can you imagine why? Because it was an exhibition of nudes! Oh virtue!

"Then Pellan returned home from Paris, bringing with him a style of painting that left us all surprised, stunned and disconcerted. His exhibition at the provincial museum was an epoch-making event in the history of Canadian painting. With his canvases, he introduced a new art form into Canada, imported from Europe, just as Suzor-Côté had initiated us into Impressionism before the First War. Many people were perplexed by these pictures, with their abstract subject-matter and their aggressive graphics, and were unsure whether to admire or criticize. While lack of space prevents our undertaking a detailed discussion of this flamboyant approach to painting, we would do well to reflect for a moment on the ill-considered opinions of certain critics who referred to Pellan's work as childish scribbling. There are in the art world two schools of thought whose single-mindedness borders on stupidity. On the one hand, we have the supporters of Braque and Picasso who consider everything that went before to be worthless; on the other, those for whom contemporary painting is the work of mentally disturbed persons who are having a joke at the expense of respectable citizens. Such attitudes can only stem from either ignorance or snobbery. What is needed is a balanced view. Just because a work of art is old does not mean it is necessarily ugly: beauty resists the ravages of time. The portraits of Hamel and Plamondon will always be beautiful, despite the old-fashioned meticulousness of their style. By the same to-ken, contemporary painting is not art made expressly for eccentric collectors. It is the result of a long series of experiments by trial and error. It reflects our times, a harsh and turbulent era if ever there was one. Art is the mirror of the society in which it develops. Painters are a product of their times and have to look at the world as it is, not as it isn't.

"One of the most pressing tasks awaiting us in Quebec, if we are to develop and encourage the public's aesthetic sensibilities, is to put more people in touch with art history. Obviously getting to know all the schools that have shaped contemporary art would require a consider-able expenditure of time and enormous documentary re-sources. It would be absurd to expect the layman to know all that the artist has to know; nevertheless, the layman should have at least a rough outline, an overview by which to be guided in his tastes and critical appreciation. We learn much about music from the radio. Nowadays nearly everyone is familiar with Beethoven's Fifth, say, or the New World Symphony. The medium of radio thus has an enormous contribution to make to the diffusion of musical culture. Such is not the case, unfortunately, for the plastic arts. Here the great achievements are known only to a small minority. We can talk for hours into a microphone about a certain picture of El Greco's or Van Gogh's, but if the audience does not have at least a good reproduction in front of them, there is little point in praising the merits of either painter or painting. It would be like giving a talk on Tchaikowsky without playing a single one of his composi-tions. The only means we have at our disposal for becom-ing familiar with the great works of art of the past are good printed reproductions, exhibitions and slide shows.

"Which brings us to a consideration of the unthink-able absence of Art History from the curricula of Quebec's convents and classical colleges, an essential element in the history of civilization which we have seen fit to ignore completely. The works of art stretching in a long line from antiquity to the present day are among man's most beauti-ful and lasting creations. Nevertheless, the outstanding figures are known only vaguely, if they are known at all. A knowledge of wars and the long list of generals responsible for unleashing them, seems to be the most important factor in understanding the development of the so-called civilized world. How many students leave convent or college knowing nothing about Egypt but the crossing of the Red Sea and the selling of Joseph into slavery by his brothers! What do they know about Greek sculpture, except that it comprised indecent objects adored by pagans? We could go on and on like this, but there is little point in laboring the obvious: the aesthetic side of history is considered by our teaching establishment to be material unworthy of attention. We can only hope that the time is not far off when every educational institution will make room for Art History in its study program. Our children's sensibilities can only be the better for such a change; they will learn to appreciate beauty in its many different forms. No cultivated man can afford to overlook the importance of the artistic imagination in the history of man, nor the powerful influence exercised by art over human destiny.

"But if there is one thing that is really detestable about Quebec, it is our preference for what comes from elsewhere, our infatuation with everything bearing an exotic name. This phenomenon is particularly marked in the field of art. We labor under the naive belief that whatever is produced in other countries must be better than anything we are capable of here. It would not be so bad if only we tended to choose the best of what is available from abroad. But by a curious twist of taste, we generally admire all that is shrill, ugly, and phony. We feel compelled to encourage any old dabbler who manages to arrest our attention, while we completely overlook our home-grown talent. We bow to the pontificating upstart and take his work as gospel, then show our disdain for those of our own artists who have the courage to take issue with the upstart, accusing them of professional jealousy. For mercy's sake, let us take a closer look at the effort being made by our own artists, who are faced with a continuous struggle against a society which not only ignores them but tends to prefer foreign cast-offs. Let's give them a chance, let's encourage the work that deserves encouragement. The painter is capable of more than just easel oil-painting. He should take his rightful place in society, where he belongs. Let him not be cast aside like a worthless object. Art is a powerful civilizing force. In every culture, even primitive cultures, the artist has always played an important role in the evolution of ideas. Let us now give the artist his due. Town-planning, tourism, traditional crafts, are just some of the fields which can profit from the artist's guidance in reaching their goals. If we want to win admiration for Quebec from abroad, for the achievements in our arts, for our standards of taste, it is the artist who must take charge in this field. There is nothing quite so distressing as seeing good intentions brought to grief by men whose artistic sensibilities are nil. This is a state of affairs which must be remedied at all costs if we are not to fall prey to a mediocrity worse than that which surrounds us already. Let's throw open the windows and let in some sunshine and fresh air, before our situation becomes unbearable. All around us, America is waking up to the importance of art in the growth of a society. Both the United States and Mexico have budgeted considerable sums for decoration and refurbishment projects undertaken by artists. Art is democratized by every means possible. At this very moment these two countries are producing works of art which will live long after the great captains of industry and finance are forgotten. It is time for French Canada to make its mark in the arts of the Americas. We count some remarkable artists and craftsmen among our ancestors, men who came to the New World and kept alive certain traditions and artistic skills which they brought with them from France: it is up to us to continue the task which they began."

In Defence of Art and Artists

At about the same time, Lemieux was drafting an apology for the artist and his role in society, particularly Quebec society. Here again Lemieux was the uncompromising critic of the Quebec cultural scene. He returned to the themes developed in his article of November 1941 and demonstrated that a teaching career which had by then lasted nearly ten years had in no way clouded his perceptions: "We produce art teachers, we give them diplomas and scholarships, then when they have been abroad to finish off their studies and are ready to make a contribution to Quebec's artistic life, we find them some meaningless little job which allows them no room for initiative or influence."

It is clear that Lemieux is here alluding to, among others, Borduas, Pellan and Omer Parent, the latter two of whom were sent by the government of Quebec to France, on scholarships, in 1926. On their return, they were to experience a great deal of difficulty in finding posts which would encourage the free exercise of their talents. The artist's influence can and must extend beyond the boundaries of his studio, the horizons of the classroom and a few receptive living rooms in order to make itself felt, as Lemieux so rightly stressed, in other fields of endeavor, to contribute to the broad tasks of transforming society. Quebec has rarely seen such an explicit and strongly-worded plea for a re-definition of the social functions of the artist.

On February 11, 1942, on the occasion of the weekly luncheon of the Quebec City Saint-Jean-

Baptiste Society, Jean Paul Lemieux, "artist and professor of the Ecole des beaux-arts," gave a talk on "French-Canadian painting and architecture." Until the middle of the nineteenth century, explained Lemieux, "painters and sculptors could live from their art," once they had liberated themselves from French influences and developed their own repertoire of plastic forms, which had their roots in the simple and somewhat naive ways of the peasantry. It was an art that flowered in the rural churches. But the compulsion to imitate, the mania for foreign borrowings, was revived again by portraitists like Marius Plamondon and Théophile Hamel, against whom there was fortunately a countervailing tendency in the scenes of traditional life so delightfully executed by Cornelius Krieghoff. Lemieux went on to quote from a book written by his friend Gérard Morisset and published a few months earlier, in August 1941. It was titled *Coup d'oeil sur les arts en Nouvelle-France* (Survey of the Arts in New France) and argued that Quebec's rich artistic traditions had been brutally cut off in the midst of their development by the Industrial Revolution, whose ill effects were first felt during the latter half of the nineteenth century. And, in this field, as in many others, things had only been getting worse since the turn of the century. Lemieux's remarks prompted *L'Evénement-Journal*, in its edition of February 12, to title its article on the luncheon address "Art backslides in Quebec for fifty years."

In March 1942, the magazine *Regards* republished "Notes sur le dessin" (Notes on Drawing), which Lemieux had already published in *Le Jour* on October 10, 1938.

An Affectionate Critic of Social Reality

While Lemieux did not paint a great deal between 1941 and 1951, he nevertheless produced a number of striking canvases, in particular *Lazare* (Lazarus) (1941) and *Fête-Dieu à Québec* (Corpus Christi in Quebec City) (1944). Lemieux was working hard to develop a personal style, one for which he would be indebted to no one. The artist's pictures were spread out over long intervals of six months or a year. Deep in his soul, in the furthest corners of his imagination, something was troubling Lemieux. He was already convinced that the pictorial perspective for which he had been searching was not to be found in the images of the avant-garde, nor in any of the then

Patineurs à Montmorency (Skaters in Montmorency), 1939, 76 x 102 cm, OFQ

fashionable styles, but rather in his enormous nostalgia for a childhood which was now receding irrevocably into the ever-thickening mists of time — time which stole up on him and then disappeared forever. The artist was obsessed, bewitched by the overriding realization, that there is an unbridgeable gap between present, lived reality and what he felt as his deepest source of inspiration — his childhood.

Canvases such as *Lazare*, *Le Pique-nique* (The Picnic) or *Fête-Dieu à Québec* did little or nothing to dispel his obsession; they could only provide a momentary diversion in their light-hearted look at a certain social reality. They made no inroads on Lemieux's essential artistic dilemma: his search for a personal aesthetic which would enable him to translate into plastic terms, and therefore to some extent resolve, his most heartfelt longings.

Patineurs à Montmorency (Skaters in Montmorency) (1939) is, from one angle, just a lively

Ville (City), 1940, 15 x 15 cm

watercolor of children at play, with its mass of detail sketched from life: the skaters caught in all their enthusiasm, the landscape stretching out over the river, spanned by the bridge which links the mainland to the Ile d'Orléans. At the same time, however, there is a striking feeling of nostalgia about this picture, a nostalgia on the part of the artist for that period of his childhood spent in this very area, on the cliffs downstream from Cap Diamant. A childhood seen through rose-colored glasses or perhaps, more appropriately, through the sepia-colored photographs of old family albums. Around the same period nostalgia of another kind, this time more sombre, had taken hold of Lemieux. This is evidenced, for example, in *Paysage de ville* (City Landscape) (1940). Here the message takes the form of a violent critique of the urban environment of the day, an environment which has been stripped of all its charm: an alley is depicted littered with debris; trees have been replaced by hydro-electric poles and chimneys spewing out their dense smoke; in the place of mountains there are only brutal concrete monoliths; and finally, in this French-speaking context, even the verbal message has its alienating connotation. The "diagnosis" written across the middle of the picture — "Repairs" — appears, ironically, in English. If it is not already too late, the damage must be undone, and we must start again from scratch with trees and greenery and nobler intentions.

Lemieux would often have occasion again, in both images and words, to return to this attack on the city — or at least on what the growth of industry and technology had done to the urban landscape. Some thirty years later, he would go so far as to imagine Montreal destroyed by an atomic holocaust. But in 1940, it was enough for him to let his harsh rendering of an all too prevalent reality evoke the sadness he felt when he hearkened back to the parks and gardens of his childhood.

"Notre-Dame Protégeant Québec" and "Lazare"

In 1941, two paintings opened up new perspectives in Lemieux's work. While *Notre-Dame protégeant Québec* (Notre Dame protecting Quebec) takes its basic starting-point from old-fashioned religious tradition it is also packed with elements of a very unusual sort. The presence of war planes and

Notre-Dame protégeant Québec (Notre Dame protecting Quebec), 1941, 61 x 48 cm, OFQ

paratroopers in the sky does not in itself have a very great impact on the ex-votive orthodoxy of the rest of the picture, since "Notre-Dame" is holding them in check with her left hand while she extends a protective right hand over the city of Quebec. Yet much of the sacred tone is dissipated by other, less serious departures from the main theme, such as the graphic disproportion between people and buildings, which is most certainly a calculated rather than "naive" effect. The architectural delights of the Old Capital are given considerable emphasis, as is the central role of the clergy, which is further heightened by the contrapuntal effect of secular sign-postings.

Notre-Dame protégeant Québec serves as a kind of introduction to another picture which, though in the same spirit, is much more complex in its composition: this is *Lazare*, also dating from 1941. Lemieux takes the biblical tale of the resurrection of Lazarus as his point of departure this time, and builds around it a series of images full of wit and contrasts. The winding streets and grouped figures which had already been key thematic elements in *Notre-Dame protégeant Québec* are here greatly refined and, in a number of paintings to follow, would become the foundation of an extensive architectonic for Lemieux. *Lazare* brings together three pictorial ideas:

In the upper left-hand corner we find a war scene (the reader should keep in mind that the picture was painted in 1941, at the height of the Second World War), in which a dark sky is made to appear all the more sinister by the inclusion of black airplanes and paratroopers, who are firing on a group of civilians caught unprotected in the middle of the countryside. A young girl lies bleeding beside her kneeling mother, while a man who has been shot in the back crumples at her side. Nearby, two women and two children huddle desperately behind a man armed with a gun, who is returning a paratrooper's fire.

The whole right side of the picture is taken up by a funeral procession which is about to enter a cemetery, where Christ, dressed in modern attire, is in the process of raising Lazarus from his coffin—a Lazarus who evinces less astonishment than the grave-digger in his suspenders, who drops his shovel. Above them the sky is clear, while out at sea a sailing ship cruises peacefully along (in contrast with the

71   *Lazare* (Lazarus), 1941, 102 x 84 cm (Art Gallery of Ontario, Toronto) OFQ

raven who is acting as a familiar escort to the mourners and the hearse, in the lower right-hand corner).

The centre of the picture is taken up by a church whose roof the painter has removed and in which a priest is recounting an edifying tale for the benefit of his less than attentive congregation. The tale in question is the parable of Lazarus, here given new life by the stark reality of war. A plump little cherub is poised by one foot on the roof of the pulpit and holds a miniature trumpet to his lips, in an attitude which certainly does not suggest that the Apocalypse is about to be unleashed. The sixty-odd parishioners who fill the nave and the balcony show a striking variety of expressions and attire.

The picture achieves a remarkable degree of unity, in spite of its three distinct narrative fields. The painter has shrewdly reinforced this unity by having the road act as a link through the separate spaces occupied by the cemetery, the church and the shoot-out with the paratroopers; in addition, part of the wall which surrounds the cemetery can be seen peeking through the balcony window of the church, while one corner of the cemetery, duly occupied by a gravestone, protrudes to the left of that part of the church roof left intact by the painter. The tripartite subject-matter of *Lazare* — life-death-resurrection — is developed with a verve not often encountered in this style of painting. The work has elicited a number of different reactions, such as this one from Charles C. Hill, in his excellent catalogue for an exhibition titled *Canadian Painting in the Thirties* (National Gallery of Canada, Ottawa, 1975, p. 117):

"In his own work he turned away from landscape to anecdotal and satirical depictions of country life, the most successful of which is *Lazarus*....In composition and theme this work has many parallels with Jack Macdonald's *Indian Burial, Nootka* (1937)....Jean Paul Lemieux allegorizes by the combination of multiple events in one composition, as in the Sienese works he so admired ....In this work Jean Paul Lemieux raises the anecdotal genre of social realism to the level of religious symbolism. It is unfortunate it was never incorporated in a church decoration."

These remarks show to what extent some features of Quebec's social reality are misunderstood by the outsider, for *Lazare* could never have graced the walls of a Quebec church! So facetious and playful is its tone that it would never have been allowed past the front

Study for *Emmaüs* (Emmaus), 1942, 25 x 20 cm

Le pique-nique (The Picnic), 1944, 66 x 48 cm MQ (color p. 103)

door. (It is interesting to recall, moreover, that this painting was finally purchased by the Art Gallery of Ontario, rather than by a Quebec gallery, public or private.) The similarities which Hill sees between *Lazare* and Macdonald's *Indian Burial* are based on a very loose interpretation of the two pictures, for *Lazare* is no more bound to the conventions of social realism than it is to the strictures of religious symbolism. It is a sweeping parody, almost a farce, executed in the spirit of the burlesque, but impregnated with the artist's distinctively ironical sense of humor. Nothing prevents us, on the other hand, from reading a certain earnestness into Lemieux's depiction of the atrocities of war; but any real concern with social realism or religious symbolism is sacrificed to the unusual theatricality of the picture and the comic details with which it abounds.

One can undoubtedly find connections between *Lazare* and the work of the Sienese school, specifically in the processions and architectural treatments of Ambrogio Lorenzetti, not to mention the paintings of Giotto. Some of the typical compositions of fifteenth-century Florence, those of, say, a Paolo Uccello, a Masolino, a Ghirlandajo, also gave the onlooker a view of some ceremony or event that was otherwise inaccessible behind a roof or facade. But the most important aspect of Lemieux's picture remains its diverting, ironical tone, which allows the painter to bring together in one imagined, pictorial space a series of wholly disparate scenes. In Lemieux's rendering these scenes manage to co-exist in a credible fashion, despite the distances between them in both time and space, which ordinarily would have militated against any sense of unity. What might have been grotesque in the hands of another artist here becomes a good-natured parody of one aspect of cultural and spiritual life in Quebec, thanks to Lemieux's quiet but knowing ability to synthesize such unlikely subject-matter. But no cleric from his own province would have countenanced such a picture, let alone seen it displayed within the confines of his church.

In 1942 Lemieux undertook to paint another religious subject, one which he again molded to his own purpose. Executed in a style of disarming simplicity, his *Disciples d'Emmaüs* (Disciples of Emmaus) shows two men, dressed like farmers or lumberjacks, conversing ingenuously with Christ in the middle of a Quebec village whose rustic splendor is emphasized almost to the point of caricature. A snaky road once again lends a dynamic aspect to the composition; the nuns and schoolchildren located in the bottom half of the picture were to become the chief subject of a 1944 canvas entitled *Le Pique-nique*, another picture in which the artist would rely on a curvilinear motif in his organization of the visual space. At the top of this latter picture, the local village is clustered piously around the church steeple, which to some extent functions to divert our attention away from the little girls in the foreground who have their skirts pulled up far enough to allow them to go wading in the river (the composition chooses not to give undue emphasis to the girl whose derrière is turned to us as she plays innocently with her sailboat in the foreground of the picture).

"Fête-Dieu à Québec"

Fête-Dieu à Québec (Corpus Christi celebrated in Quebec City) was the rich and majestic crowning achievement in the series of paintings completed in the early forties and characterized by curvilinear composition and the processional motif. Based on a gouache study which is remarkable in itself, the picture abounds in graphic detail and provides another typically critical glance at Quebec society. Again it is social and moral criticism of a sort that avoids weighty pronouncements and gnashing of teeth in favor of the light-hearted innuendo, the incongruous juxtaposition, the sly jibe.

The procession in this picture is S-shaped and gives the impression that it continues forever because we can make out neither the head, which is lost in front of a small church in the bowels of the Basse Ville, nor the tail, which is still emerging from the entrance of a much larger church higher up in the picture. The procession thus solemnly links up two places of worship, even as it winds its way past some of the more worldly features of this urban scene. One of these is to be found prominently situated in the foreground of the picture, a business whose name makes clear its less than pious purpose: "*Taverne du Peuple.*" The three words might even have sprung from the lips of the Madonna who floats above the procession on a huge banner and is exalted by a contrasting inscription more appropriate to the immedi-

Study for *Fête-Dieu* (Corpus Christi), 1944, 25 x 20 cm (color p. 85)

ate context: "*Ave Maria, Gratia Plena.*" Following along behind the banner and, as it happens, situated directly in front of the tavern, is a group of young girls in black dresses and white veils who are being chaperoned by two nuns. They also are dressed in black, with a white head-dress to set off the rest of the uniform, but in a style still more severe. The owner of the premises stands on his doorstep behind them, his arms folded across his chest and his expression indicating that he is not too happy about having had to put a "closed" sign ("*Fermé*") on the door of his establishment during the religious festivities. The tavern-keeper's name is plainly written, for all to see, on the facade of the building: "J. P. Lemieux, Prop."

To heighten the joke even further, the artist has painted in another man near the tavern-keeper: sporting a black hat and a moustache, he would have been identified immediately by all who knew him as Gérard Morisset, notary, expert on Quebec art and a great friend of the painter's. There is no end of colorful detail to be discovered on close scrutiny of *Fête-Dieu*. In one of the upper front windows of the tavern, between the name of the establishment and the name of its pseudo-proprietor, there is yet another notice: "Madeleine Desrosiers, modiste" (M.D., milliner). Having thus drawn his wife into the pictorial comedy, the artist goes on to represent Commander Paquette as an officer of the papal Zouaves; then transforms priest and writer Félix-Antoine Savard into a singing teacher by posting his new profession on the door in the lower right-hand corner of the picture; catches a little boy in the midst of urinating behind a tree located in the upper right-hand corner; and, in the same general area, depicts a couple of tourists in a calash (who would appear to be indifferent to the colorful religious ceremony unfolding nearby), as well as a couple of priests strolling through the spacious grounds of their seminary.

The city of Quebec plays a leading role in *Fête-Dieu*, as it would do again in many other paintings over the course of the artist's long career. Here he captures not merely certain physical aspects of Quebec, its geography and its architecture, but also something of its underlying spirit. Lemieux gives us a penetrating look at the mentality of the simple folk who inhabit his native province: in the context of a suitably reverential religious ceremony, they are shown to be divided between their traditional at-

Fête-Dieu à Québec (Corpus Christi in Quebec City), 1944, 152 x 123 cm, MQ

Vase de fleurs (Vase of Flowers), 1968, 36 x 26 cm

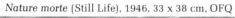
Nature morte (Still Life), 1946, 33 x 38 cm, OFQ

tachment to the litany, and their irrepressible sense of good fun, between, as it were, altar and tavern. A sense of humor seems to dominate, though some thirty years after its completion the artist wished to clarify the motives that lay behind the work, in the course of an interview with the author at the Ile aux Coudres during the summer of 1972. "I didn't intend the picture to be a criticism, a caricature or an object lesson. I simply wanted to show things and people as they were at a time when Quebec was still dominated by the clergy. I wondered how I might represent our little universe in a single image, how I might capture the colorful daily life of these people, with their mode of dress, their ideas, their feelings. The processional motif intrigued me visually and in those days, two big processions, for Saint-Jean-Baptiste Day and the Fête-Dieu, were high points of the year. I finally chose the second."

Lemieux approached his subject from a very high angle by planting his easel on a kind of promontory, thus giving the picture an unusually cinematic feel. Perhaps the artist had recalled that in 1916, D. W. Griffith used dirigibles to shoot some of the sprawling scenes in his film *Intolerance*. Lemieux has suggested though that his inspiration was drawn more strictly from his own medium: "I was fascinated by Bruegel at the time."

Traditionalism and American Realism

Apart from certain large canvases such as *Lazare* and *Fête-Dieu*, Lemieux painted several dozen smaller works between 1940 and 1947. They, like the former, were for the most part concerned with humorous observations on life in Quebec. He also executed a number of large nudes, which show a greater preoccupation with pure form than with programmatic or anecdotal aspects of the subject-matter.

In 1946 he completed a painting called *Nature morte* (Still Life), of great beauty and originality. Somewhat reminiscent of certain still lifes of Braque (we have in mind especially the 1925 painting held by the Tate Gallery), this work by Lemieux is highly distinctive, despite the great popularity of the genre during that period. Lemieux would never, in fact, paint many still lifes himself, unless we include those pictures in which objects arranged on a table play some role in a larger composition.

79 *Le fruit noir* (The Black Fruit), 1943, 102 x 75 cm

Scène d'enterrement (Burial Scene), 1945, 30 x 36 cm, OFQ

Les chasseurs (The Hunters), 1946, 91 x 71 cm, MQ

From 1944 to 1947, Lemieux painted a number of canvases with typical aspects of Quebec life as their subject — *Beauport, Scène d'enterrement* (Burial Scene, in which the processional motif is adapted to a particularly sinister situation), *Les Chasseurs* (The Hunters). The 1947 picture titled *The Birds I Have Known* (original English) is a study of a group of Anglophone bird-watchers in the midst of what appears to be a formal meeting. Mid-way between a sketch for a family portrait and full-blown caricature, and with its impact stemming from this very ambiguity, this little picture forms part of a series of notebook studies which range from the reading of a will in a notary's office to an embarkation for the Quebec City-Lévis crossing. Full of good-natured humor, these minor works balance off irony against indulgence, the condemning glance against the conspiratorial wink. They bear witness to the painter's generous feelings towards the colorful realities of life in Quebec City, a social microcosm with which he was on such intimate terms, and which he preferred by far to the contrived hurly-burly of life in Montreal. In contrast to the avant-gardist pretentions which pervaded the Montreal art scene under the inspiration of Borduas and Pellan, Lemieux clung to the earthy realism of a more traditional way of life and to the old-fashioned vision of the rural story-tellers.

A number of these works were more or less connected with an art movement that had been very prominent in the United States between 1920 and 1940 known as the "American Scene." While it flourished in New York, it also spread to Boston, Buffalo, Philadelphia, Chicago and right to the West Coast. The "American Scene" painters were the heirs to an earlier movement known after 1916 as the "Ashcan School." This group included the American painters, Henri, Sloan, Bellows, Shinn, Glachens, Luks, who were students of the seamier side of city life, of urban ugliness. They in turn had their roots in the realist strain of American painting which developed in the late nineteenth century. The chief task of all three of these schools was to describe various aspects of daily life among the working classes, without any embellishment of their material. Indeed, they were resolutely opposed to any attempt to glorify reality, cover up poverty, or transform the down-to-earth realities of daily life into a shiny, antiseptic and artificial showcase. These painters felt duty-bound to

The Birds I Have Known, 1947, 23 x 26 cm

give an honest eye-witness account of what they saw around them, even if this meant a brutal and disturbing final product. They were not however above an occasional humorous observation.

Lemieux had had the opportunity to see a number of canvases of this sort during trips to the United States. He frequently acknowledged his fascination with the American realists and the Ashcan School, in particular, with certain exponents of the American Scene such as Edward Hopper, Grant Wood and Thomas Hart Benton, as well as the Social Realism painters of the dirty thirties, Ben Shahn, Reginald Marsh and so on. By examining closely a picture of Lemieux's like *Lazare* or *Pont-Lévis*, we find more similarities with, say, *Tenement* (1935) by George Biddle or *Vanity Fair* (1946 and thus later than *Lazare*) by Henry Koerner, than we might with the altar in *The Seven Sacraments* by Rogier van der Weyden, *The Passion of Christ* by Memling (Turin), the *Temptation of Saint Anthony* by Bosch (Lisbon), the *Triumph of Death* by Bruegel the Elder (Prado) or with the *Tower of Babel* by ''Monsù'' Desiderio.

Over the course of the 1940-50 period, Lemieux thus found satisfaction in creating humorous studies of the social environment which surrounded him and for which he showed great fondness. But he would subsequently be compelled to leave these familiar surroundings in order to free himself from the easy enticements of the picturesque and anecdotal style. Though Lemieux had already begun to feel the urge to explore a different form of art, he would not find the key to a new pictorial vision until much later, when he found himself far from his native land, as is often the case with those whose business is to create artistic forms. Constant immersion in one environment makes appreciation of any other rather difficult. The artist who keeps his nose too close to the canvas cannot expect to see very much. Or as Rembrandt is supposed to have put it: ''a picture is not made to be sniffed at; besides, there's nothing pleasant about the smell of oil paint . . . . ''

Lemieux would more than once feel the need to step back, to put some distance between himself and all that was most familiar. He had this laconic, but far-reaching remark to make about the turning-point which occurred in his work in 1955-56: ''I had to leave Quebec before I really discovered things about myself. . . .''

Ferment in Montreal, 1945

It was in the latter half of the 1940s that Quebec's artistic revolution really took hold. The prime movers, Pellan and Borduas, who were located in Montreal, were soon pitted against each other and added fuel to the fire of their debates by lining up sympathizers on both sides.

After his return to Quebec in 1940, Pellan was refused a teaching post at the Ecole des beaux-arts in his hometown, Quebec City, where as far back as 1938 he had been judged ''too modern.'' In 1943, he was hired by Montreal's Ecole des beaux-arts to teach painting and he soon touched off a conflagration in the explosive atmosphere of the fusty old academy. The school's troubles spilled over into public confrontations and the Director was finally forced to resign his job in late 1945. Borduas, for his part, became involved in a series of broad social and cultural issues and in 1943 organized a group of militant artists, his Automatists, who were to remain a more coherent body than the group which gravitated to Pellan. Borduas and his friends exhibited in New York from 1946 on, in Montreal in 1946 and 1947, and in Paris in 1947.

The most telling aspect of these sweeping changes in Quebec's artistic climate was perhaps the over-hasty, and therefore largely unthinking, shift from slavish academic conformity to a kind of frenzied avant-gardism — which to all appearances was no less hide-bound itself. One may well wonder, as did Lemieux himself at the time from his vantage point in Beauport, a comfortable distance from the commotion in Montreal — what point is served by leaving behind the slavish imitation of artistic forms held to be obsolete, for the equally slavish imitation of allegedly "progressive" forms. Lemieux, in any case, kept his distance from what went on in Montreal between 1945 and 1949. He remained sceptical, and convinced that complete personal freedom was the only ideology worth serious consideration by the artist engaged in the perilous adventure of creation. Confronted with the frenzied and intolerant outlook of the fashionable artistic movements which were then sweeping Montreal, Lemieux felt entirely indisposed to plunge headlong into the fray. He preferred to fall back on his own devices, to follow the course he had marked out for himself, to follow it at his own pace, slow and plodding as it might be, and to proceed within the context of his own values — values which would not bend to external influences or to the impact of fashionable new trends. Fifteen years earlier he had deplored the stuffy orthodoxy of Montreal's Ecole des beaux-arts; now, in 1945, the stuffy orthodoxy of the "revolutionaires" prompted a similar reaction from Lemieux. He watched with curiosity, but a certain indifference, as the manifestoes *Prisme d'Yeux* (Prism of Eyes) and then *Refus global* (Categorical Refusal) appeared, the first in February 1948, the second in August of the same year. They led to Borduas' immediate dismissal from his teaching post at the Ecole du meuble in Montreal.

Lemieux's reaction to the stir created by the Paris School in 1936-37 was not to rush to his easel and begin producing canvases conceived in more or less the same style, in spite of his deep and passionate admiration for what the School had accomplished. In other words he had sufficient respect for these new works to refrain from aping them in a crude and slavish manner. He was of the opinion that everyone had to set his own goals; it was an idea he often aired in his painting classes. Indeed, he seemed at one point to turn his back on the accomplishments of the Paris School and divert his attention to concerns which had grown purely out of Quebec's artistic traditions. Thus he borrowed from Krieghoff a warmth of style that informs many of his studies of rural Quebec life. Lemieux absorbed his recent pictorial discoveries as he went on with painting rustic scenes characteristic of the province that was his home.

Quebec City in Transition

In 1945, Lemieux took part in an exhibition mounted by UNESCO in Paris designed to illustrate the development of painting in Canada. Meanwhile, life went on as ever in Quebec City until the war which had been drawing to a close, terminated abruptly with the world's first atomic holocaust. At the Ecole des beaux-arts, some of the ex-servicemen who had not been killed on the field of battle attempted now to reintegrate themselves into a so-called normal life. During the Second World War, Quebec society had undergone certain changes: women could now be seen working outside the home; the unions waged battles which, while they did not always swing the advantage to the workers, nevertheless began to shake up the traditional distribution of power; and the colleges and universities were somewhat more accessible to children from working-class backgrounds. The seeds of the "Quiet Revolution," which did not begin in earnest until 1960, had already been sown.

———

Study for *Fête-Dieu*, 1944 (p. 75)

Port-au-Persil, 1950, 26 x 21 cm (Mme. Lyse Picher)

In December 1947, Lemieux published an article in a special issue of *Canadian Art* devoted to Quebec. Entitled "Quebec City and the Arts," the article provided a broad overview of artistic development from the first sketchers of Cap Diamant to Pellan, Dallaire and Claude Picher, and took in the English-speaking military watercolorists, copyist Chevalier Falardeau and portraitists, Plamondon and Hamel. For all that he was a careful and perspicacious student of cultural life in Quebec, Lemieux continued to steer clear of the troubles that engulfed Montreal's artistic community between 1947 and 1949. He observed the events of this period with detachment, never losing his sense of perspective, or his sense of irony. He would later explain to the present author that he had been left "completely unaffected" by the noisy protestations for which Pellan and Borduas were responsible. While he could perfectly well understand their motives, he took issue with the idea of employing such raucous means in the name of art. Sooner or later, Lemieux realized, this boisterous rebellion would be put down . . . "I watched it all from the sidelines and never let it influence my work." (*La Presse*, April 13, 1963)

For a period of about two years, in fact, Lemieux had abandoned his easel and it was not until the summer of 1950, during his vacation at Port-au-Persil, that he picked up his brushes again and executed a rapid series of paintings. From October 29 to November 6, 1950, he exhibited these fresh, unpretentious little pictures in his home. The product of two months' leisure spent happily by the banks of the Saint Lawrence, these works captured various moments of the artist's life, fragments of his surroundings. They quickly found buyers; but above all else, they succeeded in reconciling Lemieux with his painting once again.

During the same period, Lemieux gave a talk to the University Women's Club of Quebec City on the history of European painting from the end of the Gothic era. Using the four seasons as a structural metaphor and drawing inspiration from Spengler's *The Decline of the West*, Lemieux situated the springtime of European painting in the fourteenth and fifteenth centuries; the summer around the blossoming of the great works of Leonardo da Vinci, Michelangelo and Raphael; the autumn in the period

La croix (The Cross), 1950, 25 x 20 cm

Paysage de Saint-Antoine de Tilly
(Landscape in Saint-Antoine de Tilly), 1950, 20 x 25 cm
(Galerie Le Parrain des Artistes, Quebec)

Port-au-Persil, 1950

up to the nineteenth century; and the winter in the period of "modern" art. Lemieux concentrated particularly in this talk on developments in color technique, and paid special attention to the Venetian and Florentine schools, David, Delacroix and the Impressionists.

The Turning Point

The years from 1951 to 1955 mark that period of Lemieux's long career when his art underwent its most profound transformation. He pursued his teaching assignments at the Ecole des beaux-arts, except during 1954-55, when he spent nearly a year's sojourn in France. On his return, he put aside the visual memories of his trip and suddenly embarked on a whole new pictorial enterprise — or so it would seem from a rapid perusal of the evolution of his painting from one year to the next. But spontaneous generation is as foreign to art as it is to biology, and what might appear in 1956 to be an abrupt departure in Lemieux's work had already been brewing for some time, especially since 1951 and a picture entitled *Les Ursulines* (The Ursulines).

In January 1951, an article by Lemieux appeared in the Montreal magazine *Arts et pensée* which decried "the unhappy history of foreign junk in our province." Once again the painter reveals to us an important side of his artistic personality, that of the passionate devotee of traditional art and handicrafts and of the countless sublime pieces of work that make up Quebec's national cultural heritage. Writing at a time when his subject was rarely broached in such outspoken terms, Lemieux levelled a scathing attack on the degeneration of public taste; the "infatuation with things produced abroad, to the detriment of those created at home"; the flood of mass-produced statuary and the shabby, trumped-up ornamentation which had overrun Quebec's churches. He went on to denounce the manner in which the province had been swamped by junk of all sorts, from tacky color prints to tasteless devotional objects, many of which had travelled a great distance to reach their final destination. As "our fine old wooden statues and wardrobes with the characteristic diamond-shaped peaks" are being sold off at ludicrous prices to American dealers and tourists, who come rushing up to Quebec looking for spoils, "we are unwittingly selling off our past, a whole tradition handed down from father to son over the centuries, the legacy of our history.... Nowadays, our fascination with the exotic, with whatever comes from afar, has diminished a little [...] Let us stop lavishing unthinking admiration on what comes to us from elsewhere and take a look at what can be accomplished here at home. This will enable us to create an art of our very own, which, as Canadian as it may be, will eventually win world-wide recognition."

It was on this challenging note that Lemieux brought to an end the series of articles which he had published intermittently from 1935 to 1951.

"Les Ursulines"

An important new work soon began to take shape on Lemieux's easel. Titled *Les Ursulines*, it had been carefully laid out beforehand, first in a sketch, then in a painted study. In November 1951 this picture secured for the artist the grand prize for painting, and a $1,500 scholarship, in a province-wide artistic competition. It was chosen from among 305 submissions, 130 of which were put on exhibit at the Musée de Québec. Pellan, Dallaire, Léon Bellefleur, Denys Morisset and Raymond Lasnier were among the artists honored by the jury. Lemieux himself, in a statement made at the Salon opening, declared that "French Canada [would] make its mark in the world not so much by its commercial as by its artistic achievement."

Recognition for *Les Ursulines* and the painter's election to the Royal Canadian Academy of Arts as an associate member, fired up Lemieux's enthusiasm for painting once again. Another 1951 picture, entitled *Portrait de Gabriel* (Portrait of Gabriel), shows the artist moving towards a pared-down style, but this process of pictorial simplification is still more evident in *Les Ursulines*, particularly when we follow the evolution of the work through its three stages of execution. Accessories, embellishments, vegetation disappear, giving way in the finished work to a wholly new dynamic which reflects the achievement of Cézanne and, in its disarmingly simple handling of figures and setting, offers a fresh approach to the use of form and color. Although the final version of this composition may appear at first glance to be rather static, closer inspection reveals the internal tension

Sketch for *Les Ursulines* (The Ursulines), 1951, 20 x 26 cm

Study for *Les Ursulines*, 1951, 20 x 26 cm, OFQ (Dr. Amyot Jolicoeur)

Les Ursulines, 1951, 61 x 76 cm, MQ (color p. 104)

Portrait de Gabriel (Portrait of Gabriel), 1951, OFQ

which governs the carefully controlled, orderly, systematic layout of its various elements, clear evidence of the consummate skill of a painter who has reached his prime (with experience accrued through both his own work and his teaching), and has now rediscovered the unfettered vision of childhood.

Les Ursulines is imbued with an air of serenity, a feeling of oneness between beings and things. Here in the walled-in garden of the convent, the sense of disquiet which lies just beneath the surface is resolved by the sure hand of the artist, who imparts a delicate balance to this innovative pictorial syntax. Lemieux would later explain to the author that he has always been struck by the astonishing self-assurance displayed by the earth's creatures and even more so by the fact that this quality is displayed by objects, which do not move, and yet seem to watch us make a fuss and then pass on with perfect indifference. Thus the inanimate world seems in a sense, because of its relative permanence, its utter placidity, and its stillness, to dominate the unsettled, disquieting world of human beings, who are haunted by time and its inexorable forward motion. A double temptation results: to undo the stolid rule of objects and at the same time to provide living creatures with a greater semblance of stability. Again, the sheer proliferation of objects can be viewed as a challenge to the artist, a kind of aesthetic threat, which he may try to meet by eliminating from his work the largest possible number of objects and details, by representing the world around him in its most essential way. Naturally, the artist cannot reduce the objects in his purview to naught without also eradicating the imprint left by man on the things around him, without eradicating the patina that life imparts to objects as they are used, well or badly — to say nothing of what would happen to the object that owes its very existence to the artist, the painting itself.

The evolution of *Les Ursulines* reveals much about Lemieux's new outlook. As we move from the original sketch to the painted study, then from there to the final canvas, we observe a ruthless weeding out of objects and details. Between the sketch and the intermediate picture, windows, chimneys, architectural decorations (shutters, detail from the arches), even a statue and two of the nuns, all disappear; the final canvas then eliminates the tree on the right-hand side, the nun standing in the doorway, the

sidewalks, the gables, a covered walkway, the flowers
to the left of the nuns, etc. All this suggests that the
painter sought to reduce the content of the picture to
its most simple and concentrated form, in order to
give it greater unity and wider scope. The artist has
attempted to arrive at an understanding of the inner
workings of the creatures and things with which he is
confronted, then has stripped them of superfluous
accessories and much of their detail—and indeed of
part of their very essence—all in order to wring some
ultimate secret from them, to force entry into their
very soul and spirit.

The 1951-54 Period

The artist could already see troubling implications developing out of this departure in his work, for
it meant an end to any easy, pleasurable communication with other creatures, as well as to the charm of
humorous, anecdotal renderings of social reality. In
1951, the year Lemieux painted *Les Ursulines*, he also
created *Portrait de Gabriel* (alluded to above), in
which he captures the perplexed, almost dazed expression of a young man isolated, lost in his solitude.
Solitude would in fact be the title of a 1953 picture

shot through with a similar feeling of absence and desolation. A woman abandoned to her thoughts is seated in a room in front of a window which is so nearly opaque that even the eye cannot penetrate to the outside world. The universe has closed in around the confines of her little cell and around the "prisoner," whose sense of anguish is exceeded only by the desolation of the setting. The painter's use of converging lines reinforces the impression of a person feeling "cornered." In another 1953 work entitled *Les Servantes* (The Servants), the artist takes up the theme of the difficulties of communication between people, of lives which, despite being in day-to-day contact, pass each other by like ships in the night. Later still, in 1966, Lemieux would use his pared-down style to great advantage in a work entitled *La Servante* (The Servant) (see p. 233).

Beginning with *Les Ursulines*, and excepting a few mural projects which we will discuss later, Lemieux became a painter concerned with states of the soul, and the organization of color and volume would now serve the interests of theme, of affective content, of the very spirit of the picture. As one might expect, it was with a certain trepidation that Lemieux undertook to develop further the new perspectives opened up by *Les Ursulines*, perspectives which would not reach their full potential until some five years after the first insights of this picture. Meanwhile, as though he might be feeling a touch of vertigo in the face of this new adventure, he was taking care to sound out the mysteries of time and solitude which lie concealed behind the apparent permanence of things, waiting to be discovered by the efforts of human consciousness.

In 1952, a few months after completion of *Les Ursulines*, Lemieux seemed to experience a period of serious hesitation, and turned back for the moment to less unsettling subject-matter. With the picture entitled *Québec* (Quebec City) the artist rediscovered the spirit of *Lazare* and *Fête-Dieu*, in which there is a concern with the picturesque daily life of his fellow citizens, rendered in an anecdotal fashion and spiced with a little innocent social commentary.

The vast horizontal panorama of *Québec* was executed as a study for a mural, which was itself never undertaken. The first thing we notice about this

Québec (Quebec City), 1952, 102 x 25 cm, OFQ (Queen Elizabeth II)

composition is its solid, thoughtful architecture, which tends to be somewhat formalistic in the right half of the picture. This is Quebec City in winter, dominated by snow-covered Cap Diamant, and bustling with activity in its every neighborhood, to the extent that we may fail to appreciate the careful layout of architectural and scenic elements and let ourselves be caught up in the pictorial hide-and-seek with which the painter has amused himself. The master of ironic humor has here given us a mischievous look at the Old Capital in a naive or ingenuous style. So we would gather at least from the gross disproportion between people and buildings, the overlapping planes, the systematic simplification of related elements, the deliberate curtailment of perspective and color effects. This painting of Lemieux's would later be purchased by the Chaudière Regiment and given

as a gift to Queen Elizabeth II on the occasion of her coronation in June 1953.

———

In 1952, Lemieux took part in an exhibition organized by the Vancouver Art Gallery entitled "Retrospective of French-Canadian Art." That same year he took part in the "Canadian Group of Painters" exhibition at the Montreal Museum of Fine Arts, and during May he appeared in an exhibition mounted by a Quebec City bookstore (Librairie Tardivel), along with nine other Quebec artists. Among the artists were Benoît East, Albert Rousseau, and two younger men, Denys Morisset and Denys Matte.

In 1953, Lemieux took part in a group show at the National Gallery of Canada, in Ottawa, and then had his first one-man show at the Palais Montcalm in Quebec City, from April 15 to 25. Landscapes dominated the forty-five or so canvases presented, most of which were painted in the area of Charlevoix and near the Saguenay.

Paysage des Laurentides (Laurentian Landscape), 1954, OFQ

The spring of 1954 inspired some of Lemieux's finest work, landscapes of great sensitivity whose every stroke bespeaks the artist's delicate touch. In one of these, titled *Le Printemps* (Spring), a woman

Le Printemps (Spring), 1954, 38 x 61 cm

Le déjeuner (Lunch), 1954, 47 x 61 cm

and her young daughter are walking through a park alive with new blossoms. The artist renders their somewhat riotous delights in a scene of extravagant rebirth, in defiance of the time not long past when nature was buried beneath ice and snow. The style of the work is rapid, pulsating, with a hatching effect in the brushstrokes, a direct response to the scene nature has presented to the painter's eye. The colors strain at the earth and the vegetation and explode into the air like a kind of wild perfume. The cycle of nature's birth finds an echo too in the figures of mother and daughter.

Later on in 1954, Lemieux turned back to the cloistered garden of *Les Ursulines* and, as though he regretted having eliminated from the painted study and final work of 1951 the statue which occupied the right side of the original sketch, the artist now planted his statue in the middle of a new picture, appropriately entitled *La Statue* (The Statue). The greater part of this work is taken up with a striking view of the Château Frontenac, Cap Diamant and the Saint Lawrence River, but the picture as a whole suffers from a failure to recapture the exquisite serenity of *Les Ursulines*. But Lemieux was not to be stopped here. In 1955 he undertook a fresh assault on the cloister, so to speak, and completed a painting called *La Fête au Couvent* (Convent Feast). It managed to retrieve the pictorial vitality of *Les Ursulines* and at the same time add a touch of humor, with a somewhat condemning ring to it (the painter would later admit to an admiration for Voltaire). It shows seven priests seated at table in the convent garden, while two nuns, taken straight from *Les Ursulines*, are busy serving up a banquet which they have prepared.

La Statue (The Statue), 1954, 107 x 130 cm, OFQ

La Fête au couvent (Convent Feast), 1955, 108 x 143 cm, NGC

An "Abstract" Leg-Pull

An important event in the artist's life separated *La Fête au couvent* from *La Statue* and *Les Ursulines*, namely an extended stay in Europe with his family. This was preceded by a series of other events worthy of mention.

From April 20 to May 4, the Galerie Antoine, located in Victoria Square, Montreal, mounted an exhibition entitled *La Matière chante* (The Material Sings). It brought together work by twenty-four painters, including Marcel Barbeau, Fernand Leduc, Rita Letendre, Jean-Paul Mousseau and Jean Paul Lemieux. Disguising himself under the pseudonym Paul Blouyn, Lemieux had contributed a work from Quebec City which amounted to an "automatist" hoax. Titled *L'Oiseau roc* (The Rock Bird), it managed to capture the attention of Paul-Emile Borduas, who had come especially from New York (where he had been more or less in exile since September 1953), in order to select and mount paintings for the exhibition.

A violent polemic then got under way, notably in the newspaper *L'Autorifé*, between Claude Picher, a leading figure in Quebec's artistic community, and Claude Gauvreau, the fiery spokesman of Montreal's Automatist group. Picher would later take a more lenient attitude towards non-figurative art, but Gauvreau was never anything less than peevish in regard to Lemieux's practical joke. Even the passing of fifteen years did nothing to temper the poet's obsession and in 1969 he would attack Lemieux for the "disgustingly morose and antiquated rubbish that rates him a highly tenuous local reputation."[11]

For Lemieux, the spring of 1954 was to be the only time that he attempted a non-figurative work, though this did not prevent him from developing an inventive style of his own. Nor did this lead him to spurn the undertakings of Borduas and his Automatists. Indifferent he may have been, but not disparaging. In the end, therefore, the leg-pull perpet-

---

[11] In *La Barre du Jour*, special number on "Les Automatistes," 1969, p. 95. See also G. Robert, *L'Art au Québec depuis 1940*, pp. 103-106.

rated by the "Blouyn" canvas turned out to be nothing more than a pleasant moment's diversion for a community which tended to take itself far too seriously.

The Sojourn in France, 1954-55

From September 1954 to September 1955, Lemieux was on leave from the Ecole des beaux-arts, and, after an unbroken stretch of teaching lasting twenty years, a scholarship from the Royal Society of Canada allowed him to spend most of this sabbatical in France with his wife and their daughter, Anne, then about ten. The Lemieux family went first to Paris. By November they were in Cannes; they travelled up the Riviera and stopped in Menton, a pretty little town full of flowers overlooking one of the most beautiful bays in the Mediterranean, close to the Italian frontier. From December 1954 to April 1955, Lemieux painted a series of watercolors and oils, twenty-eight of which would be exhibited a year later in Quebec City.

Lemieux paid close attention to the beauties of the Côte d'Azur, which had already had a luminous and luxurious rendering at the hands of Bonnard and Matisse. He also explored the inland side of the region, Provence, which he knew from Cézanne's striking reconstructions. Like Nicolas de Staël, Lemieux might well have complained about being forced to tour this "marvellous region with Cézanne and Bonnard underfoot every step of the way."[12] Lemieux's brilliant young student Edmund Alleyn had drawn his attention to the work of the then little-known de Staël. The restrained landscapes executed by de Staël in the early fifties, which would come to resemble the beach scenes at Varengeville painted by Braque late in his life, set Lemieux to thinking about the possibilities of an altered pictorial space. But his new vision would only develop with time, as his watchful eye was sharpened and brightened by the unaccustomed splendor of the South of France through the spring of 1955.

---

[12] André Chastel, *Nicolas de Staël*, p. 210. In his preface (p. 23), Chastel dates this comment 1950, but the letter containing it was written at Bormes-les-Pins on June 7, 1952.

Terrasse sur la Côte d'Azur (Terrace on the French Riviera), 1955, 36 x 28 cm, OFQ

La Promenade des Anglais, 1955

La Jetée à Menton (The Jetty at Menton), 1955, 27 x 34 cm, RG

In the interim, the artist's hand hesitated, seduced by the sensuous charms of the Mediterranean. In *Terrasse sur la Côte d'Azur* (Terrace on the French Riviera), the painter captures the feeling of luminous warmth which pervades his room. In *La Promenade des Anglais à Nice* (The *Promenade des Anglais* in Nice), he sets off in startling relief the particular way in which each element catches the sun and the eye of the beholder. In *La Jetée à Menton* (The Jetty in Menton), he rubs shoulders with de Staël.

Lemieux's scholarship, paid in French francs drawn from funds provided to pay off France's war debt to Canada, prevented him from travelling around Europe as freely as he might have liked. During the summer of 1955, he left the Côte d'Azur and went up to Brittany, stopping to paint in Saint-Gildas, and around the Gulf of Morbihan, a short distance from Carnac. The watercolors Lemieux executed around Saint-Gildas, such as *Paysage de Bretagne* (Brittany Landscape), remain among his finest pictures. They show wide-ranging freedom of style and give evidence of the pleasure the artist must have felt in seeing his approach change so radically, like a rite of passage. And indeed, he would point out later on that it is often by going abroad that an artist finds himself, or at least discovers in himself a certain potential hitherto undetected and unexplored and which had been held back by the demands of a daily routine. For Lemieux this did not in any way amount to a betrayal of his homeland, towards which he now felt a greater sense of accommodation than he had before 1955. It was as though leaving had given new life to roots too long stifled in the confines of an imagination which had become short-sighted due to lack of stimulation.

Return to Quebec City; the Société des Arts Plastiques

Immediately on his return to Quebec City in September 1955, Lemieux took up his teaching once more at the Ecole des beaux-arts; meanwhile his enthusiasm for painting had been rekindled by his stay in France. He pressed on with his work, but a picture like *Eglise de Menton* (Church at Menton) left him dissatisfied. He was looking for something else. At fifty-two Lemieux had the weight and solidity of his

Paysage de Bretagne (Brittany Landscape), 1955, 38 x 46 cm

Eglise de Saint-Gildas (Church at Saint-Gildas), 1955, 38 x 46 cm

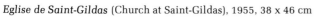

Saint-Gildas, 1955, 38 x 46 cm

Eglise de Menton (Church at Menton), 1955, 38 x 46 cm, OFQ

artistic maturity to fall back on; now he strove to reach new heights, to achieve a certain serenity, to put some distance between himself and his milieu without however slipping into an attitude of indifference.

The result was that Lemieux became involved in the work of an activist artistic association, one of the only times in his long, solitary career that this would happen. The artists of Quebec City were conversant with Lemieux's opinions on the role of the artist in society and with the demands he had made on behalf of his colleagues in various published articles. These opinions marked him out as a natural choice to lead the association which a number of Quebec City artists were busy trying to organize in 1955.

This project, inspired to a large extent by painter Claude Picher — then director of exhibitions at the Musée de Québec — answered an indisputable need acknowledged by nearly all of Quebec's artists, namely, to unite them "as a cohesive group in order to gain wider recognition in the community at large."

From January to October 1955, there were interminable discussions which resulted finally in a Society charter, the creation of a twelve-member board of directors and the election of an executive committee, of which Jean Paul Lemieux became the first chairman — much to his surprise.

An article which appeared in January 1956 in the first issue of the magazine *Vie des Arts*, provided a clear statement of the goals that the president of the Société des arts plastique, and his secretary Claude Picher, had set themselves. They first raised the point, often raised before, that the public regarded artists with altogether too much indifference, and they went on to deplore the "traditional individualism" that isolated most artists. The first executive committee wanted above all to "imbue artists with a sense of solidarity, so that they might join forces and undertake to protect the interests of one and all." The Association was prepared to welcome artists working in any plastic medium: painting and sculpture were naturally included, but so too were weaving, ceramics, enameling, photography, engraving, graphic design and so on.

Le pique-nique (The Picnic), 1944 (p. 74)

Les Ursulines (The Ursulines), 1951 (p. 89)

Quebec's artists, according to the executive council, had to learn to rid themselves of "a certain inferiority complex," which too often resulted in "an undiscerning admiration for what came from abroad" and a disdain for domestic artistic production. These were ideas, of course, that had been expounded previously by Lemieux, especially in the article discussed above which appeared in January 1951 in *Arts et pensée*.

The Société's program envisaged the creation of an exhibition circuit which would allow its members' work to be shown in all regions of the province. The intention was to decentralize the association's activities and set up a number of regional offices throughout Quebec. A concerted campaign had to be undertaken to persuade the government to earmark 1 per cent of its public works budget for the beautification of public buildings. A continuing battle had to be waged against the tide of bad taste which now left its mark in almost every domain. The association felt it would be desirable to have at least one exhibition of their members' work travel to the major cities of Canada every year, an effort which the National Gallery in Ottawa might collaborate on. Finally, a permanent collection of work might be built up which could go abroad, on loan, in order to promote the cause of Quebec culture outside the borders of the province.

A number of the proposals contained in the Société's program of action had been outlined in the writings and speeches of its first president as far back as 1938. This thoughtful and remarkably coherent program placed Quebec's artistic problems in a dynamic socio-cultural perspective. It demonstrated that Quebec City had not only followed fifteen years of turmoil in Montreal with great attention (from the creation of the Contemporary Art Society in 1939 to the battle waged by Pellan at the Ecole des beaux-arts and the undertakings of the Automatists), but also intended to avoid the bellicose approach of the Montreal community. The Quebec City artists were also determined to repatriate to the capital the cultural initiative that Montreal had arrogated to itself.

This perfectly legitimate ambition was facilitated by the fact that the two leading lights in the field of the plastic arts were absent from Montreal in 1955. Borduas had gone into self-exile in the United States

Children's class, Quebec City Ecole des beaux-arts, 1956 (Photo Antoine Dumas)

in the spring of 1953 and left for Paris in September 1955; Pellan was in Paris from December 1952 to December 1955 and in any case had withdrawn from the public forum as far back as Borduas's dismissal in September 1948.

Thus the Société des arts plastiques, presided over in Quebec City by Jean Paul Lemieux, undertook to redefine the function of the artist in contemporary Quebec society through a program of well-organized activities. If this program did not achieve all the success the executive council of the Société had hoped for, this was largely because too few artists chose to participate fully—especially those from the Montreal area — while certain others became discouraged too quickly and simply lost interest.

Nevertheless, the original program of the Société des arts plastiques is still admirable for its vitality, its toughness and its lack of bellicosity (the quality that, from the very beginning, doomed the *Refus global* to failure in 1948). Twenty years after its publication, we are in a better position to appreciate its breadth and relevance, though we may note with a certain chagrin that its goals still have not been achieved and that virtually every year one or another of these goals is set as a new priority for Quebec's artistic community.

The "Côte d'Azur" Exhibition of 1956

Let us return now to Lemieux's own work as a painter. From March 1 to March 14, 1956, the Quebec City gallery L'Atelier, located at 12 rue Sainte-Anne, presented an exhibition of twenty-eight pictures completed a year earlier in the South of France by Lemieux. Claude Picher, who in addition to working as an exhibition organizer for the Musée de Québec and as the secretary of the Société des arts plastiques, wrote art criticism from time to time, published his comments on this exhibition of work by his friend Lemieux, entitled "Côte d'Azur." Picher stressed the originality of Lemieux's approach, which managed to avoid the pitfalls of both the picture-postcard style and mere variations on the supreme pictorial achievements of the celebrated painters who had worked in the same beautiful countryside. What the writer appreciated particularly about Lemieux's work

En haut de Menton (Above Menton), 1955, OFQ
Opening of the "Côte d'Azur" exhibition, 1956

was "the vistas drenched in blues, mauves, emerald greens, a world in which the color is never fixed, in which tints shade off into one another, in which the earth seems as light as the leaves of an olive tree." (*Vie des Arts*, March 1956, pp. 24-25) Picher spoke highly of Lemieux's artistic integrity, his refusal to borrow from those who had already so effectively sung the praises of the South of France and the quality of the light in Provence; or from those who were already listed in the "dictionary of avant-garde academicism." He congratulated the painter for having "the courage to rethink [both] nature" and his painting at the same time, using the stimulating influence of the Mediterranean light, which allowed him to discover "an enchanted world, which seems to belong to the realm of dreams."

The "Côte d'Azur" exhibition, which had been opened by Gérard Morisset, curator of the Musée de Québec and intimate friend of Lemieux, provoked a very different set of remarks from those of Claude Picher, in *L'Evénement-Journal* of March 2, 1956. The reviewer, identified only by the initials R.B., had the following to say:

"One has the impression that the painter saw the clement shores of the Mediterranean under wild, tormented and disturbing conditions, which made them reminiscent of a late spring in Canada or Scandinavia. Only a few of his canvases are relieved by a ray or two of sunshine. His work would seem to be more concerned with stylistic experimentation, an almost mystical use of color, communicating certain subjective and occasionally effective ideas. The wild aspects of this region, the wind, torrid sun and riotous rock formations that typify Haute Provence where it verges into the Alpine foothills, show up in a number of vigorous examples. The beauty of these rolling hills, so often described by Jean Giono, evokes the serenity of the mountain-dweller of Provence, who is so different from his city-dwelling counterpart. M. Lemieux invites us to daydream on balconies and terraced gardens a few miles from Nice or Menton. He has also recorded scenes from the daily life of the simple folk of the region, as well as of the summer visitors come to indulge in the luxury of idleness. In the distance, our eye is caught by the dull green tones of olive trees bowed to the tramontana."

Le Chemin qui mène nulle part (The Road That Leads Nowhere), 1956, 46 x 61 cm

The Road that Leads Elsewhere

Lemieux was inspired by his efforts on behalf of the Société des arts plastiques, the success of the "Côte d'Azur" exhibition, and the rumors of a pending mural commission for the new campus of Laval University. He felt close to a new way of seeing the world, a new vision. He felt himself becoming more receptive, more transparent, but without losing his reserve, his habit of solitude, his dislike for any confrontation. His contribution to the Société des arts plastiques was thus limited to a few key addresses at meetings and the drafting of the program for action with Claude Picher.

Even his stay in France through 1954-55, for all its significance in the evolution of his art, was often difficult for him. His wife Madeleine had to exercise her wits in the many different lodgings they occupied over the course of their journey, in order to create an atmosphere the artist would find reassuring and to some extent familiar. Lemieux is the first to admit that he has a great need for routine and that any change in his habits always proves traumatic for him: "I was completely lost in France. Anything I was able to paint there was reminiscent of Monet or Bonnard. On the Riviera, I worked in the shadow of Matisse and Cézanne. As soon as I was back in Canada I began to paint in a very different fashion."

In the summer of 1956, we can mark the emergence of the "new" Lemieux, in the picture with the paradoxical title *Le Chemin qui mène nulle part* (The Road That Leads Nowhere). This work opened up a universe radically different from anything the artist had created before, even though this profound metamorphosis had begun to work its effects on his imagination at least as far back as *Les Ursulines* of 1951.

———

In his postscript to the book left unfinished by the death of its author, Maurice Merleau-Ponty, Claude Lefort described the philosophical spirit of the celebrated phenomenologist this way: "It is precisely because philosophy is, in his eyes, continual questioning, that it each time enjoins us to presuppose nothing, to neglect the acquired and to run the risk of opening a route that leads nowhere." (*The Visible and the Invisible*, trans. Alphonso Lingis, p. ixx, editor's foreword). This "route that leads nowhere" is the kind of peril that must often be faced by him who would travel beyond the boundaries of acquired knowledge. This may be the trial, the challenge, the "wager" (Pascal) of the artist or the philosopher, the nuclear physicist or the historian, the surgeon or the engineer. Creation in any domain requires that a certain price be paid. Making progress means setting out on an uncertain journey, on a road that seems to cross the threshold to nowhere, to the land of discovery.

———

Liberated now from insidious self-doubt, from the shy nature that had caused him to camouflage his vision of the world behind the sense of humor that sustained *Lazare* and *Fête-Dieu*, Lemieux at last felt comfortable with the imaginative superstructure that is part of every person's memory and is shaped by certain aesthetic affinities drawn from the broad sweep of art history. Music, literature, painting: all have their role to play in providing food for the soul.

Until 1955, Lemieux had painted in a descriptive way, codifying the underlying anecdotes in more or less complex images, which might at first seem merely clever or humorous, but which in fact are often charged with a critique of the social reality depicted and interpreted in the picture. From 1956 on, Lemieux's painting did not altogether forsake the descriptive mode, but did alter its range considerably. The anecdotal aspect, which had been closely tied to the concern with detail, now gave way to another figurative dimension, which until then had played only a small part in the painter's work: the "atmospheric" dimension, the underlying emotional mood of the scene or situation. From now on this underlying mood, rather than external details, would be the artist's chief preoccupation. It would give to the "figurative reality" (Francastel) of the picture its meaning, its value, its charm, in a word, its aesthetic foundation. The witty anecdote, the quaint detail were abandoned in favor of the subtle and mysterious play of transference, first hinted at in *Le Chemin qui mène nulle part*. This picture was soon followed by several other strong examples of the "new" Lemieux style. *La Ville lointaine* (The Distant City), *Le Train de midi* (The Noon Train) and *Le Visiteur du soir* (The Evening Visitor) (see pp. 179, 190 and 209), give clear expression to the new pictorial syntax and establish in a much more masterly way both the "scenic" aspects of the picture and its intellectual or affective tension. Something about the painter's vision had changed profoundly. His long and patient endeavors in learning how to see had brought him to a leap of faith. Maturity and serenity combined admirably in the new works, which began to appear now with a certain regularity.

Five years later the artist would explain[13] that a journey abroad can create a sense of uprootedness that has the salutary effect of later allowing the traveller to rediscover "his own country with new eyes." Lemieux would return to this same theme a number of times in the course of interviews we had together in 1968, 1972 and 1975: "After 1956, and a year spent in

---

[13] In an interview with Lyse Nantais, published in *Le Devoir*, January 28, 1961. See below, pp. 116-117.

France, I no longer saw things the same way. A totally different vision had developed, a horizontal vision above all, one that I had never had a hint of before. I had never noticed until then just how horizontal our country is. I had to leave to be able to appreciate this fact. How true it is that you have to go elsewhere to discover yourself...."

Indeed, it is often only through distance, absence or death that we come to see the importance or virtue of certain beings. Some dimensions of reality can grow dim in our consciousness through the wearing effects of habit and proximity. Often it is only when we are forced to do without that which we have taken for granted before, that we are in a position to rediscover its value.

Whereas Lemieux seems to have discovered something about himself by going abroad, or discovered at least a new, and until then, little explored pictorial perspective, it was in his native land that he learned to shape, define and extend his discovery. This would not be easy, nor would it ever be easy. Each picture represented for the painter, as he was well aware, a new challenge, a new danger, a new gamble; witness for example, *Les Champs blancs* (White Fields) of 1956, completed between *Le Train de midi* and *Le Visiteur du soir.*

Les Champs blancs (White Fields), 1956, OFQ

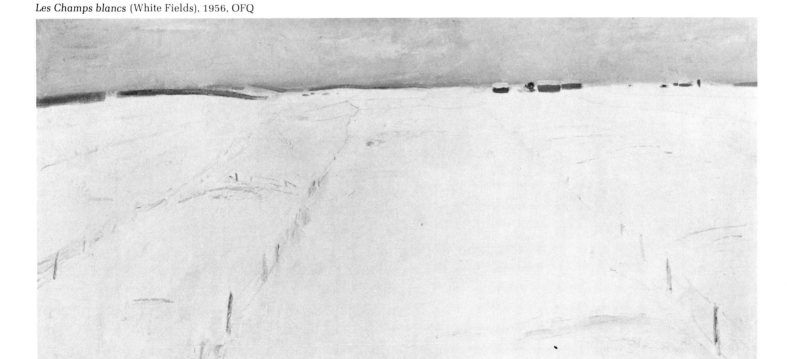

A Mural on Medicine, 1957

In 1957, a number of Lemieux's paintings found their way to the São Paulo Biennale, as well as to the second Canadian Biennale, held in Ottawa. That same year, the Canadian government held a competition in order to select a mural design for the Canadian pavilion at the Brussels World's Fair, scheduled for the following year. A relief by the young Mario Merola was the winner; Lemieux's submission was a monumental and boldly structured project, whose design certainly deserved better than this comment by Guy Viau: "Lemieux's study shows a town in which the perspective elements become increasingly compressed towards the background, all rendered in the grey tones of a winter's day. The town in question is Quebec which, with its Château, its square, its ramparts, its bleakness, evokes some distant feudal past. With a mandate to illustrate Canada as a nation from sea to sea, Lemieux, who is Québécois through and through, could see fit only to glorify his own hometown." (*Vie des Arts*, summer 1958, pp. 39-40)

Yet reviewer Guy Viau would be quite content, less than ten years later, to assume the directorship of the art museum in this very town, where Canada's fate was decided a little more than two hundred years ago. In Quebec City's Latin Quarter, meanwhile, Laval University was bursting at the seams, as it had been for some time. By 1957 a new campus was under construction in suburban Sillery, and Jean Paul Lemieux, a painter native to the city and professor of its Ecole des beaux-arts, was asked to paint a mural to grace the foyer of the university's medical sciences pavilion.

Why was Lemieux commissioned to illustrate the subject of medicine, rather than any other? There would appear to be no particular reason; in any case, this was the artist's first mural commission and he accepted it enthusiastically. He began by executing a small-scale study, then carefully transferred his model to canvas and finally, in September 1957, mounted the work on the slightly concave wall of the new pavilion foyer. The picture measured three metres high by five-and-a-half metres long and was signed at a point about midway from either end, on a little kiosk behind Château Frontenac. A famous quo-

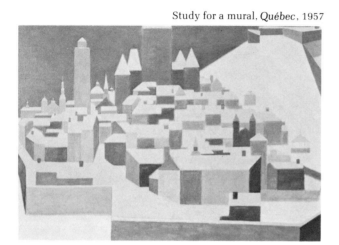

Study for a mural, *Québec*, 1957

Study for a mural, *Médecine* (Medicine), 1956, 107 x 203 cm

tation of Hippocrates could be seen in the foreground of the mural: "Science is long, but life is short." (During the winter of 1973, a breakdown in the building's heating system caused boiling water to gush out over the mural; it was later restored with great care by a cleric chosen personally for the job by Lemieux himself.)

The mural is narrative in style and concerns the place of medicine in Quebec City life. In the foreground of the composition is a row of eighteen human figures. Their faces are devoid of features — eyes, nose, mouth—for the painter has stressed the nature of the role performed by each of the various characters, rather than particular traits of the characters themselves. We find surgeons and nurses; a group of students and interns at the extreme right-hand end; and several nuns, who still had an important part to play in hospitals at that time. Behind these figures the painter creates a panoramic view of Quebec City, reducing buildings to simple geometric shapes, rectangles and triangles, punctuated by a few trees and church steeples thrusting skyward.

La Médecine à Québec (Medicine in Quebec City), 1956, 300 x 550 cm (Laval University)

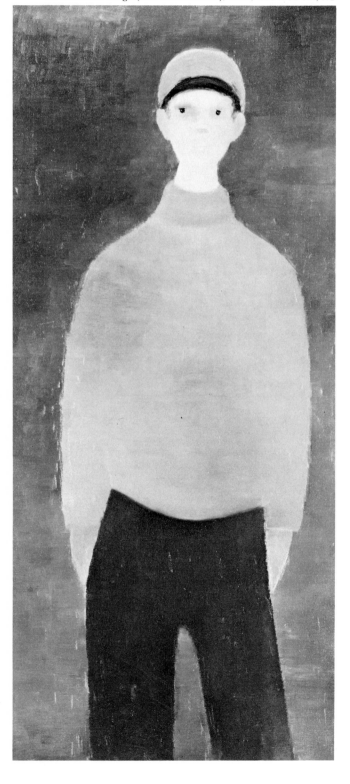

Le chandail rouge (The Red Sweater), 1958, 119 x 52 cm, RG

A Busy Schedule

In the course of an interview published in the magazine supplement to the Montreal newspaper *La Patrie* on April 7, 1957, Lemieux proffered an opinion on several aspects of the contemporary artistic climate: "Our country has unlimited resources for painters and there is certainly no need for anyone to leave in order to become a great artist. Here in Canada we have all that's needed for training painters of talent." Lemieux the art teacher, who had just benefited greatly from a one-year stay abroad thanks to a government grant, went on to explain his meaning: trips abroad were no doubt a good thing, but would be even more profitable if the grant recipients were better prepared to use them effectively and less inclined to fall into the "temptations of bohemian life." This was one of the first public denunciations of "cultural tourism" and other abuses of a grant system seemingly more concerned with concealing favoritism than requiring proof that grants had been put to good use.

During the summer of 1958, Lemieux ran a painting workshop at the University of British Columbia, in Vancouver. A female student enquired of him at one point whether he had been painting during his stay out there. The painter replied: "The mountains are too high, the sea is too vast, the sky too distant. Nature has the same colors here as in England and England is a place where I could never get any painting done...."

In 1958, works by Lemieux were exhibited in the Canadian pavilion at the Brussels World's Fair, as well as at the Pittsburgh World's Fair. The University of British Columbia also staged a one-man show of Lemieux's work in Vancouver.

During the period from 1956 to 1961, Madeleine Lemieux was busy giving drawing and art classes to small groups of children on Saturday mornings, and occasionally on a weekday afternoon, in the kitchen of the lodgings she occupied with her husband in Sillery-Québec.

In 1959 Lemieux took part in the third Canadian Biennale, in Ottawa, as well as in the Stratford (Ontario) Festival exhibition. He was trying to get as much work as possible done outside the classes he

L'été (Summer), 1959, 53 x 126 cm (Public Library and Art Museum, London, Ont.) OFQ

Marine (Seascape), 1957, 82 x 46 cm, OFQ

continued to give at the Ecole des beaux-arts. From 1957 to 1959 he painted winter landscapes, seascapes, urban scenes, solitary figures, all in the new style he had discovered in 1956 and which was winning him notice among greater and greater numbers of art lovers. Two canvases, both done in 1957, stand out from others of the same period in their pictorial intensity — *L'Orpheline* (The Orphan Girl) and *1910 Remembered* (see pp. 237 and 200 respectively).

Even as sensitive and experienced a critic as Rodolphe de Repentigny was somewhat taken aback by Lemieux's first one-man show in Montreal, held at the Galerie Denyse Delrue, on Crescent Street, from March 17 to 29, 1959. Taking as points of reference the work of Seurat, Utrillo and even Claude Lorrain, the writer jumped from one to another of the twenty pictures in the exhibition, noting here "a not unlike-able naiveté," there "a tiny detail that arrests the attention" and again, "the ennui, the vast ennui of the cities of the North, with its overtone of despair." De Repentigny went on to observe of a particular paint-ing that "the distance in space of the figures suggests a distancing in time as well," then remarked that the painter had abandoned the traditional formats in fa-vor of canvases which were either "very wide or very high," which led him to conclude, in spite of a certain ambivalence, that this was "an exhibition not to be missed and that Lemieux has a real contribution to make to the art scene in Canada. In his work, tech-nique is subordinated to personal expressiveness." (La Presse, March 19, 1959)

To Be Oneself

In 1960, Canada participated in the thirtieth Venice Biennale with an exhibition of works by Al-bert Dumouchel, Edmund Alleyn, Graham Coughtry, Frances Loring and Jean Paul Lemieux, who also had a one-man show in the spring of the same year at the Roberts Gallery of Toronto.

In the course of an excellent interview pub-lished on January 28, 1961 in Le Devoir, Lyse Nantais asked Lemieux what he thought of Canadian painting and whether "as a whole, it represented the nature of our climate." Lemieux answered by first dividing the country into two spheres of influence: Quebec, which fell under European influence, and the provinces west of Quebec, which fell under American influ-ence. He went on to deplore the "over-eager tendency to imitate," the process of levelling encouraged by the international art scene and the more and more com-monplace habit painters had of working in closed spaces under artificial light.

"On the contrary, what they ought to be doing, if only to clear their heads a bit, is taking a look at the country they were born in. I have trouble understanding, for example, how a painter born in Chicoutimi and brought up with the north wind, can express himself in the style of a Mediterranean artist. In the old days, Canadian painters were isolated; they hardly travelled at all, they looked at what was around them and expressed that. In the final analysis, the best art has always been done in isolation.

"We grovel before anything that's new, to such an extent that we have a compulsion to accept whatever's handed to us, for fear of making a mistake and overlooking an important piece of work. This is a complex that often makes us applaud art forms which inside we really don't like. [...] You have to be sincere, be yourself and not try to be something you aren't. Our biggest single problem is perhaps an inferiority complex, and that might be the source of our mania for imitating others, which comes from a kind of deep-seated anxiety. As we are a new country with strong rural roots, we feel we're behind the times and our collective touchiness is another manifestation of this inferiority complex. We feel like outsiders and therefore try to gain acceptance by imitating, rather than seeking to be ourselves, a course that could lead us to greatness, but also carries the risk of failure.... That takes courage, because often what one is is not as glamorous as what one pretends to be!"

Lemieux continued with his thoughts on fashionable artistic movements:

"It's much harder to go against the current than to let yourself go with it. I've got nothing against travelling abroad, if the point is to shake up an artist's habits and allow him to see his own country with new eyes when he returns home. The province of Quebec is not lacking in talent. The only thing is, the path to success is not very clear and a lot of young people seem to lose their way. Once we have taken stock of our own values and overcome our inertia, once we have learned to look around us, we will create art that will play a role of world-wide importance...."

The following week the same newspaper published a "reply" to Jean Paul Lemieux, in which Jean-Paul Guay undertook to qualify some of what he alleged to be the painter's more extravagant remarks. These he ascribed to the artist's facetious sense of humor, which he saw as related to a deliberately unsophisticated pose—"pretending to be the country

Les glaces au bord de la mer (Ice by the Seashore), 1962, 69 x 109 cm

boy he always was." Guay was then moved to comment in the following vein: "The idea of an autonomous, national school of painting, in the age of the supersonic jet, is a traditionalist's daydream, as Jean Paul Lemieux knows perfectly well." For Guay, Lemieux "may have become a painter, but he was born a sceptic"; the author of the reply also admitted that he had just as much of a "phobia about the cold" as did Lemieux: "Our winters are long and trying. But to argue from that observation to the conclusion that Canada is a Nordic country, is sheer sophistry. The Saint Lawrence valley is no more Nordic than Flanders, Holland, Prussia, Poland or the Moscow region. I cannot allow that German Expressionism is the exclusive mode of expression available to these countries, which, though they may be far from Mediterranean, are not exactly sub-Arctic either. . . ."

This reply of Guay's was useful at least in breaking the gloomy, dare we say "Nordic," silence which too often greeted writings as lively and provocative as Lemieux's article, published the previous week in the same newspaper thanks to the initiative of interviewer Lyse Nantais, and in which, as we have seen, he returned to a number of themes first broached in his own published writings a generation earlier. Jean-Paul Guay, for his part, saw in the fact that Quebec painting was the product of "a people whose culture was still only half-formed, unsettled, coming into its own," an argument in favor of embracing foreign art. Lemieux, on the other hand, used this same observation to warn against the dangers of slavish imitation, which too often prevents artists from expressing what they really are themselves, and therefore from contributing to the growth and flowering of their own culture.

Throughout the sixties, Lemieux held scrupulously to the principle of authenticity in the development of his painting, as art-lovers and curators could attest for themselves by studying the considerable number of canvases that cropped up in various exhibitions and collections. The painter's reputation grew quietly, without fanfare, and the fact that he had forged a painting style different from any other in the country naturally contributed to his success. It was a style, moreover, that had nothing mechanical or mannered about it and allowed the development of a thematic field rich in possibilities. These the artist prospected with skill and patience, exploring all the seasons of the year, a whole range of tensions between human figures and landscapes, figures in close-up, group studies, seascapes, urban scenes, rustic scenes. The work seemed to suggest that the artist felt a need to compensate for the spare quality of his style and the particular emotional ambience informing this style, by marshalling both a great variety of subject-matter and an inexhaustible number of thematic combinations.

During the Easter vacation of 1962, Lemieux took a trip around the Gaspé and a year later, on April 13, 1963, he had this to say about his trip in the pages of *La Presse*:

"For a long time I painted from life, but I don't anymore. I paint in my studio, an inner world. I've stored up a great deal. Painting out-of-doors I find tiring and unrewarding, but I do get out to see things. Last year, for example, I took a trip through the Gaspé. It was all sunshine and snow. When I got back I painted things like *Le Lac Matapédia* (Lake Matapedia). I find I get better results like that: I get rid of the details, but retain the main image. The same goes for people, I paint them from memory. What haunts me most is the dimension of time. Space and time. Time slipping by, and man in space confronted by this. Of course, I don't always succeed, but that's what affects me most of all. The past fascinates me! I'm very fond of old yellowed photographs. I suppose I sound a bit Proustian! I don't keep up with what goes on in Paris. I'm not working in the mainstream. I don't even try to do so, because it just wouldn't be honest for me to work any other way."

As we can see once again, Lemieux is very concerned with the questions of sincerity and authenticity: these come at the summit of his hierarchy of values in the development of his work.

Spring 1963 and Two Exhibitions

During the summer of 1962, some of Lemieux's pictures found their way to an exhibition of Canadian painting held in Warsaw. Little by little, the artist was finding a wider audience, even if the demand for his work was still not great. The sketches that had been put on display at his house in November 1950 had quickly found buyers, but that was in large measure

La jupe rose (The Pink Skirt), 1960, 100 x 32 cm, RG

Quebec City studio, April 1962 (Photo Rosemary Gilliat)

because of their ludicrously low prices. A number of his more important works had been purchased by museums: *Lazare, Fête-Dieu, Le Visiteur du soir, L'Orpheline*. But it was not until 1963 that success really began to come Lemieux's way. The artist was not far from his sixtieth birthday; he painted slowly and produced relatively few pictures, only a few dozen a year. The once low prices fetched by his work began to climb gradually from one exhibition to another, and the attention drawn by the originality of his style shifted the balance of supply and demand in his favor. Canvases were soon beginning to change hands discreetly, with a sharp increase in price each time.

In 1963, Lemieux took part in the fifth Canadian Biennale in Ottawa, in an exhibition of Canadian painters organized by New York's Museum of Modern Art and in the "Eleven Canadian Artists" show at the Tate Gallery in London. In December, he joined Pellan, Jean McEwen, York Wilson and Joe Plaskett for an exhibition at the Musée Galliera in Paris, entitled "Cinq peintres canadiens." But 1963 was particularly successful for Lemieux because of his very well received one-man shows in Montreal and Toronto.

In April 1963, the Galerie Agnès Lefort of Montreal exhibited twenty-eight works by Lemieux, thirteen of which were not for sale, either because they already belonged to a particular collector or else because the artist himself did not wish to part with them. The other fifteen canvases found buyers in the first two days of the exhibition. Among them were works like *Chacun sa nuit, Petit Arlequin* (Little Harlequin), *Hiver gaspésien* (Gaspé Winter), *1910 Remembered, Miss Knight, Matin* (Morning), *Paysage de ville, Le Ruban de velours* (The Velvet Ribbon), *Ville enneigée* (Snow-covered City), *Le Cavalier* (The Rider) and *Etoile du berger* (The Evening Star). As the list of titles shows, the artist was at pains to develop considerable thematic variety in his work.

From the time of this exhibition in Montreal, Quebec's dealers and collectors were aware that Lemieux's work would henceforth be in demand, that it would become harder and harder to obtain and would fetch higher and higher prices. Those who were anxious to purchase his paintings would soon have to hope their luck was good, put their names

La grande terre (The Big Earth), 1960, 65 x 104 cm

patiently on the artist's waiting list, or on those of the few galleries who managed to secure a canvas from time to time, watch for an opportunity and then seize the occasion without hesitation ... assuming of course that the pocketbook permitted. From the very beginnings of this relatively sudden success, this surge in the popularity of his work, the painter professed to be quite surprised and felt as though he had had no hand in it. Had he not always shunned publicity, lurid or otherwise, or indeed any manoeuvres designed to catch public attention? He stood back and watched this abrupt change of fortune from a certain distance, greeting those who lined up to buy one of his paintings with a knowing smile or a witty remark. Meanwhile, he continued to live frugally and thought more and more about retiring soon from teaching in order to be able to devote himself full-time to his painting.

The Lemieux exhibition of 1963 was generally met with praise by the Montreal critics. An exhibition

Quebec City, April 1962 (Photo Rosemary Gilliat)

L'anse sauvage (The Wild Cove), 1963

of his work held around the same time at Toronto's Roberts Gallery, however, did not prompt the same praise from Brydon Smith. This critic claimed to be unimpressed by a painter who was content to "rework a few formal ideas in an attempt to give them final expression." Pointing to "the romantic portrayal of the infinite and immeasurable in nature" and "the intense feeling of loveliness" which characterize Lemieux's work, Smith concludes that "as a figurative painter using a somewhat naive style, Lemieux depicts subjects that come from within and are only later confirmed in the outside world. His succinct statements, although mainly pessimistic, are easily related to the human situation." (*Canadian Art*, July 1963, p. 205)

Remarks on Painting

In an article published by *Weekend Magazine* in March 1963, writer Patrick Nagle proved to be somewhat more appreciative of Lemieux's work. He refers straightaway in the subtitle of the article to the "mystical quality" that pervades Lemieux's canvases and goes on to quote remarks made by the painter which, taken together, constitute a kind of aesthetic credo. Many are remarks which have appeared before, in one form or another, in various articles on Lemieux. Here, grouped under certain themes, are some of the highlights of his conversations with Patrick Nagle.

On his painting in general: "What I seek is the feeling of time. I try to do it by space and distance....I try to convey a remembrance, the feeling of generations. I sometimes see myself as the central figure, but as a child in the continuity of generations. I like the feeling of summer in the old days, the feeling of old newsreels or photographs. You get the feeling of fading away."

Painting landscapes and figures: "I like the feeling of vast spaces. I like the plains of Western Canada, although I have only painted them once.... I'm not a landscape painter. Don't call me that. I like painting figures too much. When I get tired of landscapes I paint figures. I never use models; I couldn't." **122**

On cities: "I am fascinated by cities. I see the cities as empty. A large city completely empty would be fascinating to paint."

On light and color: "I don't like blue. I can remember any sky but a blue sky. But in one of my new works I have tried a blue sky. It's quite unusual for me....I can't paint at night [because] artificial light is no use to me."

The horizon: "My horizons are not a trademark. There is no fixed formula I use. When I use a slanted horizon, it's because that's the way it looks to me. I like the feeling of motion. For example, when you are walking, the horizon doesn't stay level; it moves up and down with you."

Working methods: "Painting is not easy for me. I never get a thing right the first time. I'll paint away for a while and I get fed up. When I don't feel like painting, I don't paint. I may start with a landscape, it may turn into a figure, then back into a landscape. Sometimes I'll turn a canvas sideways or upside down to get a new angle."

Le long voyage (The Long Voyage), 1963, 102 x 145 cm, RG

Abstract art: "A painting, if it is good, can be abstract or representational. But there's too much trash these days. Personally, I couldn't be abstract. I'd get bored with it. A good abstract gives me a shock, but I don't get continuing pleasure from it. The feeling fades as you realize the substance of the painting is limited."

Lemieux, who gave these 1963 interviews with Patrick Nagle in English, expresses himself with little difficulty in his second language, as the reader can see. The painter would seem to attach a good deal of importance to the emotional aspects of life, for the word "feeling" crops up frequently in Nagle's article. This is how the writer sums up Lemieux's accomplishments: "A true artist, Lemieux has idiosyncrasies that are not really trademarks, but nevertheless defy copy cats, because they are his own ideas."

Elsewhere in his article, Nagle broaches the invariably delicate subject of influences, about which most artists are very touchy: "I think the confused ideas of today's young painters are perhaps caused by the confusion in the world. Young people are influenced by the world. I was influenced by all sorts of things when I was young. But when you grow old it's not easy to be influenced any more. When I look at anything now, it's like looking through the wrong end of a telescope. Everything seems smaller than it is."

In yet another interview, published by *La Presse* on April 13, 1963, Lemieux replied to a similar question concerning influences, though this time in a more subjective way: "In the beginning, like any other painter, I very much admired Suzor-Côté and Clarence Gagnon. And, apart from them? Gauguin for a while, then I lost interest. I was once quite fascinated by German Expressionism. I always found Impressionism superficial, whereas I think Expressionism offers a vision of sorts. I've been charmed, too, by the Italian painters of the 13th century. But it's German and Nordic painting that still impresses me most."

———

Study for *Charlottetown Revisited*, 1964, 33 x 64 cm

Charlottetown Revisited, mural, 1964 (Charlottetown, PEI)

Quebec City, 1963 (Photo La Presse)

Meanwhile, Lemieux's career moved on. In 1964 he painted a large mural for the Canadian Confederation Centre in Charlottetown, P.E.I., the cradle of the Canadian nation. He was also turning out a number of important easel works at the time, at a steady, if not rapid pace. These included *Les Mi-carêmes* (Mid-Lent), *Les Patineurs du soir* (Evening Skaters) and *Les Parques* (The Fates), in 1962; *La Fête* (The Celebration), *La Mort par un clair matin* (Death on a Clear Morning), *Le Long voyage* (The Long Voyage) and *Les Promeneurs* (The Strollers), in 1963; *L'Enigme* (The Enigma) and *Charlottetown Revisited* in 1964; *Amélie et le temps* (Amélie and Time), *Les Temps passés* (Times Past), *Eté 1914* (Summer 1914) and *Julie et l'univers* (Julie and the Universe) in 1965. (Most of these are discussed in detail in the next section of this book.)

Lemieux Turns Sixty

On November 28, 1964, the newspaper *Le Soleil* published an article in celebration of the painter's sixtieth birthday. Titled "Jean Paul Lemieux, a Québécois painter whose art never stops improving," the article provided an interview with the artist, briefly described the man, reviewed his dual career as artist and teacher, emphasized the sudden growth of his reputation and recorded the teacher's heart-felt desire to retire from teaching in order to allow the painter to devote all his time to painting.

In connection with Lemieux's method of work, the author of the article, Gaston L'Heureux, refers to the artist's tireless efforts to perfect each painting and goes on to quote Lemieux's own words on the subject of his use of color: "I'm not a colorist, I'm a *tonalist*." When confronted with the subject of his success, which had already exceeded the boundaries of his home province, since his work was more and more frequently exhibited abroad, Lemieux had this to say:

"Riopelle is the only Canadian painter on the international market. The art market is a huge organization. When a painter goes international, he puts a rope around his neck. The big galleries grab him up, the international journals publicize his work. The

Rayon de soleil (Shaft of Sunlight), 1964, 76 x 112 cm

painter is then obliged to keep renewing his inspiration, because a lot is expected of him. He soon has everybody breathing down his neck and his work ceases to be creative and inevitably develops into a commercial exercise.''

Here we touch upon one of the reasons why Lemieux has never expressed much interest in seeing his work reach the international market, whose principal nerve centers are to be found in New York, Paris, London and Zurich. At this stage, Lemieux's success in the province of Quebec, in Canada, was such that there were already long lists of buyers helping to push up demand, and therefore prices, for his work. In such circumstances as these, why bother looking elsewhere for what was already close at hand, on the very threshold of his studio, and in addition, inviting needless worries and complications? Lemieux saw in his own lucid, if rather severe, way that an international career could be a kind of strait jacket for the artist, who was liable to become a victim of his own publicity and "trademark," and the pawn of the international dealers.

The article went on to give a forum to two other opinions of Lemieux's, on criticism and democratization of art. As far as criticism was concerned, the painter was perhaps recalling his own published statements when he made the following remarks:

"As far as I'm concerned, criticism leaves me cold. I wonder to myself if it should even exist. How is it possible to criticize a painting, if it's something new? Judging a work and evaluating a painter's ideas require a vast knowledge of the subject. Still, when something's really bad, like the commercial exhibitions staged by certain galleries, then no amount of bad press is too much. But it's difficult to judge, or even to really understand, a work of art."

Lemieux's ideas about criticism are echoed almost word for word in the writings of Paul Gauguin, whose influence over Lemieux's thinking became evident with his 1938 lecture. In the interview published on April 13, 1963 and quoted above, Lemieux was perhaps dismissing a little hastily the influence exercised by Gauguin over the Quebec artist (in both the literary and pictorial domains). There are a large number of points on which their respective ideas coincide almost perfectly. These would include the following: each and every work constitutes a new risk, which creates anxiety for the artist; academies and fashions are detrimental to creative activity; painting does not consist in describing, but suggesting, transposing; nothing is ever final for the artist, whose mission is to keep pressing on with his explorations, if he is to penetrate the mysteries of the universe; Impressionism is too decorative and superficial; it is preferable to paint from memory in order to give free rein to the imagination; color adds to drawing a kind of musical dimension and translates to some extent the mysterious inner force that the artist feels and tries to interpret; feeling is the most important element in art and gives substance to the idea (or "concetto," as Michelangelo would have said); the artist must be profoundly himself and work only from inspirations of his very own. Not all of these artistic principles could be solidly corroborated from Gauguin's writings alone; some have been extrapolated from his pictorial aesthetics. But by making a side-by-side comparison between Gauguin and Lemieux, we can bring out the close similarities that exist in their respective preoccupations, without there necessarily being a concrete textural justification in any particular case.

———

Over the course of the 1960s, one question that was often discussed among members of the artistic community was that concerning the availability of works of art to the general public and, as a corollary, the democratization of culture. Here is Lemieux's opinion on the subject in 1964, an opinion which had changed somewhat over the years:

"I don't think art can be popularized. Those interested in serious painting will always form a kind of élite. People find that art is too costly. Only those with money are in a position to buy. The public should perhaps be educated, informed, encouraged to appreciate art, but this would be wasted labor, because Art will never be democratized, history is there to prove it."

———

A few weeks later, in January 1965, Lemieux had two exhibitions of his work running concurrently. One was held at the Galerie Zanettin in Quebec City, and comprised about twenty pictures, all of them belonging to collectors, a fact which frustrated a good number of those willing (and able) to buy. At the Galerie Agnès Lefort in Montreal, where Lemieux had had a highly successful show in April 1963, a line-up formed on the opening night even before anyone was being admitted, and this was despite the seasonal cold and snow.

From this time forward, the law of supply and demand began to work seriously in Lemieux's favor, at least in Quebec and among certain groups of collectors across Canada. Inevitably, prices climbed and speculation set in. Some of Lemieux's works would realize five to ten times their original selling price in the space of less than ten years.

Paysage avec deux personnages (Landscape with Two Figures), 1965, 107 x 165 cm, OFQ

La cravate rouge (The Red Tie), 1965, 33 x 18 cm, RG

Quebec City Ecole des beaux-arts, April 1962
(Photos Rosemary Gilliat)

Lemieux Retires from Teaching

On August 1, 1965, Jean Paul Lemieux turned in his resignation to the Quebec City Ecole des beaux-arts, after a six-month period on sick leave. With this, his thirty-year career as a teacher of painting and drawing came to a close, and he could now devote all his energies to painting. Our task in the next few pages is to give a summary of this practical side of Lemieux's work and of the relationship between his pedagogical ideas and their day-to-day application in the classroom.

The reader will recall that it was in the spring of 1934 that Lemieux received his diploma from the Montreal Ecole des beaux-arts, after having interrupted his studies in order to travel in Europe and the United States, and then attempt a business venture in the ill-fated commercial art studio, JANS. Lemieux was close to thirty when he left the Ecole in 1934 and decided to earn his living as an art teacher. This would have the advantage, he thought, of keeping him in close touch with the artistic community, while allowing him to take long holidays, during which he would, of course, be free to paint. At that point he could not guess the extent to which his teaching job would absorb him (even without the wearing administrative duties, the perpetual meetings and paperwork which have burdened teaching more and more since the late sixties); nor how difficult it would be to pursue a dual career as teacher and artist. On the other hand, what the young Lemieux did know in 1934, with the world plunged deep into economic crisis, was that teaching would provide a secure living and a haven from commercial experiments like JANS.

He was not particularly proud of his diploma, which he looked upon as a mere work permit, more as a passport to the teaching world than a résumé of creative credentials. Indeed, he would later be heard to quip: "Isn't there something ridiculous about giving a painter a *diploma*?" Lemieux was well aware of the mysterious aspects of all creativity, which are not reducible to formulas or the technical tricks easily taught the apprentice in a classroom. And though Lemieux would remain a teacher of painting for some thirty years, he was often at pains to make his pedagogical principles absolutely clear. Before we look at some of the landmarks of this side of his **130** career, we might sum up the key ideas contained in his concept of teaching:

Each and every student possesses certain aptitudes, which are peculiar to him and which the teacher must recognize and respect, and whose development he must take pains to encourage.

The teacher must not, therefore, impose any doctrine, aesthetic or credo on his students; his task, on the contrary, is to give every student the widest possible latitude for personal growth, in the direction appropriate to each case.

The teacher must not tell the student what he is to do and how he is to go about doing it; rather he must talk with the student, observe closely his methods of working, attempt to discover with him his personal strengths and inclinations, show him—or, better still, help him discover for himself—what his most obvious weaknesses are.

Finally, the teacher must encourage each student to explore his own ideas and help him, in effect, to outgrow any need for teachers as soon as possible!

One does not have to look far for the implications of such pedagogical principles. Tinged with the delicate irony we have seen to be characteristic of Lemieux's temperament and his painting, these were unusual ideas for the Quebec of his day. They suggested that teaching an art class would become an exercise in the Socratic method and that the teacher could measure his success in terms of the distance which separated his former students' work from his own. In this sense the thrust of Lemieux's particular pedagogy is very similar to that of Gustave Courbet, who summarized his thinking on this matter in the famous letter to his pupils of Christmas 1861: "I do not, and cannot, have pupils under me. I believe that every artist must be his own master. I cannot teach my art, nor the art of any school, because I repudiate the teaching of art or, to put it another way, I consider that art is entirely an individual matter, and for each artist amounts simply to the talent deriving from his own inspiration and his own studies. [...] The art of painting begins and ends with the representation of visible, tangible objects. [...] Beauty, like Truth, is relative to the time in which one lives and to the individual who conjures it up. [...] There can be no schools of painting, but only painters."

Other similarities exist between opinions pro-
ferred by Lemieux and certain ideas expressed in the
writings of Courbet, as with Gauguin. As we have
already seen, Lemieux continued to keep his distance
from abstract and non-figurative art ("The art of
painting begins and ends with the representation of
visible, tangible objects," said Courbet, as we have
just seen above). The thing that most seemed to irri-
tate Lemieux in this regard was the degree to which
abstract and non-figurative painting had become
fashionable, a kind of conditioned reflex or epidemic
which had seized upon many young artists, who suc-
cumbed to slavish imitation without so much as attempting the salutary and essential exercise of self-
expression, who turned their backs on a serious examination of their own talents. Lemieux the teacher
was fond of pointing out, however, that the majority
of his former students had taken enthusiastically to
abstract and non-figurative work, evidence of the
great freedom he allowed them at the Ecole.

It is interesting, also, to compare Lemieux's
pedagogy with that of Pellan and Borduas, since these
three leading painters were also the three most important *teachers* of painting in Quebec over the course of
the 1940s. Despite certain similarities in their teaching styles, their respective personalities led them in
quite different directions. Borduas developed a group
of devoted followers around him, the Montreal Automatists; Pellan, with his lively temperament, could
not help but exercise a powerful influence over his
students; Lemieux, for his part, would fall back on his
sense of humor and on what might have been interpreted as indifference, in order to avoid intervening
directly in the delicate process of each student's artistic apprenticeship.[14]

Lemieux's pedagogical outlook may explain in
part the slow development of his own artistic production. From the beginning of his teaching career in
1934 until his one-year sabbatical leave in 1955-56,
his output was not copious and was even punctuated

---

[14] For more details on the teaching careers of Borduas and
Pellan, see G. Robert, *Borduas*, pp. 68-92, 233-236 and
288-310; G. Robert, *Pellan*, pp. 40-52; and G. Robert,
L'Art au Québec depuis 1940, pp. 18-20, 65, 73.

by long periods of pictorial silence. It was during this year's leave that his work took an important new turn. Lemieux discovered a new pictorial universe and immediately set about exploring it at a pace unknown in his career before. Meanwhile, he waited impatiently for the day when he would at last be able to retire from teaching and concentrate exclusively on his painting.

For Lemieux, teaching painting amounted to trying to show his students how to *see*. As far back as 1940 he had written about his own development: "In Paris in 1929-30, I visited the museums. Looking is still the best way to learn. Museums are worth any number of professors." — At least for those who already know something about "seeing."

In the course of an interview with the author held in 1972, Lemieux discussed his long years as a teacher: "I've never believed you could show someone how to paint. You can teach the rudiments of painting, the techniques, the tricks of the trade, but not painting itself. In my classes I would watch the students, thinking of them as apprentices in an old-fashioned studio. Everyone did what he pleased, according to his own judgment. We talked, we discussed things together. I was dead set against trying to influence them. Instead I would try to strike up a conversation and make discreet suggestions. We would talk about all sorts of things, whatever came into our heads. One thing for sure, my classes were anything but strict. . . ."

Lemieux went on to comment about something he had said ten years earlier: "I gave my students a completely free hand. I didn't see myself in the role of a team captain or school master. I never had any urge to tell them what to paint or how to paint and I certainly never wanted to try persuading them to work in my style! I already had my hands full just showing them what they *shouldn't* do and explaining to them how they might avoid the pitfalls of fashionable style, of plagiarism. . . . As far as I'm concerned, a good painting could just as well be abstract as representational, even though abstract work never holds my attention for very long, or touches me very deeply, and even though I've never done any abstract art myself. And yet a large number of students who were once in my classroom were then doing, or later did, abstract work."

Caricature of Lemieux by Raoul Hunter,
Le Soleil, Quebec City, January 15, 1965

In her introduction to the little catalogue accompanying the first retrospective of Lemieux's work at the Art Gallery of London, Ontario, in 1966, Clare Bice corroborates this observation by the painter: "Lemieux is a quiet, modest man, completely bilingual. He is never aggressive yet holds his own definite opinions. In the years when he taught in Montreal and at the Ecole des Beaux Arts in Quebec City, he strongly believed in the development of his students' own personality and approach and refused to impose his own ideas and style on them."

In 1963, a young painter who had taken classes with Lemieux at Quebec City's Ecole des beaux-arts, explained his former teacher's unusual enthusiasm for wet, dreary fall days: "He liked that kind of weather because colors come out better when it's really wet! Like agates, which look more beautiful when they've been moistened, dull, humid weather brings out colors you never see when it's sunny. That's why Lemieux was always in such good spirits on rainy days: he saw the advantages to being all wet!" (*La Presse*, April 13, 1963)

Painting, a Full-Time Occupation after 1965

Since going into retirement in 1965, Lemieux has divided his working year into roughly equal halves. During the summer, from May to November, he takes up residence on his Ile aux Coudres property, where the patio juts out over the tiny village of Saint-Louis and provides a sweeping view of the Saint Lawrence and the steep coast of Charlevoix. Behind the house the ample grounds provide yet another view, as breath-taking as the first, of the south shore and an ever-widening expanse of the river downstream from the island. In the house itself, which has been modernized and decorated with fine period furniture and other Quebec antiques, can be found the painter's tiny attic studio, on one wall of which he fastens the canvas in progress.

During the winter months, Lemieux lives in an apartment in Sillery, in the suburbs of Quebec City, where he uses a small, cluttered room for his studio. Here too one can always find a canvas tacked up on the wall. On each canvas the artist first sketches out a rough design in pencil; the original idea will then undergo numerous transformations before it finds its

View from the terrace at the Ile aux Coudres, summer 1972

way to another wall for drying. Even then the new painting may not be safe, for chances are good that it may be called back to the main working wall to undergo a few final alterations. The tiny studio accommodates a rocking chair, which happens to be the painter's favorite spot for meditating in front of a work in progress, and, near the door, a large country wardrobe which contains the yellowed photo albums of Lemieux's childhood, an inexhaustible source of inspiration and nostalgic memories which the painter is constantly turning over in his mind.

Lemieux has never been very fond of the rigors of the Canadian winter and admits without hesitation that he tolerates it less and less the older he gets. He and his wife therefore flee every year in February-March for a few weeks' vacation in the Florida sunshine.

Painting has thus been Lemieux's chief preoccupation ever since 1965. Yet it still takes little to disrupt his artistic inspiration, which, as we have seen, is slow in taking shape. The very idea, for example, of getting ready for a retrospective such as those held in 1967 and 1974, is enough to upset

Chemin en hiver (Road in Winter), 1966, 58 x 135 cm, OFQ

The island studio, summer 1972

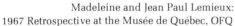
Madeleine and Jean Paul Lemieux:
1967 Retrospective at the Musée de Québec, OFQ

Lemieux for months, and almost keep him from painting. The present author saw some of this first-hand while preparing the 1968 book on Lemieux's career, practically every time he met with the painter in Quebec City or on the Ile aux Coudres. Similar difficulties arose for Lemieux during the filming of a half-hour documentary on his work — which was unfortunately a long, drawn-out process — as well as during the research stage of the present book, in 1974-75.

In order to create, Lemieux needs something approaching absolute peace and quiet. He leads a secluded life. He is said to be retiring, tight-lipped, difficult to get to know. He values his privacy very highly, as one would expect, and relies on his wife Madeleine to help keep intrusions to a minimum. Otherwise, they would have a steady stream of visitors at their doorstep, from students doing research on Lemieux's work, through academics, journalists, critics, art-lovers, collectors and dealers, to former students and friends of every stripe. Every artist who reaches a certain level of repute is eventually forced to protect himself from curious outsiders if he is to get on with his work and set aside time for a private life. Sculptor Alexander Calder summed up his feelings on this subject with the following witticism: "One of the problems confronting me is to get enough free time to work and not to go around talking about it." This author has heard Zadkine, Miro, Giacometti, Lardera, Riopelle and many other artists say more or less the same thing. Albert Dumouchel found a solution of his own when he shared a farm and studio on the banks of the Richelieu with Monique Charbonneau in the late sixties: he posted a sign on the front gate reading "No Visitors."

The Beginnings of Fame in 1967

In 1966, Lemieux took part in an exhibition titled "Chefs-d'oeuvre de Montréal" which toured seven American cities. In February 1966, the Art Gallery of London, Ontario presented the first retrospective of Lemieux's work, comprising forty pictures dating from 1937 to 1965. The exhibition then moved to the Kitchener-Waterloo Art Gallery in March.

In 1967, Lemieux took part in a National Gallery of Canada exhibition titled "Three Hundred

Julie et l'univers (Julie and the Universe), 1965 (p. 239)

La Nativité (The Nativity), 1966 (p. 139, 150 & 219)

Years of Canadian Art," on the occasion of the centenary of Canadian Confederation. A large Lemieux retrospective was arranged that same year at the Montreal Museum of Fine Arts. It later went on to Quebec City and Ottawa.

It was the beginning of real fame.

An album containing six color reproductions of Lemieux's paintings was published by the Galerie Agnès Lefort of Montreal. A numbered edition of this album, signed by the artist, soon became a much sought-after object of financial speculation. During the same year, 1967, UNICEF reproduced a beautifully composed painting entitled *La Nativité* as a greeting card, part of the series used to raise money for needy children. The figures in this work, which bear a family resemblance to the 1475 work of Piero della Francesca (National Gallery, London), are deployed in a setting which is one of Lemieux's most striking, not least because of the droll, restrained landscape perched on the horizon line near the top of the picture.

In December 1967, Lemieux received a medal from the Canada Council along with a $2,500 scholarship.

The retrospective held in 1967 deserves further comment. Both the Montreal Museum of Fine Arts and the National Gallery of Canada had already held retrospectives to honor Pellan, Borduas, Riopelle, Morrice, Lismer, Milne, Cullen ... and it was certainly no coincidence that Lemieux was chosen during the year which saw celebrations for both Canada's Centenary and Montreal's Expo.

Lemieux's work, as the evidence shows, is deeply rooted in the magical labyrinth, the fertile soil of memory, and the nostalgia which pervades many of his canvases suited the spirit of the Centenary ideally. Furthermore, Lemieux's political opinions favored the idea that Quebec should continue to play its role within Confederation, while ties of friendship put him in direct touch with a number of high-ranking officials in Ottawa. It was indeed Pierre Elliott Trudeau, the then federal Minister of Justice and future Prime Minister of Canada, who presided at the opening of the Lemieux retrospective in Montreal on September 14, 1967.

On the Ile aux Coudres, 1967, OFQ

The retrospective became, in fact, the occasion for a kind of official sanctioning of Lemieux's work, with all the tributes that were to be expected. There were few discordant notes in the symphony of praise, although a review of the event written by Richmond Jones shows all too well the radical disjunction that may exist between a particular artist's vision and the *interpretation* of that vision by a particular reviewer, critic or historian. Jones was at pains to reduce Lemieux's world to the most negative terms: gloom, confinement, senility, helplessness, corpses, even death itself. Lemieux, he writes, "seems to paint not with oil but with mortician's makeup." In other words, the reviewer deplored the fact that Lemieux's work was not a frivolous and flattering depiction of the Folies-Bergère. Jones continued by tossing out a few names in support of his argument (Munch, Francis Bacon, even Faulkner) and then finished venting his spleen by declaring that the "frequent reiteration of his visual metaphor of hopelessness becomes tiresome despite the clarity of his philosophical assertion." (*The Gazette*, Sept. 23, 1967)

Another Montreal reviewer, writing in a short-lived magazine called *Sept Jours*, attributed Lemieux's success as a painter to the unthinking and indeed reactionary taste of the "middle-class élite" and a handful of "leading citizens of greater or lesser importance." Lemieux was made out to be the "artistic promoter of a quaint, backward-looking Quebec, portrayed in those good-natured images so beloved by the natives of this province; nostalgia for the good old days is alive and well, and it goes hand in hand with the new-found urge to rediscover our roots, not to mention all that fine old furniture." Then, with what seemed to be a characteristic about-face, the reviewer suddenly began to heap praise on the selfsame painter for the restraint, the modernity, the originality, even the topicality of his work, and concluded in a rather improbable burst of generosity that the exhibition was "not to be missed!"

The various commentaries which appeared in print at the time of the 1967 retrospective were for the most part in agreement on the originality of the painter's work and the aptness of this homage, which brought together 106 works dating from 1929 to 1967, as well as two from 1917 and 1923. The exhibition ran at the Montreal Museum of Fine Arts from September

15 to October 11; at the Musée de Québec from October 18 to November 22; and at the National Gallery in Ottawa from December 6 to January 7, 1968. In each of the three cities large crowds turned up to see the painter's work. The bilingual catalogue contained a biographical note, and introduction and 92 illustrations, seven of which were in color. It opens with this highly appropriate phrase: "In this Centenary of Confederation and in full awareness of the immense dimensions of Canada and the diversity of Canadians...."

The Reputation Confirmed, 1968-70

In the spring of 1968, Lemieux contributed to the "Ten Painters of Quebec" exhibition presented at the Montreal Musée d'art contemporain, then later at the Musée de Québec. In June he was named to the Order of Canada.

In an interview published by the Toronto magazine *Chatelaine* in March 1968, Lemieux explained he had removed blue from his palette altogether because it did not harmonize well with the other colors used in his pictures and upset their chromatic balance. "If I want a blue effect, I now mix black and white." (As we have already noted earlier, Lemieux is affected by color-blindness in the blue range.) Lemieux went on to say in the same interview, which was conducted in English, that he was influenced by films and television, particularly in regard to layout or disposition of the pictorial elements. He also added that he no longer painted from nature or life models, but from memory, and had been doing so for a long time.

October 3, 1968, marked the launching in Quebec of the first book ever written about Lemieux. The work, entitled *Jean Paul Lemieux, ou la poétique de la souvenance* (J.P. Lemieux, or the Poetics of Remembrance), was well received, especially by Claude Daigneault of *Le Soleil*, by *Le Devoir*, *Vie des Arts*, and Jean Royer, writing in the Quebec City journal *L'Action*: "This is a beautiful book, beautiful for what it tells us about one of Quebec's most important painters, beautiful for the warm, fervent admiration Guy Robert evinces in regard to the painter and his work. This is the book's chief virtue, that it is able to acquaint us with Lemieux the painter and his long road to success, his moments of grace, his most expressive canvases."

Exhibition of "Ten Quebec Painters" at the Montreal Museum of Contemporary Art, showing two paintings by Lemieux and three by Pellan (Photo La Presse)

Le temps d'hiver (Wintertime), 1968, 128 x 164 cm (Air Canada, Montreal)

Illustration for *La petite poule d'eau*
(Where Nests the Water Hen), 1971

In 1969 Gilles Gascon made a ten-minute National Film Board documentary called *Québec en silence*, in which color shots of some of Lemieux's paintings alternate with shots of Quebec landscapes in black and white.[15]

In 1970 Lemieux received honorary doctorates from both Laval University in Quebec City and Bishop's University in Lennoxville, P.Q. In June 1971, he received the Louis-Philippe-Hébert prize awarded by the Saint-Jean-Baptiste Society of Montreal.

Commissioned to illustrate a deluxe re-edition of Gabrielle Roy's *La Petite Poule d'eau (Where Nests the Water Hen)*, first published in 1950, Lemieux executed a series of pictures of which twenty were

---

[15] In 1944, Lemieux was the subject of an 18-minute National Film Board documentary called *Sept peintres du Québec*, along with Suzor-Côté, Clarence Gagnon, Marc-Aurèle Fortin, Alfred Pellan, Henri Masson and André Bieler. In 1967, another short film was made about Lemieux for television broadcast in Toronto.

Indian River, 1970, 23 x 30 cm

chosen for reproduction. The resulting album was printed in a mere 230 copies and published in Montreal during September 1971. The illustrations, signed by the artist, soon became the target of speculative buying, to such an extent that some of the twenty reproductions would later sell individually for the original price of the entire album.

Ever since the 1967 retrospective, Lemieux has been producing new pictures on a regular basis, and a number of these have been included in the next section of this book, where we will be examining the recurrent themes that lie beneath the surface of the varied and complex subject-matter of the artist's work since 1956. The structures of time and space which inform the architecture of these paintings will be the subject of our final section. Here we shall limit ourselves to brief comments on a few representative pictures executed over the years.

Sketch for *Les citadins* (The City-Dwellers), 1973, 34 x 41 cm

Washes and Drawings since 1970

Since 1970, Lemieux has returned contentedly to his sketchbooks, whether to draft ideas for paint-

143

ings, try out variations on themes already attempted in previous works, execute a finished study or take pictorial "notes" of a particular scene on-the-spot (as, for example, with *Indian River*, executed in Florida in March 1970).

Lemieux has frequently put aside the lead pencil and pen and ink for the felt pen, especially since 1972 and in particular for large-format drawings — some of which go up to two metres in size. The felt pen imposes a particular technique on the artist, and the subtleties of wash must be left out of consideration. Each stroke is much like the last and hatching replaces gradation in the tones. Some of the drawings take on the stark simplicity of an X-ray photograph yet, even without being fleshed out, they bear the artist's characteristic stamp.

Lemieux's pen-and-ink drawings naturally preserve his characteristic poetic moods better than the felt pen, although it, in turn, gives a skeletal rendering which the artist has striven for in certain drawings. And the feelings of anguish which underlie much of Lemieux's work are thereby brought to the surface in a more brutal and penetrating fashion, unmollified by the gentle and affecting ambiguity that pervades several of his most remarkable paintings, those which depend for their effect on his characteristic *sfumato* technique.

During the summer of 1972, Lemieux executed a series of washes that brought a breath of fresh air to the thematic structures he had been developing over the previous fifteen years. Wash technique encourages spontaneity, in fact demands it; a heavy-handed approach with the brush can only spoil the picture. Yet for Lemieux spontaneity does not mean licence to lose control or indulge in a Dionysian frenzy, as an artist with an utterly different temperament — like Michelangelo or Van Gogh — could afford to do. The washes done in 1972 shrewdly combine inspirational bursts with careful control of the pared-down style. This can be seen in both the economy of line and the range of the palette, which is dominated by greys and blacks laid on white sheets of paper, punctuated here and there by bits of vermilion or emerald green. In some of the pictures the line almost becomes a kind of calligraphy, with patches of color and brushstrokes providing discreet trails for the wandering eye to follow. Figuration becomes, as it were, diaphanous and again it is the theme of time that dominates, time in all its delightful ambiguity, which leaves us uncertain as to whether it is oriented to past or future, or even to some indefinable parallel present, gently torn between reverie and hallucination in the artist's mind. There is something very familiar about the images Lemieux employs: they seem somehow to be a part of our own imaginary life, perhaps a once-buried layer, now brought to the surface by the sweep of the artist's brush, to reveal profiles and faces, horizons and reefs.

A Film, and the European Retrospective of 1974

The marks of official acclaim continued to pile up around Lemieux and his work. In 1973 he received the $15,000 Molson Prize. On January 27, 1974, the painter attended the première of a film titled *Tel qu'en Lemieux* (As with Lemieux) held at the Musée de Québec.

La chevauchée (The Ride), 1972

Le chapeau noir (The Black Hat), 1972, 61 x 182 cm (color p. 156)

This was a color documentary 25 minutes long produced by the Office du film du Québec. The project was first conceived as far back as 1968, although the bulk of the work was done in 1972. The script and direction were by Guy Robert, the electronic sound track by Micheline Coulombe Saint-Marcoux, photography by Paul Vézina and editing by Dorothée Brisson; Jean Paul Lemieux gave his willing co-operation and recorded a commentary. Here is what the film critic of Quebec City's *Le Soleil*, Claude Daigneault, had to say about it two days after the première:

"Here in Quebec, or in Canada for that matter, we cannot boast a fine collection of films dealing with artistic expression, any more than the radio and television networks can take pride in the interest they have shown in the visual arts. For this reason the première of the documentary *Tel qu'en Lemieux* takes on particular significance. In spite of more or less obvious shortcomings (a sound track that sometimes grates on the ear, the almost total absence of lap dissolves, shots blurred by an unsteady camera, cutting sometimes moving at a much faster pace than the speed of camera movement warrants), this short manages to convey some idea of the gentle pace at which paintings are created, especially these paintings, images of a past that the painter takes time to interpret, but also documents of a geography dominated by white silence. *Tel qu'en Lemieux* is a kind of corollary to Guy Robert's book *Jean Paul Lemieux, ou la poétique de la souvenance*. One of the film's most striking qualities is the way in which it expresses the painter's preoccupation with time, in particular the transience of the life cycle. There is a beautiful sequence in which the camera moves over the picture entitled *Les Noces d'or*: after slowly taking in each of the characters, it moves in a long travelling shot to bring out with some intensity the feeling of silence and isolation

146

Lemieux retrospective in Moscow, July 1974

being experienced by the two old people. All in all, this is no conventional documentary, with long pronouncements by the artist (here we get only a few sentences from the painter, accompanying big stationary close-ups), or carefully chosen passages of classical music between sections of an authoritative-sounding commentary. What we have instead is a personal view of Lemieux's work and its significance."

The year 1974 was especially significant for Lemieux's career because of a large retrospective of his work which brought together 70 pictures dating from 1956 to 1973. Organized by the Quebec Ministry of Culture, in co-operation with the Russian, Czech, Belgian, French and Canadian governments, the exhibition ran in Moscow from July 1 to 21, Leningrad from August 1 to 21, Prague from September 13 to October 6, Anvers from October 16 to November 6, and Paris from November 14 to January 5, 1975.

The Musée de Québec prepared an 80-page exhibition catalogue which contained 67 illustrations (9 in color), biographical and bibliographical notes and an introduction by Anne Hébert. The Musée d'art moderne de la Ville de Paris published a slightly different version, this one 58 pages in length and containing 40 illustrations. The Russian version was shorter again (40 pages) and contained 22 illustrations, seven of which were in color.

This full-scale European retrospective failed to stir up as much commentary about Lemieux as might

pessimism" to "severe solemnity," from "enchanting color" to remarks on the artist's sense of humor, and including a number of rather more prosaic considerations: "The artists' union absolutely must have an air-conditioning system installed in this gallery!"

In Prague, the Communist newspaper *Rude Pravo* reproached Lemieux for the infinite sadness of his work, while the Moscow newspaper *Gudok* had praised the rich nuances of Lemieux's colors. The journal *Russkaia Literatura* noted that "in these canvases, silence and concentration are kings," an unusual metaphor in a country where the czarist royalty was ruthlessly liquidated.

In Belgium, the retrospective was presented in Anvers. On October 25, 1974, *La Libre Belgique* carried an article signed J. P., which made the following remarks, among others: "Lemieux is as fine an artist as Chekhov! Just as the Russian playwright did for the theatre in his native Russia, this Québécois painter has managed to capture the heart and soul of his wintery province and to magnify all its little shivers, all its harmonics. With subtlety. Without fanfare. [...] To sum up, a whole world from the past, from the era of Duplessis, hardly able to match the excitement of life in present-day Quebec, yet presented with love, faithful to the memories, suffused with melancholy as well as with a highly romantic affection. For all that he is a regionalist, Lemieux is still a universalist, and art-lovers of all countries will certainly find these canvases stirring familiar emotions as they relate them to their own past."

CHRISTMAS/NOËL
Jean Paul Lemieux
Canada 6

150

Lemieux retrospective in Leningrad, August 1974

towards the end of September. Seventy artists were allowed to display their work to a crowd of visitors for a period of four hours.)

But let us return to the Lemieux exhibition. In Moscow yet another visitor regretted "not having had the urge to visit Canada and learn how its inhabitants live." With this remark, dated July 20, 1974, the visitor in question, a Mr. Znozenko, unknowingly pointed to one of the principal virtues of Lemieux's work, which is so fundamentally different from Krieghoff's, or, for that matter, from the typical Canadian postcard or the publicity brochures published by the Ministry of Immigration in Ottawa! An engineer from Perm was able to discover Canada through Lemieux's paintings and someone from the Leningrad Academy of Fine Arts wrote: "This is not just Canada, these are the very horizons of consciousness!"

Dozens of other Russian visitors filled the visitors' books with their comments, their feelings, their joy in discovering this "magical song without words." There were naturally a few dissenting opinions. On July 19 someone wrote: "I found nothing good about it, everything is abstract, without any intensity of thought or expression," while his immediate neighbor commented: "Why aren't there more exhibitions of this calibre? They have a beneficial effect on those visitors whose taste leaves something to be desired...."—To which someone added: "I like everything!"

"De gustibus et coloribus non disputandum," as the adage has it....And indeed, Lemieux's work prompted a wide range of reactions from the Russians, running from "the great delicacy of the pastel tints" to "a mess painted with mud," from "dreadful

Lemieux retrospective in Prague, September 1974

pessimism" to "severe solemnity," from "enchanting color" to remarks on the artist's sense of humor, and including a number of rather more prosaic considerations: "The artists' union absolutely must have an air-conditioning system installed in this gallery!"

In Prague, the Communist newspaper *Rude Pravo* reproached Lemieux for the infinite sadness of his work, while the Moscow newspaper *Gudok* had praised the rich nuances of Lemieux's colors. The journal *Russkaia Literatura* noted that "in these canvases, silence and concentration are kings," an unusual metaphor in a country where the czarist royalty was ruthlessly liquidated.

In Belgium, the retrospective was presented in Anvers. On October 25, 1974, *La Libre Belgique* carried an article signed J. P., which made the following remarks, among others: "Lemieux is as fine an artist as Chekhov! Just as the Russian playwright did for the theatre in his native Russia, this Québécois painter has managed to capture the heart and soul of his wintery province and to magnify all its little shivers, all its harmonics. With subtlety. Without fanfare. [...] To sum up, a whole world from the past, from the era of Duplessis, hardly able to match the excitement of life in present-day Quebec, yet presented with love, faithful to the memories, suffused with melancholy as well as with a highly romantic affection. For all that he is a regionalist, Lemieux is still a universalist, and art-lovers of all countries will certainly find these canvases stirring familiar emotions as they relate them to their own past."

150

While the Lemieux retrospective was prompting this diversity of comment in Europe, the Canadian Post Office was busy with a Christmas printing of 130 million stamps which featured Lemieux's 1966 painting *La Nativité*, the very one previously honored by inclusion in the UNICEF greeting card series in 1967.

The Pleasures of Retirement

As we have already noted, Jean Paul Lemieux has a great need for quiet and solitude. "I dislike travelling intensely, especially by plane!" While en route to the opening of his retrospective in Moscow, in June 1974, Lemieux had to stay over in Copenhagen for medical reasons, exhausted as he was on the brink of his seventieth birthday by all the hubbub that went with the preparations for this major cultural event—of which he was naturally the centre of attention. He was undoubtedly quite relieved to get back to Quebec and away from the burden of social duties. In November it was his wife Madeleine who represented him at the Paris opening of the retrospective.

Lemieux has never been fond of publicity, ·lurid or otherwise, nor of being lost in a crowd. Any amount of commotion is enough to set his nerves on edge, and he will take the slightest excuse to slip away to more peaceful surroundings. Discreet, self-effacing and sober in all things, he is quite happy to avoid receptions and social functions, and is of the opinion that being past seventy is another strong argument in favor of a life of peace and quiet. "The slightest disruption in my daily routine is a very trying experience for me."

Nevertheless, Lemieux does not live an entirely cloistered existence. When he is not in the grip of feverish creative activity, harassed by whichever picture he happens to be working on, the painter is happy to receive friends and relatives, provided of course that everyone respects his desire for moderation. For some years now the present author has had the privilege and the pleasure to meet with the artist at length, and he has always been open and animated in his conversation. Naturally, like many artists, he is not fond of being interrogated ruthlessly or assailed by photographers. In a two-way conversation, however, he speaks freely when given the chance. He loves to tell stories, and does so with great style and a characteristic elf-like quality detectable in his speech and twinkling eyes, which sooner or later explodes into hearty laughter.

It would be easy, and unfair, to make too much of Lemieux's dark pronouncements. By taking a remark out of its context in a conversation or article we can of course turn it to any tendentious purpose. To give a complete account of Lemieux, we would have to make room for his sense of humor, his irony, his mischievousness, his skill in repartee, his fondness for story-telling and much else besides. Once an avid reader of Voltaire, and of Spengler's *The Decline of the West*, Lemieux has taken a certain sceptical outlook from them, seasoned on occasion with a sarcastic contribution of his own. For Lemieux *is* known to evoke the *taedium vitae* in his more sombre moments. Some of his remarks may therefore appear peremptory and exaggerated, when taken out of context and quoted without the nuances of tone in which they were originally delivered. As a rule, however, even Lemieux's darker observations tend to have a carefully modulated and cheerful quality in their conversational context.

Lemieux sometimes gives the impression of a man consumed by sadness, haunted by grief, tortured by pessimism, obsessed by the idea of decadence, imprisoned once and for all by overwhelming solitude. But to reduce his world to such a bleak vision of things would be to misread altogether both his person and his art, and to mistake the part for the whole. There is no real bitterness in Lemieux's outlook. And his sense of humor, which is as lively as ever, often bubbles to the surface in the midst of an otherwise very bleak series of remarks, something he seems to take considerable pleasure in. In other words, this is not a man whose every remark should be taken too seriously!

The pace of present-day life leaves Lemieux dizzy, indeed it can make him quite literally sick (though one doesn't have to be a celebrated painter or a septuagenarian to feel a similar revulsion!). On other fronts, the artist cannot help feeling a certain distrust in regard to the daily bombardment of news of every sort, which is manipulated and distorted (or

View from one end of the property on the Ile aux Coudres, summer 1972

"processed" as the euphemism goes), before it is thrust at us. And while he is of the opinion that our civilization is in a state of decline, his diagnosis has a subtlety about it:

"We are living in a period of decadence, or at least of transition, a little like in Alexandria when hundreds of schools and camps were thrown together and battled one another for supremacy. These are times of great unrest. It's as though we were at the bottom of the trough between two waves. But even in the most decadent period, there is always hope, there are values that survive to save us from the catastrophe, from the darkest hour. Will we pull ourselves out this time? Will we see a new Renaissance? I don't know. I often feel we're living in a century in which machines and technology are suffocating everything else, especially art. All people can talk about is mass production. I'm not suggesting we should be listening to Beethoven or Vivaldi all day long! What makes a beautiful piece of music or art appealing is precisely not overdoing it, keeping it as something special. That's why I don't believe in the democratization of art, because that inevitably means the cheapening of art. Art will remain the privilege of a minority, of an élite who have a taste and a need for it, because men are quite simply not created equal and never have been equal, are different from one another in their tastes, as they are in other respects."

153

Lemieux went on to point out that some people are more muscular than others, some are better at maths, others at pole-vaulting. There are people who are crazy about military parades, hockey games or the music of a particular singing star. Others prefer cross-country skiing, the music of Stockhausen, books of philosophy or historical novels—or, for that matter, the paintings of Jean Paul Lemieux! And we are told by the sociologists who have made culture their field of study that the democratization of art often leads to a lowering of standards.

"Let's not forget," continued Lemieux, "that an élite was responsible for the Renaissance. It's also quite possible to live without art, completely detached from works of art. Billions of people do it every day, while others are content to admire calendar or postcard art and find themselves perfectly happy!"

As far as the kinds of art being produced today, since 1970 in particular, whether in Quebec or in Canada or elsewhere in the world, Lemieux makes no attempt to conceal his puzzlement and his profound scepticism. Conceptual art, Kitsch, hyperrealism, anti-art, anti-anti-art, all seem to him to be overblown and ephemeral fads, the stuff of avant-garde academicism, perils he had already warned of as far back as the mid-1940s.

"At my age I don't have much patience for novelties of that kind any more. They leave me cold. Why is there so much *negation* of art around these days?"

When he talks, Lemieux likes to fall back on anecdotes, unusual observations, amusing situations, as he once did in his drawings during the thirties and in his paintings in the decade following. Ever since 1956, however, his painting has ruthlessly stripped away all superfluous decoration, retaining only the bare bones of nostalgia, which is carried by the personages and landscapes of his pictures. His is the art of decanting, filtering, maturing an idea until it reaches a point at which it can express some aspect of the great mystery which is the human condition.

L'orée (Edge of the Forest), 1975, 38 x 50 cm

Les mi-carêmes (Mid-Lent), 1962 (p. 196)

A Living Memory

Having crossed the watershed of his seventieth birthday, Lemieux has tended more and more to keep his eye on the distant past, on a childhood shining with the miraculous light of happiness, made all the more intense for having been idealized in the artist's heart.

"The past is very important to me indeed, as I have often pointed out to you. It can never be completely forgotten. It's there and won't let you forget. It exists, whether you want it to or not, it clings to you like a shadow."

Or like a memory, a living memory. Like something nostalgic, nostalgic yet still full of wonder. Like remembrance, with its poetry translated so faithfully, so tirelessly by the paintings, through inexhaustible pulsations and variations. Like the old wardrobes, which can be found in every room of the painter's house, old wardrobes full of reminiscence and legend, about which Alain Grandbois has written:

Fermons l'armoire aux sortilèges
Il est trop tard pour tous les jeux . . .
(*Let us close the wardrobe full of sortileges, It is too late for all the games.*)

Lemieux on the contrary opens his wardrobes and as if by magic makes his pictures come forth, so that we can experience them as one would an album full of images touched by the mysterious alchemy of his art.

A great pleasure still awaits the painter every spring when he travels down to the Ile aux Coudres. Once thoroughly picturesque and unspoiled, the island has suffered somewhat from the less than unmercenary interest taken in it by numerous journalists and filmmakers. But Lemieux and his wife have little to do with the locals and stick pretty well to their own property, which casts a fond look over the sweeping panorama of Charlevoix and the river. Jean Paul and Madeleine Lemieux have spent the fine summer months here for some forty years. Lemieux has always been fascinated by the history of this little island, as well as by that of old Quebec, a subject with which he is quite conversant having learned to read

157

Le chapeau noir (detail), 1972 (p. 146)

The Lemieuxs in the island studio, summer 1972

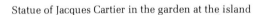

Statue of Jacques Cartier in the garden at the island

Madeleine and Jean Paul Lemieux on the island in 1966

Madeleine and Jean Paul Lemieux on the island, summer 1972

in the patina of its old and often desecrated walls the story of a great and bygone era.

The Lemieux house bears witness to this pious attachment to tradition and heritage. Seventeenth-century French relics keep company with Levasseur wooden angels, sculpted gilt candlesticks, antique engravings, armchairs from the seigneurie de Neuville and painstakingly restored country wardrobes.

The Ile aux Coudres, like any island, is awash with legend. Along the thirty-kilometre road which encircles it live less than two thousand souls with about as many porpoises living off-shore. It was on this island that Jacques Cartier and the crew of his three sailing ships caught their breath on September 7, 1535, intimidated as they were by the rapids opposite what would later be called Baie Saint-Paul. Two centuries went by before families from Tremblay and Savard in France arrived to establish a village. In 1759 the English put up there for a few months before going on to assault the fortress of Quebec, which the French had forsaken some time earlier and which was virtually handed over to the conquerors.

A long sandbank protects the island from high tides, while the Laurentian range deflects the north wind. And Quebec City is always there in the distance, a little more than an hour's drive through Charlevoix. This is home to Lemieux, a place where the painter can take refuge, where he can pursue the quest taken up in various forms with brush and paint ever since the great turning point of 1956. This is also the place where he turns inward to the unfailing inspiration given by the luminous memories of childhood.

We will now discuss a number of thematic "sequences" in the following section of the book, before going on to suggest the central "convergences."

SEQUENCES

This section of the book is concerned with Lemieux's work as a painter since 1956. This period covers the emergence of the new style which has made a name for Lemieux in the world of contemporary art, and through which he has reached a wide audience and achieved a great deal of success. Lemieux's paintings will be examined thematically and the reading will be based on a more extensive framework than that employed in the first book to appear on the painter, in 1968. Instead of delineating a single thematic spectrum, the solitude-others-encounter constellation between the space-time and pictorial magic poles, we shall deploy four rather more complex grids, illustrated much more copiously. They will be detailed in a long series of visual "sequences" and laid out in double-page spreads in order to demonstrate various dimensions and perspectives of the underlying thematic structure.

The text thus becomes analytic and breaks down into component parts — or at least into series more or less distinguishable one from another—what otherwise is presented very coherently in Lemieux's pictorial output as a whole. This approach to a discussion of Lemieux's work becomes necessary when we realize the difficulty inherent in trying to explain and illustrate everything in a single context. Once this analytic dismemberment has served its purpose, the coherence of the work will be restored by a process of synthesis in the final section of the book, appropriately titled "Convergences."

This thematic reading of Lemieux's work does not, of course, claim to be exhaustive. The underlying method is strictly empirical: some four hundred works, produced by Lemieux in the twenty-year period between 1956 and 1975, were compared and classified according to certain thematic lines as they emerged during the study. Secondary variants were then eliminated, prior to the establishment of a relatively simple thematic schema. A more elaborate or differently assembled sampling would probably not yield a substantially different profile, though it could cause the incidence curve or classification breakdown to end up in a somewhat different form.

Lemieux's Work since 1956

The work of Québécois painter Jean Paul Lemieux occupies a special place in North American painting since 1950. His pictures have remained apart from the schools and fashions that have swept the Western hemisphere since World War II. The artist has kept his distance from any camp or movement and has commented without reservation: "I am not in tune with Paris fashion. I am not part of the general current. The trends of contemporary art do not stir me. I look at these works, I read what is said about them but I feel nothing in common with them, even though I am sure they have a good deal of merit." (Quoted in the catalogue to the 1967 Canadian retrospective, p. 6)

Contrary to what often happens in the highly competitive world of contemporary art, where many artists achieve a brilliant but premature and fleeting success, Lemieux did not step into the limelight until the end of the 1950s, when he was already more than fifty years old. Yet with his discovery of a style that permitted ready identification of his paintings — an indispensable prerequisite for any artist who is going to rise above the mêlée of contenders for fame and fortune on today's art market — acceptance of Lemieux's work by a wide audience came very quickly.

Lemieux's work came of age, then, in 1956. Having sketched its archeology, genesis and long, slow evolution in the preceding section, we shall now undertake an analytic and thematic reading of this same work.

162

The world that Lemieux has painted since 1956 calls for a kind of dream-like approach, rather than a rigid system of deciphering whose conceptual assaults might well drive away the essential quality of the work, namely, its discreet, quiet, aesthetic texture. There is no question here of fanfare or fisticuffs, or the noisy pronouncements so common on today's art scene. In fact, some may find these works of art lukewarm or lacking in substance — but only if they are deaf and blind to the subtle discourse of a truly intimist artist. And it would be less than fair to criticize Lemieux's aesthetics or reject his work on the grounds that one does not like this aesthetic option.

The dream-like approach that Lemieux's work calls for, mentioned above, does not necessarily result in arbitrary or casual interpretations of his paintings. Rather, the method allows the viewer to identify the contours of Lemieux's affective geography which lies beyond the ordering of landscapes and personages, beyond what is visible to the eye, within the boundless domain of sentiment, feelings and states of mind.

The Thematic Approach

Among the many possible grids which can be used to shape the reading of works of art, the thematic grid would seem to be one of the least restrictive since it is intimately bound up with one of the most fundamental dimensions of aesthetics. A work of art, after all, is a repository of sensibilities, a vehicle of affectivity. But how is this connected to the concept of "theme"? And what is the usefulness of the thematic approach?

Let us question in turn several authors whose writings[1] though primarily concerned with the art of literature are readily applicable to the question of painting:

---

[1] The five texts in question are, in order of quotation: *Pourquoi la nouvelle critique*, by Serge Doubrovsky, p. 103; *André Gide*, by Jean Hytier, trans. Richard Howard (London: Constable, 1963), p. 23; *L'Entretien infini*, by Maurice Blanchot, p. 12; *L'Oeuvre et ses techniques*, by Guy Michaud, p. 53; *L'Univers imaginaire de Mallarmé*, Jean-Pierre Richard, p. 24.

"The theme, a key notion of modern criticism, is nothing else but the affective coloration of all human experience, at that point where it brings into play the fundamental relationships of existence; in other words, theme is the particular manner in which each man lives out his relationship to the world, to other men and to God. The theme is therefore the existential choice at the centre of every vision of the world: its affirmation and development constitute the mainstay of any literary work, or, if one prefers, its architectonics."

The themes of a work may, in simpler terms, constitute "the major directions of the deepest affectivity."

The concept of theme, which is not a container but the contained, always supple and open, could also take the form of a question: "Upon the background noise that constitutes our knowledge of the world and which precedes, accompanies and follows all knowledge of our own waking and sleeping, we project sentences that scan as questions — questions that speak. What are they worth? What are they saying? More questions. This concern for questioning, and the great dignity we ascribe to questions — what are their origins?"

In deciphering a thematic profile through the considerably more complex and ambiguous grid of symbolism, we could refer to theme in yet another way, as the open (and therefore questioning) dimension, and make of it a "cross-roads of meaning."

Theme is found at the root of a work, in the structural whole that informs it, a "concrete organizational principle, a scheme or locus around which tends to be constructed and deployed the world" that is put forward by the artist in his work; moreover, the "identification of themes is usually carried out according to the criterion of recurrence."

On the other hand, Roland Barthes asks: "...The *theme* (a good critical object, the 'right' object) is something that is repeated, isn't it?"[2] But to propose

---

[2] *Roland Barthes by Roland Barthes.* Trans. Richard Howard (New York: Hill and Wang, 1977), p. 71.

such a question is to confuse recurrence and repetition. The theme does not repeat itself, it modulates, assuming various configurations at different points in the same profile, progressing through its domain, at once changing and unchanging thanks to its virtually inexhaustible combinative powers. If it is, in fact, a "critical object," then theme can hardly be susceptible of repetition, copying or reproduction: these lowly tasks are left to the "Doxa," or Public Opinion, which Barthes speaks of in the same breath. Theme, on the contrary, thrives by virtue of the abundance and variety of its possible modulations.

The thematic aspect of an artist's work comprises all the contours of his vision of the world. Against this somewhat obscure and enigmatic background other congeries related to the thematic contours may also be isolated, such as characteristic symbols and archetypes. Looked at another way, the themes constitute points of affective convergence in the repertoire of images employed by the artist. They are therefore not reducible to the "subject-matter," "motifs," or "titles" of paintings. In his *Studies in Iconology*, Edwin Panofsky presents an interesting theory of picture analysis operating on three levels, none of which ever appear to be clearly distinguishable from the other two. However, by redistributing the elements of the analytic grid put forward by Panofsky,[3] and by carefully avoiding any confusion of "themes" and "concept," we can give a reading of a picture such as *Saint Anne with the Madonna and Child* by da Vinci in terms of the following four levels of analysis, classified under two main modes:

The iconographic mode, which is concerned with the description of the picture includes two levels of analysis: (a) the picture's technical data: dimensions, materials, dating, condition, artist or attribution, title, history, list of owners and places and dates exhibited, etc; (b) the picture's composition. Taking *Saint Anne* as an example: in a rocky landscape, a woman is seated on another woman's knees and extends her arms towards a child who is playing

---

[3] Erwin Panofsky. *Studies in Iconology* (New York: Harper & Row, 1967). See especially the Introduction, pp. 14-15.

rather roughly with a lamb. Details would follow concerning the landscape, vegetation, style of dress and age of the figures; underlying compositional structure; the palette and other tricks of the pictorial trade (*sfumato*, etc.).

The iconological mode is concerned with the interpretation of the work. Subsumed under it are the two remaining levels of analysis: (c) the subject-matter and its ideological and cultural environment. These are studied with the help of historical, geographical, sociological, religious, economic, political, psychological and psychoanalytical data —Freudian theories in the case of *Saint Anne*. We might note that this Italian Renaissance painting depicts a scene from Christian mythology in which Mary, seated on her mother Anne's lap, saves a lamb (mystical significance) just in time from having its ear torn off by the joyous but painful buffeting of the "gentle baby Jesus." Comparisons would follow with other works in the genre done by this and other artists. (d) Using the findings of the first three stages of analysis, the final step is to isolate those dimensions of the picture that may be described as affective or emotive: the look of tenderness shared by the three figures, the "poetic" mood of the work. In short, the goal of the final step is to grasp the thematic reality of the painting, the outline of the human condition it portrays, the vision of the world it presents, its emotive content.

In terms of an analytic grid such as the one we have just outlined, which could be adapted to almost any category of art object, whether plastic, musical, literary or cinematic, theme is given a privileged place. It is the theme that enables us to define the emotive or affective co-efficient of the work, and hence its essential aesthetic quality. After a lengthy phenomenological inquiry into the nature of a work of art, and in particular its poetic dimension, philosopher Mikel Dufrenne comments: "If we wish to define 'poetic' as an aesthetic category, then we must invoke the humanity inherent in appearances: the poetic resides in the generosity and benevolence of the tangible." (*Le poétique*, p. 194)

The poetic in fact lays the groundwork for the thematic architecture of the work, which reveals the poetic in its affective, emotive and tangible textures. Theme is thus relieved of the ideological component sometimes attributed to it and is solely concerned with the affective "impregnation" of the work and the emotional response of the beholder. This would seem to set apart a work of art from the menacing proliferation of objects in the world around it.

The Thematic Spectrum

Since 1956 the work of Jean Paul Lemieux has developed around two broad thematic concerns, those of time and of space—which also make up the axes of his emotional preoccupations. These concerns will be examined in one light here and in another light in the last section of the book. Here, they will be studied through the following two-part scenographic analysis: first, a scenography of place, which comprises four main constellations of reference, namely, the figure-background relationship, the city, places "elsewhere," and crowds or groups; secondly, a scenography of duration (this category is closely intertwined with the preceding one, and can only be isolated and defined as a separate entity for the purpose of analysis and for the convenience of discussion), which groups three thematic cycles — the seasons, times of day, and festivals or celebrations.

This two-part scenographic analysis provides the basis for another double-edged thematic approach comprising the categories of dramatic interplay and ritual. The former covers a number of Lemieux's family portraits, some depictions of the ages of man, a series on couples and several scenes of tragedy; the latter category emphasizes the strategic importance of variants in a particular thematic architecture, and it encompasses various works depicting religious scenes, nudes and women wearing necklaces.

It should be clear that what we are putting forward with this thematic schema is a simple method for "reading" a picture. The sole function of the method is to help us get behind the thematic mysteries of Lemieux's work in a manner that is neither completely arbitrary nor constrained by a methodological strait jacket. This schema does not rely on any rigid theory, system or preconceived formula; it has evolved, rather, from direct study of the paintings in question. It leaves ample room for the play of intuition and the magnetic attraction of "elective affinities" (whose subtle conjunctions Goethe explored so magnificently in his novel of the same name, published in 1809, and which is so reminiscent of the subtle shadings of mood and half-tones of Lemieux's post-1956 work). The fundamental ambiguity of Lemieux's paintings is charged with a singular sensibility. It points the way to the possibility of an interpretation which reveals both the usefulness and the limits of the thematic approach. Free rein is thereby given to the aesthetic pleasure buried in the heart of the beholder's imagination.

The present section proposes to enter into a dialogue not only with Lemieux's work, but also with a number of ideas expressed by the painter in conversation, as well as with quotations from other writers.

One last remark about the pages to follow: they will provide the reader with a breathing space at this point in the book, during which the eye will be less preoccupied with text and more agreeably entertained by the pictorial image. It is hoped the reader will interpret this as restraint rather than abdication of duty on the part of the author. He did not find it easy to rein in his pen just when the paintings seemed particularly to call for commentary.

THE SCENOGRAPHY OF PLACE

How has Lemieux represented space in his paintings in the post-1956 period? How has he organized his sense of pictorial place? The artist has had a number of different things to say about his approach to landscape, one of them being that he refuses to be considered a landscapist pure and simple. The human figure is such a pre-eminent force in his painting that even a seemingly uninhabited landscape becomes a person in itself and is treated by the artist as though it were a state of mind.

Lemieux's scenography cannot be reduced to a particular system of perspective or code of representation; it simply constitutes a "meaningful space." This concept was arrived at, after many twists and turns, by Jean-Louis Schefer in his book, *Scénographie d'un tableau* (in connection with *The Chessplayers,* by Paris Bordone). Though somewhat overwrought, this study makes such useful observations as "the figure can only be understood by means of the trap it sets for us (an image of things)." This brings us back to the theme, lying more or less concealed behind the subject, and to the total affective quality of the painting. The theme lends meaning to the many spaces delineated by the painter throughout his work, not merely for the purpose of multiplying an individual picture's perspectives and surfaces, but rather to give sense to the overall iconography developed as each new picture appears. In other words, it translates into a diversity of images a certain representation of the universe. This representation is at first intuitive and later more or less "composed," to the extent that the artist's field of consciousness settles and becomes organized in an aesthetic mode. Jean-Louis Schefer puts it this way in the course of a long tangential remark: ". . . there are several pictures inscribed in the picture; the picture thus represents a plural system of meaning whose unification is at once an ordering principle and an object in itself; the picture becomes a diagram of the meanings it evokes." (Scénographie d'un tableau, pp. 7, 98, 169)

In other words, the depth of meaning that a work of art has relies on the availability of meaning in that work. Every "reader" is limited in his comprehension, moreover, by the output of labor of his own sense working through his sensibilities. Place in painting (not simply figurative painting but all painting, whose surfaces constitute the locale of their own scenography), becomes a structure for receiving a cluster of meanings, and at the same time is a fluid diagram of the sensations uniting within it.

Paysage avec personnage (Landscape with Figure), 1963, 56 x 109 cm, RG

Figure and Background

Let us begin with a simple example from Lemieux's work and consider a dozen of his pictures that depict human figures painted against backgrounds, i.e., a series painted by the artist representing the relationship between the figure and the landscape against which the figure is inscribed. We could let our attention wander to a consideration of physiognomy, clothing, composition (framing, cropping of faces or bodies, etc.) or the modulations in the background. Instead, let us return to the leitmotiv of these pictures, the relationship between figure and background, which for all practical purposes represents man's place in the universe and his attitude towards that place.

In classifying these dozen or so pictures, we are struck by one thing above all, namely, the almost systematic approach of the artist in his treatment of the theme — whether he did so unconsciously or by design. The paintings themselves, however, are no matter of chance or accident, but were willed and then painted accordingly. Each one has a place, independent of its date of execution, in a logical progression: from the face viewed in close-up on a more or less non-existent background, to the figure that has become a virtually negligible quantity lost in an immense landscape. The latter gives the impression of being on the very edge of non-existence — and yet its presence, meagre though it may be, gives meaning to a space otherwise devoid of that seed which makes the creative act of seeing possible.

Le ruban bleu (The Blue Ribbon), 1974, 18 x 15 cm

Jeune homme au chapeau (Young Man with Hat), 1962, 48 x 32 cm, RG

Jeune fille au bord de la mer (Girl by the Seashore) 1961, 77 x 31 cm

Mademoiselle, 1960, 110 x 74 cm

Killer Joe, 1972, 82 x 20 cm

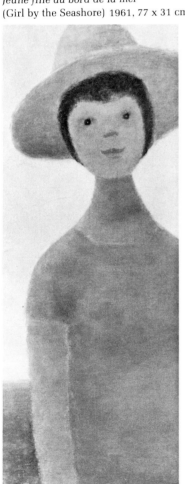

Sylvain et les étoiles (Sylvain and the Stars), 1970, 123 x 74 cm (Equinox Gallery, Vancouver)

Tête sur fond jaune
(Head on Yellow Ground), 1974

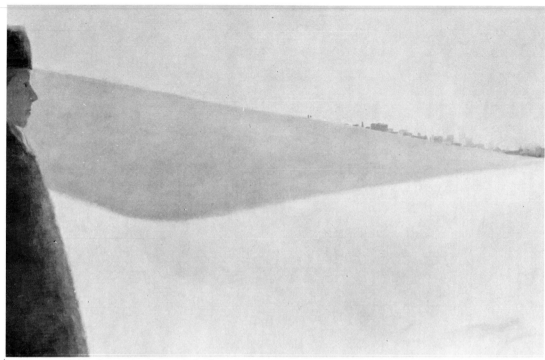

Les Hauteurs d'Abraham (The Plains of Abraham), 1963, 66 x 107 cm

"Now the scene is set on a virtually empty stage. On the vanishing line. Where attention is at its highest pitch, in all its mute density. On the crest of the wave, caught at the height of its authority. Only to sink and vanish. Let us make no mistake, life's other side is here, a powerful presence, waiting, soon to occupy the available space." (From the introduction, by Anne Hébert, to the catalogue of Lemieux's 1974 retrospective in Russia.) The very space that man and man alone can bring to life.

La semence (The Seeding), 1966, 20 x 61 cm, RG

Garçon dans un paysage
(Boy in a Landscape), 1974

Janvier à Québec (January in Quebec City), 1965, 107 x 152 cm, OFQ

The City

In his heart, Lemieux has never been a city-dweller; indeed he has always made his aversion to cities, especially big cities, quite clear. Though he has painted the city of Quebec many times, he has always depicted it as a kind of shrine, a vast museum whose outer shell bears the markings of historical incident and ancestral tradition. Earlier in his career, for example in the 1944 painting *Fête-Dieu*, Quebec City was the backdrop for numerous amusing and mischievous scenes of daily life. After 1956, the city would be observed mistrustfully, even cruelly, from afar.

Soleil sur la ville (Sun on the City), 1958, 36 x 104 cm

La nuit à Québec ouest (Night in Quebec West), 1964, 41 x 109 cm

Nuit sans étoile (Starless Night), 1964, 56 x 109 cm

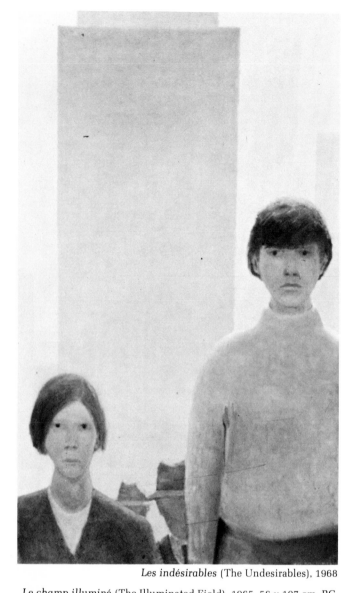

Les indésirables (The Undesirables), 1968

Le champ illuminé (The Illuminated Field), 1965, 56 x 107 cm, RG

"I've done a lot of travelling by train because it gives you a chance to see the countryside, to let it loom up, linger for a moment, then disappear again. It's a wonderful sight to behold, the countryside moving slowly past your window. When I got back from Europe in 1956, I made the trip from Quebec City to Montreal by train, and I was struck, somewhere around Trois-Rivières, by a strange spatial quality about the landscape. I felt like I kept getting closer to something elusive, that I could never reach. That was what I tried to capture in several paintings of the period." (From 1972 interview with the author)

Vent de mer (Sea Wind), 1963, 71 x 109 cm

Plage américaine (American Beach), 1973, 122 x 183 cm

Montréal l'hiver (Montreal Winter), 1965, 41 x 135 cm

Le Temps de Noël (Christmas-time), 1974,
150 x 75 cm (color pp. 1 & 192)

Crowds

Lemieux does not, of course, confine himself
solely to painting solitary figures lost in a setting that
dwarfs them, figures that look like so many contemp-
tible castoffs forever incapable of constructing for
themselves a suitable refuge in a hostile universe. A
number of the artist's most striking works are, on the
contrary, peopled by crowds. These crowds are moving at an accelerated pace towards some unknown
destiny, bearing witness to the troubled quality, the
absurd turmoil of urban life—for which, as we know,
the painter is so unsuited by temperament. Many of
the faces in these crowds are appropriately haggard,
anxious, sometimes even belligerent. Yet in most of
these works the gloom is relieved by the presence of a
child's face whose innocent quality keeps a spark of
hope alive even at the most pessimistic moments.

Lemieux's pictures of crowds are often cropped in an unusual manner, such that occasionally
figures are cut in half vertically by the edge of the
painting. These elisions seem to proclaim the unre-
lenting solitude of each person amidst the larger mass
of human beings, and they freeze the movements of
the body into strange, almost conventionally religious poses. What we have here is the sudden sus-
pension of life, a state of being, realized and captured
by the painter's eye. These images, as we know, have
not been taken directly from life, but have been constructed piece by piece in the painter's imagination.
This in no way prevents their being rooted in reality,
in that larger reality which extends beyond the in-
stantaneous—a reality of archetypal dimensions.

Terrasse Dufferin (Dufferin Terrace), 1967, 89 x 137 cm (Mr. & Mrs. W. Sofin) OFQ

Les Promeneurs (The Strollers), 1963, 107 x 147 cm, OFQ

THE SCENOGRAPHY OF DURATION

Why did Gaston Bachelard write a "dialectics" rather than a "poetics" of duration? Whatever his reasoning, the important point is that he invites us to try and understand with him "the slow adjustments of objects and time, the action of space on time and the reaction of time on space." He states, moreover, that "psychic continuity is not a given, but a task," an obscure kind of task performed in the field of consciousness, and fed by the "impulse of our origins." We translate the dynamic of that impulse using the sovereign architecture of rhythms and the "energy of existence," of which everyone carries an enormous reserve in his heart of hearts. (Bachelard, *Dialectique de la durée*, pp. viii, ix, 131)

No discussion of a poetics of duration can ignore Bergson, who wrote in *Matter and Memory* that "practically we perceive only the past, the pure present being the invisible progress of the past gnawing into the future."[5] Bergson again takes up the question of duration in his *Creative Evolution* and makes it a central concern of *The Creative Mind*: he believes that duration alone allows us to perceive as intensely as we do "the moving originality of things."[6]

Is this not, in fact, the task of the painter — to show, to bring to life "the moving originality of things"? Since November 1940, Lemieux himself has described the artist as someone who "seeks to express the visions that surge up from his subconscious with the incoherence of dreams, the perpetual movement of things and life in the world."

The scenography of duration can be delineated quite simply as a vector running from the past to the future through the shifting focal point of the present. Such a scheme cannot retain its elegant simplicity for long though, because the shifting point that represents the present turns the schema into a complex field of continual transformations.

---

[5] Henri Bergson. *Matter and Memory*. Trans. Nancy Margaret Paul and W. Scott Palmer (London: George Allen & Unwin, 1911), p. 194.

[6] Henri Bergson. *The Creative Mind*. Trans. Mabelle L. Ankison (New York: Philosophical Library, 1946), p. 124.

"I've always loved old yellowed photographs, family albums," Lemieux explains. "And when I'm in my studio, confronted by the empty canvas, something appears in my mind's eye from very far away. People appear, hazily, people from my own inner world. It's through memory that I make them my own, and eliminate the details at the same time ... I imagine that must sound a little Proustian...." (1972 interview) Proustian it does sound, profoundly so, reminiscent as it is of the idea that the immense cycle of "things past" constitutes a "search," a noble, sacred quest. This quest is never completed yet manages finally to attain a point where the "past is recaptured" and it does this (in the closing lines of Proust's monumental work), despite the vertiginous quality of "a past which already went down so far," "a place, a very considerable place compared with the restricted one which is allotted to them in space, a place, on the contrary, immoderately prolonged...in the dimension of Time."[7]

The Cycle of the Seasons

The idea of time, which constitutes the most palpable, spatial element in Lemieux's aesthetics can be seen unfolding throughout the cycle of the seasons, as well as joining certain moments of the day. The range in "scale" here is analogous to that found in the extended sequence of the human figure-background relationship alluded to earlier.

At this point we have brought together a series of pictures by Lemieux, all of which represent various seasons. The cycle corresponds to the Julian calendar and runs from January to December, beginning and ending with winter — a season Lemieux finds most disturbing: "Winter has a certain grandeur about it, but in our country it goes on too long. And the older you get, the longer it gets. Winter is traumatic. I dread snow and cold so much I would have a hard time deciding whether or not to spend the winter on the Iles aux Coudres. Reality can take on a frightening aspect, especially in winter. The artist's function is to transform life, just as Botticelli in his *Primavera* painted an extraordinary spring, a kind of ideal season." (Interview of summer 1972)

---

[7] Marcel Proust. *The Past Recaptured*. Trans. Andreas Mayor (New York: Vintage, 1971).

185

La Prairie (The Meadow), 1964, 64 x 109 cm

L'été canadien (Canadian Summer), 1965, 71 x 150 cm, OFQ

Fleurs et brume (Flowers and Mist), 1964

Mars, 1961, 42 x 82 cm, RG

Solstice d'hiver (Winter Solstice) (C.I.L., Montreal) OFQ

La Moisson (The Harvest), 1966, 28 x 36 cm, RG

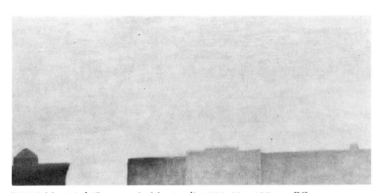

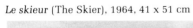

L'été à Montréal (Summer in Montreal), 1958, 58 x 127 cm, RG

Tempête de neige (Snowstorm), 1974, 15 x 18 cm (color p. 191)

Le skieur (The Skier), 1964, 41 x 51 cm

Les grands prés (Open Meadows), 1964, 107 x 147 cm
(The Royal Bank of Canada, Toronto)

Le bel hiver (A Fine Winter), 1966, 107 x 173 cm, OFQ

"When we reach April I'm always in good spirits because it's the end of winter and I know I'll soon find peace and quiet again on the island—something you never find in the city. You get up during the night and you can hear an endless low roaring, a continuous background noise; and you can't even see the sky because the streets are all lit up and there's a sort of fog always hanging over cities. To think there are actually people who want to send up satellites that would light up everything, so we'd never have night again...." (Interview of summer 1972)

Novembre (November), 1962, 51 x 124 cm, RG

Nuit d'été (Summer Night), 1962, 109 x 74 cm, RG

Midi (Noon), 69 x 112 cm, RG

Times of Day

Lemieux's work contains few depictions of sunrises, dawns or mornings — we might recall here the revealing title of a 1963 painting, *La mort par un clair matin* (Death on a Fine Morning). On the other hand, there are many paintings of dusk and night scenes, while daytime scenes seem to begin mostly around noon. Lemieux has nothing of Picasso about him, of that obsessive identification with the morning prompted by an old man's refusal to come to terms with his age. It was Picasso who hurled this scathing remark at André Malraux: "Nature has to exist, so she can be raped!" (*La tête d'obsidienne*, p. 56) On the contrary, Lemieux's philosophy does not countenance doing violence to nature, precisely so that nature can assume her full importance in his work.

Le Train de midi
(The Noon Train), 63 x 110 cm, NGC

Tempête de neige (Snowstorm), 1974 (p. 187)

*Le Temps
de Noël*
(Christmas-
time), detail,
1974 (p. 1)

Crépuscule (Twilight), 1962, 61 x 109 cm (Art Gallery of Hamilton) OFQ

Après-midi d'été (Summer Afternoon), 1971, 38 x 135 cm (M. Gabriel Gilbert) OFQ

"Melancholy can be represented by horizontal lines." (1940)

Tombée du jour (Nightfall), 1964, 107 x 165 cm, OFQ

193

Les patineurs du soir (Evening Skaters), 1962, 27 x 175 cm, OFQ

"I know the still of the night well, because I often wake up at night and listen to it. Silence for me is looking at a star-filled sky and hearing only the faint rustling of a few leaves." (Interview, 1972)

Voyage dans la nuit (Night Journey), 1963, 64 x 109 cm, OFQ

194

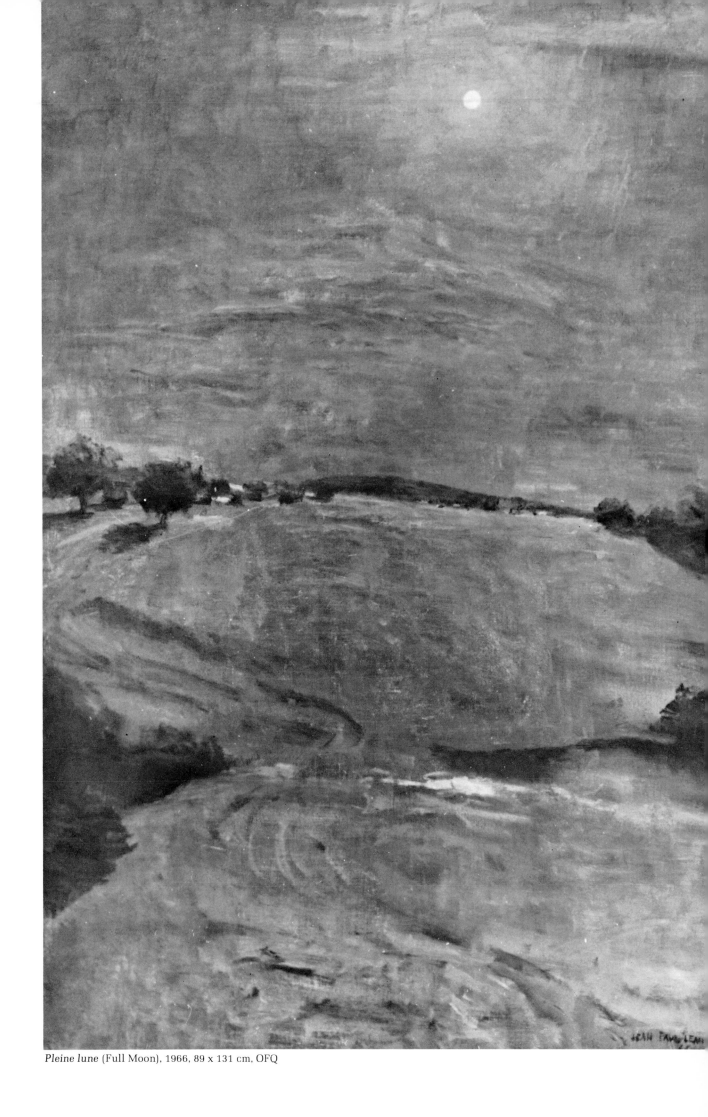

195

Pleine lune (Full Moon), 1966, 89 x 131 cm, OFQ

Les mi-carêmes (Mid-Lent), 1962, 88 x 135 cm (color p. 155)

Jeune clown (Young Clown), 1970, 34 x 24 cm

Festivals

Every morning could be considered a celebration of the sun reborn after the agony of the night. With every spring too, though on a vastly greater scale, life begins anew after the great white hiatus of winter. Sadly, the ancient, ecstatic Dionysian rites that were dedicated to the celebration of nature have disappeared from our culture, long ago harnessed by what we have come to call civilization. Modern-day celebrations have been tamed and stripped of their powers of transgression. They are even written into our lawbooks and calendars, any revels to which they give rise being carefully controlled. Even though, as sociologist Jean Duvignaud puts it in *Fêtes et civilisations* (p. 192) "our capacity to violate, to break down the restraining framework of our lives is probably the most fertile aspect of our being," it is a capacity that today is rarely exercised.

The celebration, the festival, is therefore repressed and reduced to a travesty circumscribed by a set of dates and censorial norms, to mere festivities which are radically out of touch with the mythic forces that once inspired the true festival. Those disquieting frenzies are now mainly confined within the limits of certain unabashed works of art (from the finale of Beethoven's Ninth Symphony through Rabelais and John of the Cross to *The Death of Sardanapalus*). We have lost that wild, raw instinct for the great celebration which can dissolve our inhibitions and fling us deliriously into the forbidden realms where the weight of cultural law no longer makes itself felt.

In their own way, certain of Lemieux's works are concerned with the mystery of what lies beneath the surface of things: they seem to go beyond the faces and landscapes which are their subject-matter. Once all the distracting elements have been eliminated, Lemieux's pictorial process aims at nothing less than the universal truth to be found at the focal point of all cosmic forces. The picture becomes an exploration of the labyrinthine depths of existence, and the rhythm of this search reveals the other side of our nature: that of primordial passion and the violation of taboo. Upon the frame of his themes the artist weaves a celebration, drawing inspiration from the well-spring

196

Les noces de juin (June Wedding), 1972, 114 x 178 cm
(CBC, Montreal) OFQ (color p. 226)

of his own recreated childhood which he has nostalgically invited to this fabled "eternal return."

·Here we find the harlequin and the minstrel, in
a night or winter setting. A manor house is the backdrop for *Les noces de juin* (June Wedding), about
which the artist commented: "There is something sad
about this painting, something tragic, almost grim."
A picture titled simply *La Fête* is set, enigmatically,
in a forest — the original site of man's most ancient
religious rituals.

La Fête (The Celebration), 1963, 89 x 176 cm

La Visite du Jour de l'An (New Year's Day Visit), 1971, 81 x 134 cm, OFQ

THE PROGRAMMATIC NETWORK

We must take care at this point not to over-emphasize the austere and introspective side of much of Lemieux's post-1956 work. Despite the great despair and solitude evinced by many of the scenes he has painted, he is nonetheless attempting to render his powerful desire for closeness and communication. The Quebec panorama, (are we dealing here with physical or mental geography?) wild, hostile and relentlessly horizontal as it is, comes to life under the affectionate and animating eye of the painter. Without betraying its essential nature, Lemieux converts it into an open place where time and space come together completely. They form a single continuum which moves to one rhythm and breath, suspended, united and made tractable by the artist's hand. This process is supported by a robust structure, in which the pictorial technique serves only as a measure of Lemieux's restrained eloquence and as the beginning of a seductive but perfectly discreet stylistic rhythm.

The theatrical aspect of Lemieux's pictures is strange indeed: while the bodies of his characters are fixed in hieratic poses, their souls seem to be free to pursue their longings and frustrations. The ambiguity of the scene is further heightened by the presence of a bright-eyed child. Lemieux's work balances upon points like these; he unites in one place (the child) two important planes of existence — childhood and the past.

Family Portraits

The perfect meeting ground for childhood and the past is provided by the yellowed photo albums of which Lemieux is so fond. From these, and through the alchemy of brush and imagination, he draws his family portraits. The artist's treatment of this theme extends the emotional range expressed in his work; almost all these pictures have a troubled, ambiguous air about them, as if levelling some gentle criticism. This critical aspect is very pronounced in a picture like *Chacun sa nuit* (To Each His Night), which catches three characters in profile on a cold winter's night. The mother and father stand together as one figure, almost as though one were a reflection of the other. The child, separated from his parents and perhaps pleased to be on this strange outing, is faced with the inevitable solitude which is everyone's lot in life, there being no escape from the painful fate of

Album de famille (Family Album), 1958

198

separation and loneliness. The painter has explained that in its first phase the painting depicted a field of battle dominated by a general, shouting orders to his troops. For several weeks the picture languished on the studio wall while Lemieux attempted to re-organize it altogether — as he often does with his paintings. Now, only the general survives the drastic reworking of the composition in the rather martial representation of the father, although something of the original feeling of the battlefield survives also, because *Chacun sa nuit* remains tense, tragic, distres-sing. In the final version, however, the conflict is of another, and more complex, sort: less explicit and colorful, it concerns man's struggle against the ele-ments, the cold and the dark, his struggle against time which tears apart and isolates, against deathly sol-itude, against the mute indifference that separates one human being from another.

1910 Remembered, 1962, 109 x 149 cm, OFQ (color p. 34)

The family can, of course, be a joyful rallying point for celebration and honored traditions, but Lemieux's vision of the family focuses on other aspects. His painting *1910 Remembered* represents a trip more than fifty years back into the past, a trip that is heavily charged with nostalgia. As is often the case in similar paintings of Lemieux's, the child depicted is the artist as a child. The artist is attempting to salvage at least part of his childhood from utter oblivion. The child is framed on either side of the picture by a man and a woman in profile. They stare at each other, apparently indifferent to the little boy who is the product of their conjugal union. As in *Chacun sa nuit*, the child here seems to be taking the inevitable step into a separate existence with its attendant loneliness. However, the overall feeling of this picture is less despairing than that of *Chacun sa nuit*.

200

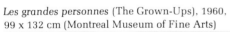
La Visite (The Visit), 1967, 170 x 107 cm, NGC

Les grandes personnes (The Grown-Ups), 1960,
99 x 132 cm (Montreal Museum of Fine Arts)

Un âge va, un âge vient . . . (One Generation Comes, Another Goes),
1972, 36 x 43 cm (color p. 52)

Une famille (A Family), 1966, 175 x 109 cm, OFQ

Dans le temps (Through Time), 1967, 127 x 179 cm, OFQ (color p. 51)

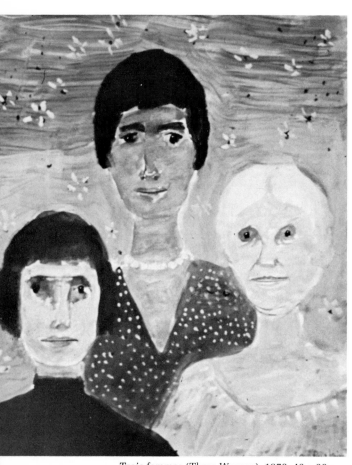

Trois femmes (Three Women), 1972, 43 x 36 cm

The Cycle of Life

A number of the family portraits touch on the theme of the life cycle, and primarily on the child-parent relationship. But Lemieux's obsession with the past does not end here. It prompts him to travel further back through the generations in search of the very roots of memory, and to go beyond the ever-present pain of time irretrievably lost. In the crucible of memory the artist finds suitable images with which to translate his burning desire for a continuity through the dark and tortuous labyrinth of life. For Lemieux though, as for us all, the facts of life remain the same: the carefree child gambols about on the very ground that must one day hold his bones. Such is life. "One changes, one evolves, but above all one ages, and one remains forever a prisoner of a past that creeps into the present, which in turn goes back into the past. . . ." (Interview, 1972)

In Lemieux's work we find people of all ages, from the newborn baby to the old man on the verge of death. Many of them seem to pose the enigmatic question which Lemieux and Gauguin ask: "Where do we come from? Who are we? Where are we going?" It is the question raised also by the Fates and by the enigma of life, to which the answer might be " a voyage to the end of time."

202

Les Parques (The Fates), 1962, 71 x 110 cm, RG

Amélie et le temps (Amélie and Time), 1965, 74 x 180 cm, RG

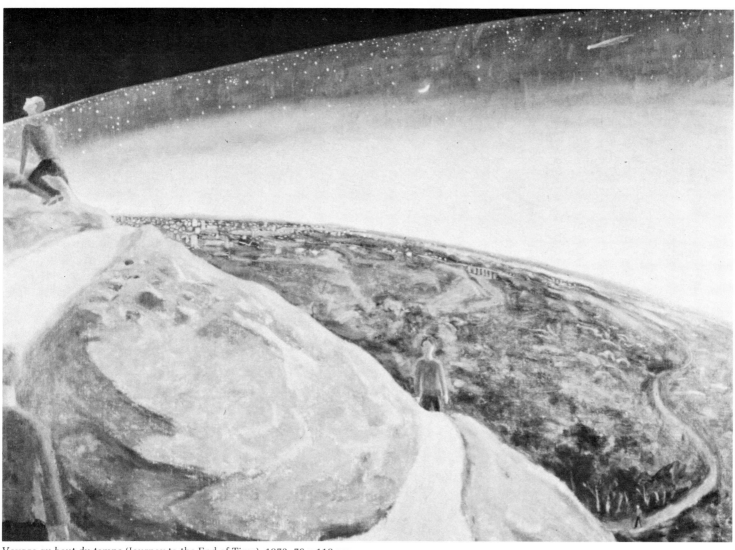

Voyage au bout du temps (Journey to the End of Time), 1973, 76 x 110 cm

Mère et enfant (Mother and Child), 1965, 74 x 51 cm, RG

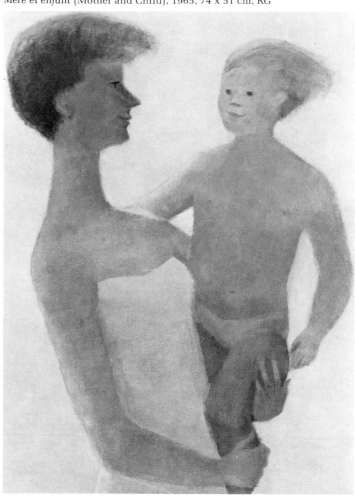

204

Rencontre (Encounter), 1968, 38 x 61 cm (color p. 225)

Deux fillettes (Two Young Girls), 1963, 102 x 57 cm, RG

Le dessert (Dessert), 1970, 68 x 46 cm

Couples

Several paintings in Lemieux's work depict couples, and this group of paintings has its own dramatic range, one which covers the relationships between two persons. The first phase comprises the theme of mother and child, though this receives far less attention from Lemieux than the relationships between two boys, two girls, two children or two adults. Often these groupings are situated in a landscape and occasionally, as in *Le dessert* (The Dessert), the two figures may be cropped and juxtaposed in an unusual manner.

A 1968 picture entitled *Rencontre* (Encounter) occupies a special place in this series because of the joyful quality that shines through it. The boy and girl face each other with a certain gravity, in a tender, yet unsentimental way, lips parted as if ready to murmur their first "I love you." They give new meaning to love, to communicating, to seeing, in the dull setting of Quebec City in the winter.

L'hiver (Winter), 1969, 188 x 131 cm

Felt pen drawing, 1973 (Photo La Presse)

More often the artist paints older couples caught up in the divisive troubles of building a shared life and yet bound together by sheer force of habit. In one picture, the man is leaving, umbrella in hand. In *La Floride* (Florida), the old couple are separated by a child who has his back turned to them. He seems ready to plunge into the sea and a life of his own, leaving his elders to warm their old bones under an intense sun which softens and melts their memories.

The picture titled *Les noces d'or* (Golden Anniversary) concentrates on this theme and pushes it to its tragic limits. The painter himself has described how this painting came about. One July day in 1966, he saw a priest seated on the balcony of a village presbytery. His domestic, wearing a polka dot dress, was seated close by. This scene soon found its way onto canvas, but in the process of being reworked (as most of Lemieux's paintings are) the priest and his domestic turned into a couple celebrating their fiftieth wedding anniversary. There is a composure here that bears witness to a half-century of loyal and mutual tolerance. Yet the two old people seated on either end of a bench look remarkably alone, at a time when they should be surrounded by teeming grandchildren; both of their faces are set in faint, sad smiles, and there is a chilling look-alike quality about them. The void that separates them is dominated by the crucifix. The old woman's arms hang limply beside her weary body, although we sense that her hands are still equal to the most thankless tasks. The old man's hands are folded across his stomach, as though holding back some secret hernia and seemingly locked in place by the handcuff-like shirtsleeves. There is, in spite of everything, a serenity on these deeply lined old faces, a serenity left by the passage of time spent together, a last gesture of life before the pallor of oblivion.

206

Les noces d'or (Golden Wedding), 1966, 130 x 173 cm, MQ

La Floride (Florida), 1965, 91 x 135 cm, OFQ

The Tragic

What is finally tragic about the human condition is precisely the passage into death and oblivion suffered by one and all, and the impenetrable mystery of what lies beyond our ultimate disappearance. Lemieux has tried to capture this tragedy in a number of his pictures. He has indicated his interest in the Expressionist school of painting, particularly as represented by Edvard Munch; indeed, the "fresco of life" painted so hauntingly by the Norwegian artist is reflected in much of Lemieux's work. In particular, both share a sense of anxiety. They despair over life and its masquerades, and over the horror of death, which the Québécois artist has shown coloring the features of a priest bringing the last sacraments to a dying man, in the painting *Le Visiteur du soir* (The Evening Visitor).

Les Temps passés (Times Past), 1965, 74 x 109 cm

Le Visiteur du soir (The Evening Visitor), 1956, 80 x 110 cm, NGC

Les masques (The Masks), 1973, 84 x 129 cm (M. & Mme. Gilles Boissonneault) OFQ

Lemieux has said that he likes "to paint old people, characters deeply marked by life," — and therefore marked by imminent death as well. Lemieux believes that the face has a message to impart all through life, and a good deal of his work has been concerned with capturing the characteristic expressions of different stages of life from cradle to the deathbed.

|Supermarché (Supermarket), 1964, 84 x 51 cm, OFQ

La vieille dame souriante (Old Lady Smiling), 1965, 109 x 71 cm

Les appartements Stanford (The Stanford Apartments), 1965, 107 x 66 cm

210

La Nouvelle-France (New France),
1972, 71 x 122 cm (M. & Mme Marius Lessard)

La Nouvelle-France in progress, July 1972

During the summer of 1972, the author watched a painting, *La Nouvelle-France* (New France), undergo a drastic transformation in Lemieux's studio on the Ile aux Coudres. The transformation was again a process of stripping away inessentials. Here are the painter's own comments about his work: "Everything about it is grim. These people are lost. They are in a land they knew nothing about when they arrived, so they are completely ill-equipped. They're trapped. The black bird beside them and the storm-cloud overhead further emphasize this tragic quality. These people will disappear, massacred by the Iroquois or carried off by some deadly epidemic. The scene is set around the time when my ancestor Pierre Lemieux arrived in New France. He must have led a similar life, trying to survive against terrible odds. When I look at them I wonder how it is that we're still here."

We move on now to another and very different work, entitled *Supermarché* (Supermarket), a "phantasmagoria in which the consumer society has wasted away and has only bones left to chew on," as Anne Hébert described it in the catalogue for the Lemieux retrospective of 1974.

Terminus, 1962, 74 x 102 cm (C.I.L., Montreal) OFQ

L'énigme (The Enigma), 1964, 104 x 157 cm

Solitude de l'homme (Solitude of Man), 1962, 48 x 110 cm, RG

La mort par un clair matin (Death on a Clear Morning), 1963, 107 x 81 cm, OFQ

"This nostalgia for time past, for a more peaceful time when things moved slowly, is a mark of serenity, akin to the serenity of landscapes. A terrible sense of fear streams from the feverish eyes of certain characters; you think you have captured their expression, but they are looking so far away, beyond you, into a terrible space without end, which seems to mesmerize them." (J. Folch, *Liberté*, Montreal, March 1963, no. 26, p. 164)

THE FIELD OF RITUAL

Let us penetrate further into Lemieux's pictorial work, into what we might call his "thematic rituals." As we have already noted in connection with his treatment of the seasons, for example, or of the relationship between landscapes and human figures, the corpus of Lemieux's work presents a series of subject areas which reveal striking coherence and complementarity. They appear to be part of a systematically conceived project. At the very least they bear witness to an obsessive continuity in thematic forms, and to the artist's perhaps unconscious desire to develop these forms to their fullest extent and in all the variety permitted by consciousness. Another important aspect of this "serialization" of subject-matter is the development of variants on particular themes. We will consider this aspect as best we can, given that we cannot see what goes on in the privacy of the artist's studio, and hence cannot observe the numerous and far-reaching metamorphoses undergone by most of Lemieux's paintings before the act of signing puts an end to their internal development.

These variants can be likened to litanies or incantations; they are closely bound up with the artist's sense of mission or his "obsessive metaphors," as the psychocritical analysis of Charles Mauron, whose goal is to isolate the "personal myth" that inspires the work of certain artists, would have it. But such a convergence on a single point of explanation, even when the point is as wide-ranging an area as that of myth, is abortive. It blocks the free flow of thematic permutations in a picture, and the interpretation of its forms and meanings. The latter two intertwine with each other and affect the emotions, which in turn links them to the ever-shifting field of consciousness. Any work of art involves a process of sedimentation whose geology and geography remain dynamic, organic and in continual transformation, though a static appearance belies this fact.[8]

---

[8] Merleau-Ponty expressed this same idea in the notes published as an appendix to his unfinished work, *The Visible and the Invisible*: "Thus the painting is a 'world' by opposition to the unique and 'real' world — In any case, it forms a world with all the other paintings — The *same* sensible elements signify something else there than in the prosaic world." ("Working Notes" p. 223) See bibliography.

The rectangle of canvas that is the painting, which the painter conquers and makes tractable, becomes a cosmogony, both a symbol of the world and a world of symbols. Meaning is at work behind the painting's architecture of forms, taking shape through them and proliferating. (Meaning here signifies the physio-psychological origins of our sensation-sentiment that the intellect strives to conceptualize, in order to grasp and express them verbally.) The symbolic character of a painting gives it its dimensions of incantation and of a complex living ritual.

In this aspect of his work the artist must look back at himself. He recognizes in himself certain profound tendencies, various intuitions and fascinations which lead him irresistibly to certain schemas, themselves inexhaustible either in one work or many because of their boundless thematic and semantic fertility ... thus the importance of the unfinished work in aesthetics, and Lemieux's pertinent observation that a painting is never finished, never quite finished.

This radical incompleteness arises from the impossibility of ever finishing anything whatsoever in a rigorously definitive manner. It injects into every new work its own justification: paintings and books are born from paintings and books, as are men from men. It is the incompleteness of this endless succession of forms that constitutes the driving force that expands the inventive faculties and pushes them on to new explorations.

Variants

The artist, turning in on himself, translates his state of mind and produces variants on his own work or on the work of others (who might well be connected with other artistic and aesthetic languages altogether). Variation and variable — at once something else and yet the same — incantation, litany, ritual. Here then are three radically different sets of variants from Lemieux's work.

Les deux cavaliers (The Two Riders) in progress at the island studio, July 1972

Les deux cavaliers, 1972, 127 x 177 cm (color p. 243)

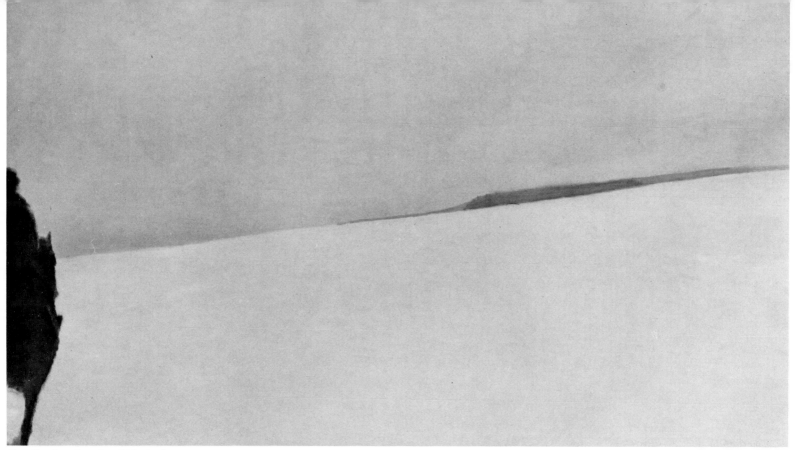

Cavalier dans la neige (Rider in the Snow), 1967, 89 x 135 cm, OFQ

First, a set chosen from the secular domain, that of the rider. Behind these images, which in certain cases border on the frivolous, or seem to amount to nothing more than so many sporting illustrations, we find the artist's obsessive theme of *homo viator*: the horseman forever seeking through the movement of his mount to give direction, if not meaning, to his existence.

Cavalier au bord d'un lac (Rider Beside a Lake), 1970, 55 x 132 cm, OFQ

Le Cavalier (The Rider), 1964

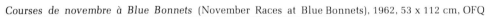

Courses de novembre à Blue Bonnets (November Races at Blue Bonnets), 1962, 53 x 112 cm, OFQ

Le manoir (The Manor), 1973, 42 x 67 cm, OFQ

La chasse à la poule d'eau (The Water-Hen Hunt), 1970, 21 x 30 cm
(color p. 244)

The second set of variants concerns hunting, and might seem equally worldly and trivial. And yet it is not, for it is linked to one of man's oldest rituals, as evidenced in the caves of Pech-Merle and Altamira.

La chasse (The Hunt), 1972

La chasse (illustration for *La petite poule d'eau*) (color p. 244)

Cortège funèbre (Funeral Procession), 1972, 36 x 46 cm

La Nativité (Nativity), 1966, 72 x 102 cm, OFQ (color p. 138)

Nativité (Nativity), 1964

The third set of variants is borrowed from the world of Christianity. Liturgy and ritual are represented very literally, if not particularly intensely or profoundly. Two "nativities" serve to introduce a long procession of religious scenes. Many of these employ a ritual setting that has been drained of its original mythic thrust by an institutionalized religious ceremony that has made it more readily subservient to the demands of organized worship.

La Crucifixion (The Crucifixion), 1957, 135 x 61 cm, OFQ

Religious Scenes

Lemieux has painted many religious scenes, particularly in 1941, 1944, 1951, 1955, and also in the post-1956 period. The artist's eye maintains the same critical discernment he brings to bear on all the thematic areas he has explored. Lemieux does not hesitate to assume a certain detachment, which to some extent accentuates the internal tension of these pictures — often to the point of pathos — and underlines the anguished sense of dereliction of duty resulting from the problems of both living and painting.

Oddly enough, Lemieux's religious works are not necessarily his most hieratic, in the sense that they best express the nature of the sacred. This we find more intensely rendered in those paintings dealing with man's place in the universe as a major theme, or those in which a child's questioning look throws the enigmatic nature of fate into relief.

Le Témoin (The Witness), 1963, 79 x 107 cm (Galerie Zanettin, Quebec City)

220

Quebec City studio, April 1962 (Photo Rosemary Gilliat)

L'Ange blanc (The White Angel),
1958, 128 x 58 cm, RG

L'Annonciation (Annunciation), OFQ

221

Les enfants de choeur (The Choir Boys), 1966, 109 x 58 cm

L'Apôtre (The Apostle), 1966, 107 x 76 cm, OFQ

Portrait d'évêque (Portrait of a Bishop), 64 x 49 cm

"Pastor et Nauta," 1973, 121 x 70 cm, OFQ

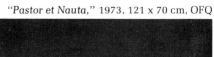

222

Les Moniales (Enclosed Nuns), 1965, 107 x 203 cm

La Soeur blanche (The White Sister), 1961, 133 x 76 cm (C.I.L., Montreal)

"We must achieve silence with ourselves, a silence of that profound sort which alone enables us to hear the prodigious silence of the universe, the austere and splendid silence of Lemieux. What lurks here is not just silence but the invisible, challenging us to capture it, as we are invited to this contemplation, to this beyond. No point in trying to dodge this pressing invitation, this summons out of time. Why attempt to flee, like certain characters from the paintings, right at the edge of the frame? Are we that attached to life as we know it?" (Anne Hébert in the catalogue of the 1974 Lemieux retrospective)

Detail from the mural *Médecine*, 1956 (p. 113)

Portrait, 1973, 66 x 51 cm

Women with Necklaces

A woman wearing a necklace has become a favored leitmotiv in Lemieux's work since 1956. *Vanitas vanitatum*....Feminine vanity has often, too often, been a target for Western painters, nearly all of them men of course. Yet without this quality, life, both public and private, would be much less agreeable—at least as far as appearances are concerned.

In Lemieux's painting, the vanity of woman is no longer a simple matter of make-up or gaudy jewellery. It becomes a refusal to submit to the ravages of time, an exorcism of the aging process and even the proclamation of a quality of being—a singular way to announce one's person, beautifully and almost poetically. Beyond what appears to be mere frivolity, we are therefore dealing with ritual once again. The ceremonials of beauty maintain a significant yet ambiguous relationship with other ceremonials and with the universe. The ceremonials of beauty become a kind of incantatory display in which the necklace serves as a talisman, a talisman of beauty such as Musset described—rare and therefore precious, like a pearl. Any attempt at liberation however, whether from aging or time, takes on a mythical dimension. And any process of liberation imposes, in a dialectical fashion, an order of its own. Thus the necklace becomes a leash and a symbol of servitude beneath the jewels' sparkle.

224

Rencontre (Encounter), 1968 (p. 205)

Le beau monde (The Beautiful People), 1969, 56 x 91 cm (Lucie & Claude Vary)

Les noces de juin (June Wedding), 1972 (p. 197)

1914-1964, 1964, 111 x 61 cm, OFQ

Portrait de profil (Portrait in Profile), 1961, 51 x 31 cm, OFQ

Miss Knight, 1961, 135 x 71 cm

Le déjeuner (The Lunch), 1965, 79 x 38 cm

Jeune fille en jaune (Girl in Yellow), 1964, 109 x 61 cm, OFQ

227

Dame en noir (Lady in Black), 1962, 51 x 36 cm, RG

Le collier (The Necklace), 1961

Les perles (The Pearls), 1963, 130 x 53 cm

229

Five o'clock, 1973, 66 x 51 cm (Louise & Marcel Lacroix)

The Nude

The nude occupies a special place in the world of art, even beyond the frontiers of Western civilization, because of the particular nature of the sentiments it arouses. Lemieux has painted a number of nudes over the course of his career, usually without a model. Ostensibly, therefore, he was following Gauguin's advice (though Gauguin himself ignored it, at least as far as the use of models was concerned): "In painting, the artist must try to suggest rather than describe, like the musician. And it is preferable to paint from memory, because then the picture will faithfully translate the artist's feelings, intelligence and outlook."

Lemieux's nudes mainly depict children, occasionally young girls with budding breasts, rarely women. Also depicted is a naked young horseman and a nude child with a bird perched on his fingers. These are chaste nudes. The painter seems to lack a taste for gross sensuality: "I find Rubens' paintings, with flesh spilling out all over the place, completely unpalatable," Lemieux explained during an interview on February 5, 1975.

There is nothing here of the erotic torments that create turmoil in the work of Leonor Fini, nor of the more placid, yet none the less powerful, eroticism that haunts the pictorial universe of a Balthus. In a picture entitled *La Servante*, we sense the beginnings of some disturbing ritual which seems to have been cut short by the artist before being allowed to develop further, as though it threatened to precipitate some dangerous transgression.

230

Le cavalier nu (The Naked Rider), 1972, 43 x 36 cm

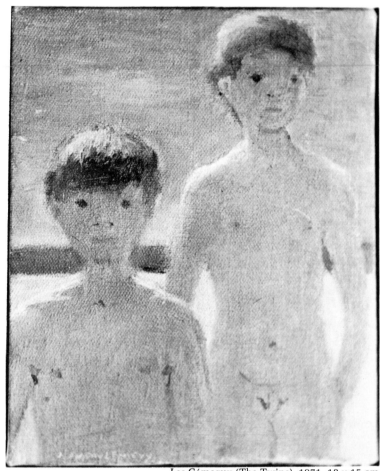

Les Gémeaux (The Twins), 1971, 18 x 15 cm

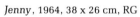

Jenny, 1964, 38 x 26 cm, RG

Petit nu rose (Little Pink Nude), 1963, 48 x 30 cm
(M. & Mme Lucien Mainguy)

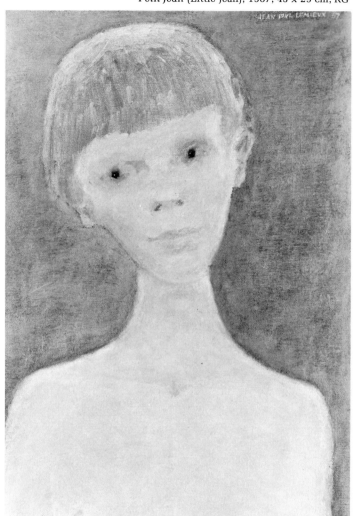

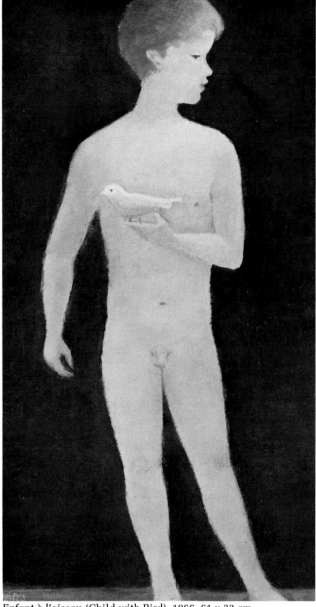

Enfant à l'oiseau (Child with Bird), 1966, 61 x 33 cm

La baigneuse (The Bather), 1964, 86 x 80 cm, OFQ

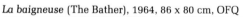

Nu sur fond bleu (Nude on Blue Ground), 1963, 110 x 61 cm, RG

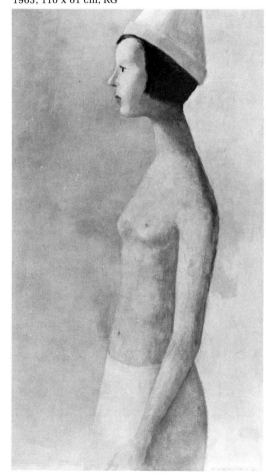

232

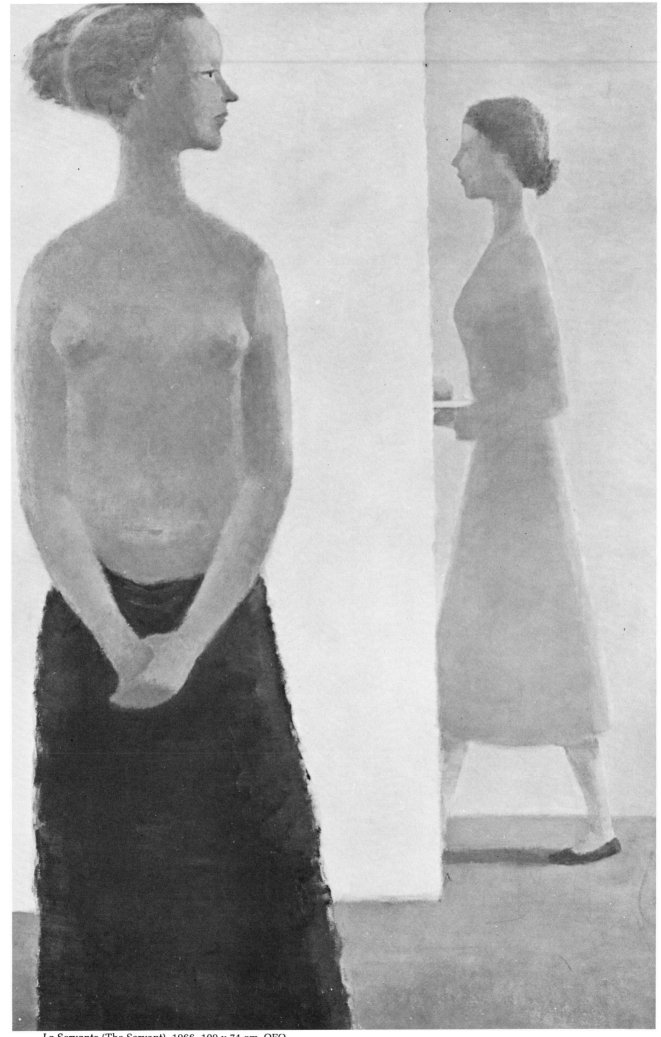

233

La Servante (The Servant), 1966, 109 x 74 cm, OFQ

CONVERGENCES

The preceding section has suggested several thematic readings of various portions of Lemieux's work. However, it remains far more complex and involved in its affective architecture than we have been able to demonstrate. It is important that we appreciate the artist's astonishing skill in uniting the emotional content of the image with its plastic context. His achievement opens up dizzying vistas on the "otherness" that is within everybody, and that makes it possible to establish a mode of communication.

Lemieux has pursued his determined quest for a means of communication through a body of work that might at first seem to fortify, rather than break down, the high wall of solitude. This observation is justified by remarks like the following, made in the course of an interview in 1961: " . . . generally speaking, the best works of art have been produced in isolation." But Lemieux's deserted landscapes and solitary human figures also constitute a powerful denunciation of solitude. They could well be interpreted as an extended critique, as well as a focal point, of the human condition.

Convergence of Solitude

The urge to communicate is the driving force behind a quest for "the other." This is a project which can only be undertaken in solitude, and for Lemieux, the project specifically calls for the "island" that is his studio. This is a solitude that remains open to the world though, in search of the other, a search which may never be satisfied yet is always attentive to the slightest hint of human warmth. We are not dealing here with a solitude that shuts itself away and withers everything around it, but rather with the profound desire to cross a barrier, beyond which the effigies of isolation lose their severity and open up the prospect of a pairing of visions — the painter's first of all and later our own.

Let us now examine a few paintings with these ideas in mind. In *L'Orpheline* (1957), the theme of solitude reveals itself in the child's social status (clearly indicated by the title), in the rigid posture of her body (truncated by the frame), her fixed stare away from the village, and in the sheer distance that separates her from the little world in the background, the village she can never call her own and which will never have a place for her. The little girl also wears the severe and sadly anonymous uniform that indicates her exclusion from society. The carefree happiness typical of other girls her age is altogether absent from her being. We can see this from her ghostly face, which manifests all too clearly an overwhelming desire for the affection and tenderness cruelly and finally thrust beyond her reach. Her hair is neither gracious nor appealing and any feminine vanity is made all the more conspicuously absent by the hastily tied and clumsy-looking white ribbon. It sits on her head like an absurd butterfly in a desolate and infinitely sad landscape where the feeling of oppression is virtually intolerable.[1]

---

[1] A painting like *L'Orpheline* carries an emotional charge which leaves it open to any number of readings, including that of Quebec as the oppressed victim of some political conspiracy, doomed to its fate, while the Québécois himself may be regarded as a kind of social orphan, estranged and uprooted....Cf. the following observation by Barry Lord: "His paintings like *L'Orpheline*....focus strictly on the plight of the Québécois, never on their ability to unite together to fight and win. The figures always stand staring meekly, their arms at their sides, engulfed in the immense landscape of Quebec, often with a town marked by a church steeple on the horizon....This is an art that tells us that people are alone, futile, orphaned in the world....As propaganda, its message clearly is that the situation is hopeless, so that the best we can do is feel sorry for these repressed souls.... From the dark days of Duplessis to the unjust society of Bourassa-Trudeau, Lemieux has depicted only the mute victims of oppression." (*The History of Painting in Canada*. Toronto: NC Press, 1974, pp. 168-69.) In regard to the many possible readings of Lemieux's work, we should not overlook the opinions of the painter himself, in particular the following, expressed during an interview in February 1975: "Politics has nothing to do with art and my painting has never been political."

236

L'Orpheline (The Orphan Girl), 1957, 61 x 46 cm, NGC

Le petit arlequin (The Little Harlequin), 1959, 120 x 60 cm

A picture from the same period entitled *Le Petit Arlequin* stands in sharp contrast to *L'Orpheline*. Here the figure is sumptuously dressed in shining costume, still breathless from some display of acrobatics. His bright, delicate face seems almost mobile under the perky, sail-like hat, and we can well picture him swinging from one trapeze to another, high above the horizon. Caught between dances, the young harlequin is alive with the pleasures of a circus or village fair, his right leg impatiently at the ready, his left hand patting his thigh, his right hand already out of the frame. The whole composition is flooded with light, except for a thin strip of ground right at the bottom of the frame, just enough to provide a trampoline for his next acrobatic feats.

L'Orpheline and *Le Petit Arlequin* — two complementary fragments of Lemieux's childhood, rescued from the realm of his most profound nostalgia. In response to a question on the author's part, the painter took the time to rummage, not without some emotion, in the old wardrobe that graces his studio, and he pulled out several yellowed photo albums, relics of a lost existence. But Lemieux has managed to recapture, through the children's faces he has created, some of the flavor of spring, the mythical season of eternal return, belonging to this past life.

237

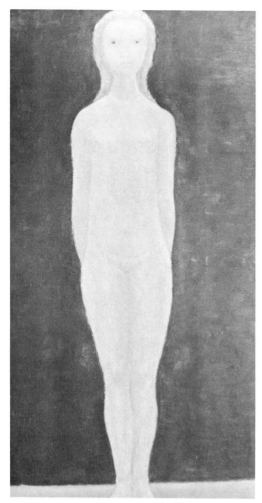

Nu (Nude), 1966, 107 x 58 cm

La vieille servante (The Old Servant), 1966, OFQ

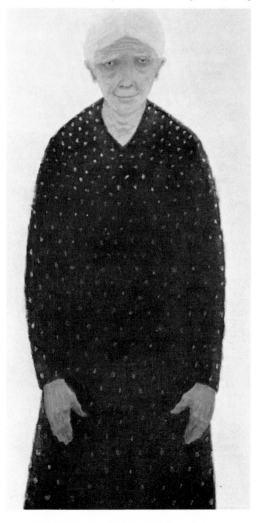

The mood is nostalgic, then, almost *fin de siècle*, imbued with the influences of Proust and Thomas Mann. In fact, the film, *Death in Venice*, made in 1971 by Luchino Visconti, with its adagietto from Mahler's Fifth Symphony, evokes a mood that has much in common with Lemieux's work. This is not merely a question of "period" fashion, but is rather a search for the eternal roots of being and the living springs of consciousness.

Let us consider a few other examples of Lemieux's representation of the theme of solitude. This will underline the range and subtlety of his thematic and affective repertoire, as exercised in a single basic type of pictorial subject-matter. The similarities between *La Vieille servante*[2] (The Old Servant) and the painting of a nude girl, provide a striking illustration of this: the former is crushed and weary from having been so long in service and, as she looks out on the world with the weight of her years visible in her eyes, she is barely capable of giving voice to the burden of sadness she carries; the latter, however, with her youthful, pale-pink skin offers herself to the caress of the light and the promise of marriage, her features free of any trace of servitude.

We move on now to two other renderings of solitude entitled *L'Homme prisonnier* and *Julie et l'univers*. The first establishes the man's claustrophobic situation within the narrow geometric confines of his cell. The character himself seems affected by the brutal dichotomization of the background which at once holds him fast and at the same time lets him float. This background divides the surface of his

[2] This painting is a reminder that Lemieux likes "to paint old people, characters deeply marked by life," as he put it to me on one occasion. It is also a pertinent illustration of a remark made by Galienne Francastel in connection with a portrait painted by Rembrandt of his mother in 1639: "A wrinkled old woman is as interesting to him as a fresh young beauty, and not simply because she happens to be his mother....As one who will render the marks of old age on a face with great fidelity, he knows that such marks do not necessarily detract from a desired effect, but add new effects of their own....He likes to paint old people or better still, people who are undergoing physical change as they move from one period of life to another." (*Le Portrait*, p. 147)

238

obsessions into irreconcilable zones of black and white and stamps the schizophrenic grid on the very wall of his cell. The prisoner has his back to the door and to any possible human communication. The door apparently has no handle, although it might be found behind the head of this Kafkaesque character for whom any idea of escape seems impossible. Despite his terrible impassiveness the prisoner does retain one link with the outside world, namely the painter, who is there to bear witness to his plight. One is reminded of the work of Giacometti and also — provided one reverses the roles of painter and model — of Van Gogh painting Dr. Gachet in June 1890. (A less risky comparison might be made with Van Gogh's rendering of a mental asylum in his picture *Prisoners*, February 1890, after an 1872 drawing by Gustave Dore. *Prisoners* hangs in the Pushkin Museum.) The magnificently composed *Julie et l'univers* would seem at first glance to be a radically different work than *L'Homme prisonnier*, yet they both pose the same question concerning our place in the universe, a question the painter works out in the thin light of a winter's afternoon. It displaces all other questions, paralyzing snow and childhood, scale and duration, in the same chilling, ineluctable evanescence.

Solitude, of course, is closely tied to the urge to communicate however communicating is not always easy. It becomes especially difficult when we charge it with certain expectations, for example, when we expect the exchange in question to defeat all obstacles, including any possible misunderstanding. This problem has been a leading preoccupation of existentialist thought and has prompted extremes of anguish and absurdity from writers such as Pascal, Kafka, Dostoyevsky, Camus and Kirkegaard.

But we must not allow ourselves to be carried away by the force of the Nietzschean vision nor by the wave of pessimism currently in fashion and so suited to the times. We ought to realize that despite the gloomy aspects of much of his work, Lemieux has managed to preserve a certain detachment through the use of irony, an irony that is always restrained and discreet, without bitterness or sarcasm, and whose principal function is to protect the artist from his overdeveloped emotional vulnerability. Prompted by an instinctive sense of decency, the painter takes pains to avoid any emotional demonstrativeness, and

Julie et l'univers (Julie and the Universe), 1965, 104 x 112 cm (color p. 137)

L'Homme prisonnier (L'angoisse) (Imprisoned man — Anguish), 1967, 135 x 79 cm

in his work he relies upon restraint, ellipsis, discreet allusion. This quality of restraint becomes for Merleau-Ponty the pivotal point of a particular aesthetic: "The sensible is that: this possibility to be evident in silence, to be understood implicitly...." (*The Visible and the Invisible*, p. 214).

This is the difficult task undertaken by Lemieux, who, as early as July 1938, put forward in a published article the notion of a thematic approach based on the affective responses of the artist: "It is interpretation, personal vision and the artist's own sensibilities that count in painting; the subject itself is only a point of departure, a base upon which one builds, a motif one uses to express one's innermost feelings." Some thirty years later, in the catalogue of his 1967 retrospective, Lemieux returned to his artistic motivations and once again mentioned solitude as his main preoccupation: "I paint because I like to paint. I have no theories. I try to express in my landscapes and characters the solitude in which we all live and, in every painting, the inner world of my memories. The surroundings in which I find myself are only of interest because they allow me to paint my inner world."

IN TIME AND PLACE

Like the Taoist artist, Lemieux paints nature with the aim of "deciphering how ... forces (work) through things, not (of) copying outward appearances," and in his attempts to render the idea of time he looks to "two chief groups of imaginative unit ... cyclic patterns of process ... and linear threads or veins."[3] However, Taoist representation has a tendency to dissolve into the metaphorical "clouds" of its own calligraphy as it tries to capture the essence of

---

[3] Philip Rawson and Laszlo Legeza. *Tao: the Chinese Philosophy of Time and Change*, pp. 18 and 13.

passing time. Lemieux, in contrast, examines time and tries to condense its energy into a revealing critique through the use of *sfumato*. In his work, time reverts to the feeling of permanence in the ephemeral, the precarious in the established. Plunged into time, which both consummates and consumes, man stands erect in the midst of that which continually fades, that which assures his existence and yet is forever beyond his grasp. Time allows man to continue in what he no longer is, and what he has not yet been. He labors under the magnificent illusion of continuity but lacks the power of true duration. The function of art would thus seem to be to rescue a few fragile images from the shadows of previous lives in order to enshrine them in the magic of Proust's "recaptured" past.

In trying to render in painting some of the properties of time and space, Lemieux has the task of reconciling tenderness and melancholy, diffidence and determination. Prompted by his deep desire for communication and seeking to delineate its possibilities in a rich yet discreet manner, the painter explores life's ephemeral side and takes refuge on occasion behind a quick smile whenever the direct arousal of his feelings seems out of order. But, Lemieux has also shown himself to be most persevering in the development of the thematic side of his work, and he is skilled at finding new modes of expression with which to surprise us. This is particularly so in the wide-ranging modulations of his pictorial language and in his ostensible indirection which amounts in fact to a denial of distance. The result is that he knows where to find the chink in our armor. As far as emotion, sentiment or affectivity are concerned, even the armor of complete passivity or moral blindness does not avail against this artist's compelling human warmth.

The Space/Time Dynamic

As time moves through the fluidity of space, it takes root and adds duration to extension. The result in Lemieux's best pictures is a feeling of being strangely out of time, as though suspended in bottomless depths where an inner luminosity with no apparent source reveals a density that is similar to the Tantra: "Tantra has always believed that our failure to

241

grasp time lies at the root of all other human failures. To see the nature of time is to understand other human failures. To see the nature of time is to understand the process of Genesis, that ladder of descending stages from the Origin through the evolution of the cosmos. . . . To reach [the] summit of intuition Tantra holds to be the worthwhile goal."[4]

Although Tantric iconography clearly bears few similarities to Lemieux's work, the importance given by both to time constitutes a common ground. It also prompts the observation that a number of Lemieux's paintings are reminiscent of icons and images eminently suitable for meditation on the origins of the cosmos, and on time, which provides its primordial energy. The following remark is typical of many made over the course of the artist's career: "What haunts me most of all is time, time passing, time past, the very dimension of time, time that flows and man's response to this flow."

Mindful of the old adage that time waits for no man, Lemieux installs his picture in time, so to speak. He looks to time for the inspirational rhythm of his artistic journey and finds in it a niche for his imagination and a source of his vision. His artistic journey, or more accurately, his quest, involves a tireless exploration of the profiles of characters and landscapes, through the perspective of memory. With this perspective, Lemieux attempts to unite the living breath of beings and objects with their acts of union, through *sfumato*. And he gives scope to this conjunction through the scale and desires of his imaginative range.

Lemieux's perception of time is manifested in a treatment of distance that makes of the pictorial space a suggested, rather than a defined, continuity. It is a continuity that is revealed but not shown. This distance roughly comprises the passage from the here-and-known to the conjured-up-elsewhere. Space is thereby opened up to its own (imaginative) becoming. The horizon serves as a focal point for the

[4] Philip Rawson. *Tantra: the Indian Cult of Ecstasy*, pp. 9-10.

Les deux cavaliers (The Two Riders), 1972 (p. 215)

La chasse (The Hunt), illustration, 1971 (p. 218)

La chasse à la poule d'eau (The Water-Hen Hunt), 1970 (p. 218)

meeting of the temporal and spatial planes, the horizon and horizon line upon which the vision falls during the progress of memory's course.

The artist constructs the space in his picture directly from memory. It is part of the actual visual experience that underlies the alchemy of painting. Alchemy is involved because we are dealing here with metamorphosis, with transmutation, as well as with the great quest that transcends all iconography. The moving finger of time reveals and warms the space, giving it its beat. "Express the visions that surface from the subconscious with the incoherence of dreams, express the perpetual movement of things and life in the world," wrote Lemieux in November 1940. The painting becomes a theatre of hieroglyphs, of signs which approach and withdraw, in an enigmatic choreography. It is not the lack of meaning (absurdity) which astonishes us but, on the contrary, the proliferation of meanings, which open the floodgates of multiple readings that delight us and enrich our experience. Beneath the simplest and often most banal of appearances, the painter invites us to look with him into the hidden secrets of human alchemy and observe some of its vital workings. And yet he does this without even seeming to have broached the question, without disturbing the slightest particle of dust, and with the most disarming simplicity.

The picturesque landscapes and human figures painted by Lemieux since 1956 may distract us from the artist's deeper vision, which utilizes horizon lines as barometers of the soul.[5] This does not imply that Lemieux's pictures have no visual roots in his Quebec background. On the contrary, the author has seen traces of these roots in Charlevoix County, on the Ile aux Coudres and elsewhere, at dusk, in the snow and even by moonlight, or again on the bleak plain crossed by the Quebec City-Montreal autoroute on the south shore of the Saint Lawrence.

---

[5] Let us recall these words recorded by Gauguin in Tahiti in 1896: "A work of art, for him who has eyes to see, is a mirror in which the artist's soul is reflected." (*Oviri*, p. 159)

Space is what first strikes us when we look at a painting. What is the nature of the space in Lemieux's paintings? How does it function? Is it static? Stereotyped? Does it lead the style into any form of stylization? Does it fall into the predictable patterns favored by the art market, rather than taking its chances on the more uncertain fortunes of a personal vision?

Space in Lemieux's work distinguishes itself by its dynamism. The artist's pictorial scenography is constantly renewing itself and undergoing metamorphoses while managing to preserve very profound connections with an integrated affective world. Time within this world acts as an axis of rotation and deployment, infusing the entire representational plane with a delicate mist. The *sfumato* opens up another kind of vista beyond the systems of visual perspective, a vista that is metaphorical and partly secret because it is unfathomable—the vista of duration. There we find the crux of a certain aesthetic, the centre of gravity of a world of mental states which bases its geography on a certain thematic grid. Instead of trying to give an extended analytic reading of this grid, let us examine phenomenologist Merleau-Ponty's perceptive comment on its "convergence": "Every painting, every action, every human enterprise is a crystallization of time, a cipher of transcendence...a certain manner of modulating time and space...it is a question of grasping this very time that is space, this very space that is time....The *Gestalt* (of time and space) is everywhere present without one ever being able to say: it is here....It is a double ground of the lived." (*The Visible and the Invisible*, pp. 208, 205, 259).

So the space-time dynamic — the inexhaustible conjunction of existential form in the field of consciousness — is represented on the canvas by a combination of the twin series: time-duration-remembrance-nostalgia; space-extension-distance-ennui. Here solitude itself becomes inhabited, if only by being perceived (first by the painter, then by us, as spectators) and absence itself becomes presence. This is of course a question of dynamism, as George Kubler observes in his *Formes du temps*: "Everything changes with time and place, and nowhere can we settle definitively on an invariable quality such as is presupposed by the idea of style. When we keep duration and context in mind, we come across shifting

Mon oncle Victorin (My Uncle Victorin), 1965, 51 x 109 cm

relationships ... and all imaginative dimensions or stable sequences like style elude our investigations." (p. 179)

It is not merely the future that teems with hypotheses; the past too is peopled with possibilities, for every past is read in the light of what else it could have been. Memory can create illusions as readily as imagination (in which it plays a role); everyone cultivates his garden of memories as he sees fit, substituting envisioned experience for actual experience. The sheer force of desire, which tends to shape the future in its own image, is able to rework the abandoned materials of the past with even greater ease and effect. Everything becomes a matter of perspective, of dimension: in a bidimensional space like that of the linear narrative, a sphere is perceived merely as a circle, and the intervention of creative imagination is necessary in order for the sphere to realize itself in space. Creative imagination is needed as well for it to take on the vertiginous dimension of time: time which at once devours (Saturn/Thanatos) and engenders (Kronos/Eros).

The existential co-ordinates of time and space are both mixed in the pulp of the painting — but which incorporates which? Space, the indispensable place of all duration, and time, the no less indispensable duration of all place — both are necessary in order that the field of consciousness may function in its dynamic aspect as a "stream of consciousness," and the imagination may invest the picture with living, breathing human beings.

Showing Less, To Show More

For Lemieux, there is nothing rigid or static about the horizon: "When you walk, the horizon rocks back and forth to the left and the right as you move along," as if it were breathing. In many of his post-1956 paintings the painter has discreetly rendered this "breathing" as though sharing a confidence with the landscape; the horizon thus reveals its most secret modulations on the seismograph, or perhaps one should say the cardiograph, created by the pictorial representation. The cosmos whispers on the edge of the horizon where sky and earth, here and elsewhere, time and space, are respectively defined and united. But all this can be seen first in the specific space delimited by the format of the picture. It is moved onto another level by the pictorial representation.

For any painter, the outline of the canvas itself is an act of shaping, a way of marking it out from the surrounding space, of giving it life and cutting it off from all other objects. Lemieux is extremely careful about his framing, far more so than most painters. The definition of the surface to be painted signifies for Lemieux not only the selection of a space on which to undertake the pictorial exercise, but also the selection, the "segregation" of a place of ritual. The surface of the picture already signifies the inscription of man's place in the universe.

In much of his post-1956 work, Lemieux has deliberately exploited the effects of strongly horizontal or vertical formats, and explains their use with some feeling: "I found the classical formats boring. Their proportions did not allow me to get across the sense of horizontality, both its weight and its oppressive effects on man." (Interview of summer 1972) It is difficult to overemphasize the strength of feeling behind Lemieux's attitude to the common, accepted formats, which he finds boring because of their conformist and characterless way of dividing up space. His attitude is an expression of two complementary notions: a rejection of conformism and a search for individuality.

248

Métropole (Metropolis), 1960, 59 x 132 cm, RG

Gaspésie (Gaspé), 1962, 23 x 165 cm, OFQ

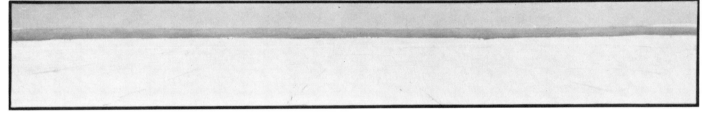

We have already seen in Lemieux's teaching and writing his complete disdain for any form of academicism, whether traditional or avant-garde, and his position of relative isolation, created by his attitude to the artistic community as a whole. But something that seems negative at first glance may take on a more positive aspect if one sees in the experience of isolation an opportunity to strive for individuality, uniqueness, irreducibility. These qualities can be viewed in turn as rare and bizarre: let us recall Baudelaire's aesthetic judgment that "beauty is always bizarre." Characteristically what is "bizarre" breaks the bonds of routine, the daily grind, the ennui that slowly poisons the painter Dino in Alberto Moravia's disturbing novel *La Noia*.

Working from his artistic instincts, then, Lemieux reformulates the question of painting in its most basic and concrete form. For Lemieux, the painter looks at the picture itself, not the scene it contains, which may in fact be absent or purely imaginary. What he sees first (since seeing is what is at issue here) is the surface, or, to be more precise, the emergence in space of the very space of this surface—the format.

Blanche, 1961, 103 x 53 cm, RG

Françoise, 1957, 104 x 56 cm, OFQ

Lemieux's penchant for horizontal surfaces appears as far back as 1952, in a picture like *Québec*. Ten years or so later, pictures such as *Paysage de Gaspésie* and *Les Patineurs du soir* (Evening Skaters), were actually painted on canvases seven times wider than they are high. In 1965, *La Moisson* (The Harvest) and *Montréal l'hiver* (Montreal Winter) became the two latest additions to an extensive series of paintings which over the years have been translating what the painter calls "the oppressive effects of horizontality on man."

Poised against this horizontal thrust, Lemieux has from time to time given free rein to his vision's curiosity about the vertical which, when exaggerated, can produce similar feelings of oppression, constraint and suffocation. Here characters find themselves trapped, compressed, torn apart and, sometimes, actually emaciated or truncated by the lines of the painting so that parts of themselves are driven out of the pictorial space. Carrying an affective reading one step further, we come upon a quality of

250

desertion that conveys the feeling of man's isolation and the loss of all divine intervention. But divinity is not merely religious, and the description of desertion relates more to a tone of myth — man abandoned in the universe and cut off from natural, cosmic forces— than to a reductionist moral code.

The vertical format is used by Lemieux particularly for portrait and character studies (nudes, women with necklaces), and for paintings such as *Killer Joe* or the moving *L'Homme prisonnier* of 1967; rarely does it encompass pure landscapes devoid of human figures.

We could draw a comparison here with Japanese aesthetics, specifically with the *kakemono* in the case of the vertical format and the *makimono* in the case of the horizontal format, but this would take us too far from the distinctive yet ambiguous aesthetics of Lemieux himself. He works both from profound sentiments, whose origins he "figures" in a restrained manner, and from very concrete pictorial "data," which he explores in order to reveal their affective relationships. Furthermore, the ascetic dimension of Lemieux's work, which prompts the comparison with Japanese aesthetics, ought not to distract us from the lucid dimension, the aspect of pictorial play and the evident, somewhat mischievous pleasure with which Lemieux's vision explores the space to be painted and gives it an unexpected and inventive shape. These shapes have evolved from squares to the ovals of the summer of 1975 by way of Lemieux's predilections towards emphasizing both the horizontal and the vertical.

Lemieux's pictorial grammar juggles masses of landscapes and human figures without recourse to stylistic crutches. No aerial perspective, cartoons, spiral arabesques or tidy diagonals are to be found in his work. Frivolous fripperies, excess and melodrama are eschewed, as are all the usual gimmicks of painters of lesser talent. Lemieux relies on nothing more than the soft breathing of a human presence, the inspiration of man seized in all its most dizzying and profound reality, the reality of memory pushed back to the origins of time. Through the magic of duration, time becomes the image and representation of the continuity of being, of its tireless renewal and its metamorphoses across space. Space becomes in turn, through the same pictorial magic, a place where the universe is continually being reborn.

The conventions of framing pictorial space have long accustomed us to seeing human figures truncated, cut off at the knees, the waist or the shoulders. But many of Lemieux's characters surprise us with an unusual kind of vertical cropping: it is as though they were the victims of some assault, some amputation to which our eye is not accustomed. This amputation can extend to the severing of bodies or faces, even when the figure is the principal character of a picture, as in *Le Temps de Noël* (1974).

We might recall here Lemieux's fascination with the cinema, and the fact that films shown on television (since the mid-1950s, in fact) often cut off the sides of the original frame because of the difference between film and TV formats. The result is that actors are often cut off or squeezed into the extremities of the TV screen, as is the case with dozens of Lemieux's post-1956 pictures. Another influence here is certainly the family album, for example, the photograph reproduced on p. 21, in which a young friend of Lemieux's is cut off, accidentally no doubt, by the framing of the camera. The painter has spent many long, nostalgic hours perusing this album.

Landscapes are of course inevitably cut off by the blinkers of vision. For centuries painters have readily used the dramatic truncation of certain elements of a picture to suggest a continuity of these elements beyond the painted surface, into the outside world, only a fragment of which is depicted by the painting itself. "The image must project beyond the frame," as Francisco Pacheco was fond of saying in his Seville studio. His pupil and son-in-law, Velázquez, applied this advice masterfully when in his painting, *Las Meninas*, he chose to eliminate most of the reverse side of the picture of the King and Queen he seems to be painting there, thus making it, in effect, a self-portrait.

This is the play of ellipsis and elision, capturing part of the subject only, retaining half in order not to let the whole slip away. Implied here is the recognition that we can never wholly and absolutely possess anything. What is absent is invoked by making the absence conspicuous. Under the guise of mutilating or cutting human beings in half, this process in fact acknowledges their radical ambiguities.

The painter divides up, sections off, and segments in order to spare the eye the illusion it might

Orion, 1967, 178 x 130 cm, OFQ

otherwise entertain while engaged with the picture, that it is seeing everything. This style is also intended to excite the desire in us to look beyond, to pursue our quest beyond the confines of the picture. The painter is, in other words, showing less, to show more.

With Lemieux, even the palette is truncated, equipped with a deliberately limited range of colors. More like a piece for chamber, than symphony orchestra, a typical work by Lemieux recalls the artist's favorite kinds of music: Gregorian chants, Vivaldi and the music played to accompany silent films, once a lively influence on the young man's imagination and now, half a century later, a nostalgic memory. "Painting should be more a matter of suggesting than describing, just as music does in its own way," noted Gauguin, for whom colors could have "vibrations like musical notes." (*Oviri*, pp. 246 & 179)

Lemieux's palette leans more towards secondary than primary colors and is rarely disturbed by a fanfare of strident reds or loud yellows. It is more receptive to greys highlighted by touches of warm brown, ochre, olive green.[6] And the economy of Lemieux's pictorial means accentuates the affective range of the work. The sensual material of the image presents its pictorial equations with discreet confidence, without fuss or furor, in the whisper of infinite secrets which have been gently taken apart, the better to reveal the whole.

A Taste for Ruins

Against this background of whispers sumptuously dominated by recollection, can be found an occasional taste for ruins. These are objects nurtured in the bewitching shadows of time past and the cult with which the painter surrounds them.

"The cancer of time is eating us away," writes Henry Miller in the opening lines of *Tropic of Cancer*.

---

[6] In his book *Concerning the Spiritual in Art* (New York: George Wittenborn, 1947), Wassily Kandinsky analyzes the "language of form and color" and discusses in detail the affective relationships between grey, green and brown on the one hand and immobility, equilibrium and silence on the other (see pp. 45-67). These colors and qualities are strikingly characteristic of much of Lemieux's own work.

It is just this feeling that inspires pen and brush, as if a work of art could ward off death or at least mollify or postpone its grim labor. No stranger to such sombre thoughts, the romantic artist tries to recapture the past and exclaims with Shelley: "Rise, Memory, and write its praise!"

We have seen to what extent Lemieux's vision is haunted by the thematics of time. One related preoccupation that has cropped up occasionally in his work over the years is the theme of decadence, which he has tended to treat ambiguously, yet with enough wit to render it less unpalatable. In his book titled *L'Atelier du temps*, Jacques Guillerme draws inspiration from Byron to make the observation that "one generation beautifies and another generation destroys; the former leaves us beautiful ruins, the latter their absence....If man's great monuments continue to stir us even as ruins, is the reason not likely to be that they remind us that our own creations are only transitory too?" (pp. 3 & 210)

Ruins have long fascinated Lemieux, and he is often deeply engrossed in reading the English and German Romantics. He recalls that Saint-Denys Garneau, who attended Holgate's studio with Lemieux around 1931, built a kind of ruin as a homage to the romantic spirit, near a river on the grounds of the main house in Sainte-Catherine de Fossambault. Ruins hold a strange fascination for us, evoking displaced worlds floating solemnly through and out of time. Lemieux also mentioned to the author a certain very mysterious Western painter, as he flipped through a book devoted to the painter in question: "We mustn't forget Monsù Desiderio...."

Building a ruin is a strange project indeed, even for a poet who has rejected the world and turned in on himself....But the fascination exercised by ruins is strong enough to have prompted many people over the centuries to do just this in situations where there were no ready-made ruins at hand. In ancient Rome people would even set aside corners of their gardens for the display of Greek ruins. And in a more general vein, does not every civilization need to build on the ruins of the preceding one?

But let us return to Monsù Desiderio, about whom Lemieux went on to say: "Ruins like his, visions as fascinating as that, don't exist and simply couldn't exist in reality." (Interview of July 28, 1972)

Québec brûle (Quebec Burning), 1967, 53 x 178 cm (Mr. & Mrs. W. Sofin)

Little is known about Monsù Desiderio except that behind this pseudonym he hid a double identity as François de Nome and Didier Barra, both of whom were from Metz and shared a studio in Naples around 1630. We are here interested only in the former, in his capacity as the presumptive author of half-collapsed, grandiose imaginary structures shaken by terrible cataclysms which are depicted on canvas as part of a vision of the end of the world. What is fascinating in the painting of François de Nome is the way it manages to suspend time while the pillars of the universe come crashing down. No pictorial style has ever managed to be more dizzying in its rendering of fantastic and apocalyptic scenes.

A few of Lemieux's works are concerned with this idea of the end of time: these include scenes of cities devastated by fire or flood, an understandable theme for an artist who has little affection for big cities. However, it is also true that urban settings have always provided more appropriate settings for the trenchant visual exposition of apocalyptic iconography.

In his March 1939 lecture on painter and poet William Blake, Lemieux made an emotional reference to the visionary's terrible prophesy in "The Marriage of Heaven and Hell" that "the world will be consumed in fire at the end of six thousand years, as I

La Ville inondée (The City Inundated), 1962

First scene from *L'An 2082* (The Year 2082), 1972, 36 x 46 cm

have heard from Hell."[7] Years later, during an interview in 1972, Lemieux returned to his morose visions:

"I've always mistrusted technology and scientists. One day, thanks to all their efforts, they'll blow the Earth to bits! Life is being taken over more and more by machines — the new gadgets found in every house, in every city, as well as the broken-down machines that have turned parts of our cities, and the countryside too, into junkyards. Automobile graveyards, heaps of scrap metal that pile up and pile up, that's what modern life amounts to, that's what they call progress! I prefer to keep away from all that, to turn my back on it and rediscover the past and its charms; at least it's still possible to paint pictures about the past that aren't too disturbing, pictures that don't run on gas and don't make any noise."

---

[7] "The ancient tradition that the world will be consumed in fire at the end of six thousand years, as I have heard from Hell." ("The Marriage of Heaven and Hell," *The Portable Blake*, p. 257)

It was in fact in 1972 that Lemieux, prompted by renewed feelings of pessimism, began a book of watercolors, writing, in English, on the first page: "Sketches taken during an expedition to the poisoned lands of Northern America in the year 2082."

This little introduction, signed "J.B.," was followed by five grim and arresting images: a panorama of Montreal in ruins, after some terrible atomic explosion; a road leading to a far-off city littered with skeletons and bordered by menacing mushrooms; a once thriving business district now peopled only by the carcasses of automobiles and former inhabitants; a visitor in a space suit picking his way carefully through the radioactive debris of a ruined city; and finally, another observer wearing protective clothing dicovering two skeletons seated at a table in what was, before the conflagration, their hotel room.

The dossier on the year 2082 is followed by a little picture entitled *Les Vieilles Rues — Emile Nelligan* (The Old Streets — Emile Nelligan), which alludes to a poem by the fiery Québécois prodigy who was so obsessed by childhood memories and a "bizarre taste

Les vieilles rues (Emile Nelligan) (The Old Streets – Emile Nelligan), 1972, 36 x 46 cm

for the grave" that he had sunk deep into a state of alienation before he was twenty:

"Que vous disent les vieilles rues.
Rêvant de choses disparues?"
(What do the old streets tell you, dreaming of forgotten things?)

Nostalgia for the past has given Lemieux's outlook a certain melancholy that sits very well with the spirit of our times, as he was already explaining in an article published in November 1940: "In a century such as ours, when traditional values are crumbling, when people are prey to anxiety and wonder what tomorrow will bring, and when material goods seem to have destroyed the life of the mind, we are in no position to hope for the emergence of a serene art." This gloomy side of Lemieux's nature would seem to have even older roots, because as far back as 1931 he had executed five drawings for a futuristic novel by Emmanuel Desrosiers entitled *La Fin de la Terre* (The End of the World). In it the author postulated that during the year 2400 our planet would break apart, a hypothesis that is illustrated in chapter VI by some striking "visions of the Apocalypse."

Hommage à Nelligan (Homage to Nelligan), 1971, 85 x 133 cm (University of Montreal)

Pise (Pisa), 1965 (p. 270)

Lemieux's work can be considered as a kind of critique of the human condition, relying sometimes on his ironic sense of humor, but more often on an allusive and indirect way of saying things. Implicated in this critique are various characters adrift in their solitude, couples locked in an endless silence, families under strain or split apart, groups eaten up by the "cancer of time," cities lying in ruins. Although Lemieux's work taken as a whole offers more than just unrelieved gloom — it is often brightened, for example, by the presence of a child's face or a "woman wearing a necklace" — it is nevertheless profoundly marked by what the painter himself calls "*taedium vitae*," a disgust with life that draws over his vision the morose veil of nostalgia.

Much of Lemieux's work obviously cannot help but be melancholic since a concern with the past is its pivotal point, its governing obsession. There is something baroque about Lemieux's art, not in the sense of a great profusion of ornamentation— his painting on the contrary is very spare and re-strained—but in this other sense suggested by Eugenio d'Ors: "At the entry to the forest of the baroque stand two tall columns bearing the names of the poets Milton and St. John the Divine: *Paradise Lost* and the *Apocalypse*." (*Du Baroque*, p. 36. See bibliography)

This is a gate Lemieux knows well and the window of his studio has often provided a view of this baroque forest. Is an obsession with the past and a far-off childhood not a kind of nostalgia for paradise lost? And does the melancholy to which this gives rise not find its logical outcome in eschatological or even apocalyptic visions? Lemieux thus joins Blake, a number of the great Romantics, and Nelligan in their flight from European civilization, and Gauguin too, who fled to Polynesia in his desperate search for some forgotten fragment of an earlier golden age.

Sharing this feeling are three great Germans, Goethe, Nietzsche and Spengler. All of these men have worked their influence on Lemieux's outlook and sensibilities by demonstrating, each in his own way, that cultures and civilizations grow old and die, just as do the men who have created and subsequently fed off them, often to the point of intoxication. Goethe reinvents Faust and translates the myth of the eternal return into "Dying and Becoming," a notion taken up by Nietzsche when he installs the "Amor fati" at the heart of his thundering *Zarathustra*. And in *The Decline of the West*, published in 1918, Oswald Spengler examines in particular a German culture of the Faustian type which leads him to his philosophy of decadence.

The feelings of sadness, melancholy and even anguish that imbue many of Lemieux's paintings have never constituted the basic fabric of his work but only a gloomy shadow cast across it. Lemieux rejects the morbid aspects in paintings such as those by contemporary American artist Ivan Albright, which depict people horribly deformed or in various stages of decomposition. While Lemieux does paint the dusk more often than the dawn and his prophesies hardly promise a shining future, we must not look for an Apocalypse at every twilight scene. Even with the gloomy shadows and a vision colored by nostalgia, there is no morbid bitterness or desperation here, for his work is informed by the warm stirrings of remembrance. Pessimism and an obsession with the past find their own redemption in the Proustian alchemy of the "past recaptured," and revealed in the miraculous emergence of pictorial representation.

In a 1968 picture titled *La Ville détruite (Aftermath)* (The City Destroyed – Aftermath), the street is overrun with mushrooms (one thinks of certain washes by Victor Hugo) and over to the extreme right, high up on the ruins of a building, are the first three letters of a word apparently truncated by the frame: CAN . . . . Is it the word "CANADA" that has been cut off? And is the painter making reference to the terrorist activities that, especially in the Montreal area, threatened the future of the country, which had just celebrated its centenary in 1967? In the course of interviews between Lemieux and the author, questions pertaining to such matters came up from time to time. Lemieux, convinced of the advantages of federalism for Canada, without however believing that the system is perfect, revealed that he is indeed concerned that terrorist activities or political unrest might do considerable harm to the already precarious network of relationships between Quebec and the rest of Canada.

La Ville détruite (Aftermath) (The City Destroyed – Aftermath), 1968, 61 x 170 cm

The Quebec Question

And so we come to the "Quebec question" as it affects Lemieux, who is at once the least and the most Québécois of the province's contemporary painters. For Lemieux, the adjective "Québécois" signifies that he was born in the city of Quebec and that he lives in the province of Quebec. In terms of nationality, Lemieux calls himself a Canadian, and it would not serve any purpose here to undertake a long discussion on what is really meant by the word "nation" or its political and linguistic implications. Lemieux's wider "landscape," which is part of his artistic vision and takes concrete form on his canvases, no doubt reaches far beyond Quebec's borders, although it is inside these borders that he finds his inspiration. Outside them, as he admits, he is unable to express himself in painting. On the other hand, the Russian retrospective of the summer of 1974 did allow us to expand our analysis of Lemieux's work, which in the post-1956 period has obviously not returned to the humorous and anecdotal approach of *Lazare*, *Fête-Dieu* and *Pique-nique*.

Are the artist's oppressive use of the horizon line and his disturbing suggestions of solitude not denunciations of the shattering of the collective bonds that are society's only hope for escaping its present impasse? Is his depiction of the sterile cold of winter not a symbol of the dispossession and exploitation of the land by outsiders? Does the mute alienation of a long procession of oppressed human beings not make us feel the atavism of three centuries devoted to tasks of an essentially negative kind, namely those of resisting and surviving? And does this not all constitute, at least implicitly, a depressing image of Quebec's present situation, as has been suggested by a number of commentators writing about Lemieux's work?[8]

Lemieux's iconography easily gives rise to confusion because it is charged with ambiguity and steadfastly refuses to give a simplified account of its wide-ranging thematic interpretations of reality. Let us therefore not do the work a disservice by reducing its scope to the level of regionalist propaganda or by reading sweeping and ethereal generalizations into it which run roughshod over its basic meaning. The artist has chosen to take a lucid and critical view of life and it is with this clear-cut attitude that he pursues his work. The result is an aesthetic whose ideological and affective bases we have already examined, with the help of numerous quotations and suggestions for a thematic architecture. Rhetoric and demagoguery are foreign to Lemieux's temperament, although this does not prevent him from being profoundly concerned about the situation of Quebec, more so perhaps than many of those who sound the alarm at the slightest provocation. There is a more consistent "description" of the realities of life in Quebec than in the writings of many sociologists, political commentators, futurists and other pundits who claim to be in calm possession of the ultimate verities. The situation is an indescribably muddled

---

[8] Here are some sample opinions concerning Lemieux's work as a representation of the more distressing aspects of Quebec life: "[He] clearly exhibits . . . the drama of our estrangement, which takes the form of an almost morbid inhibition, the temptation to take refuge in resignation and silence." (Guy Viau. *Modern Painting in French Canada*. Quebec City: Department of Cultural Affairs, 1967, p. 32.) " . . . Lemieux has depicted only the mute victims of oppression." (Barry Lord. *The History of Painting in Canada*, p. 169)

La route vers la mer (Route Towards the Sea), 1964, 34 x 48 cm, RG

one, in which a few violent demonstrations and vaguely apprehended insurrections give little hint of the profound evolution that is sweeping Quebec, which certain powers will go to any lengths to stop—be the means repression, Machiavellian machinations or insidious co-optation. For a generation now Quebec has been undergoing a slow transformation rather than revolutionary change, a process that has been paralleled in Lemieux's paintings.

What we now know as the "Quiet Revolution" has been visibly at work in Quebec since about 1960. The fight against a kind of multi-faceted colonialism has distant historical precedents, though, in the rebellions of 1837 and April 1918. Later, the *Refus global,* propounded by Borduas and his young anarchist followers in 1948, continued the fight. Lemieux's contribution to the recent changes in

Quebec society clearly comes under the "quiet" rather than the "revolutionary" side of this well-worn catchphrase. The first stage of this ground-swell movement was an attempt to define and give an identity to the Quebec situation, the landscape of here and now, no longer in the traditional terms of folklore and the picturesque, but in terms of a new and profound authenticity. All manner of poets, novelists, playwrights, singers, sociologists and politicians committed themselves to this task both in public and in private. In the realm of painting, it is Jean Paul Lemieux who has made the most prolific on-going contribution, in his discreet but determined way. More than anyone, he has long known that this search for identity, which always operates at the personal level before it becomes collective, is never at an end. This is particularly so in a society that is still developing, and in which new struggles crop up as fast as the old ones are resolved.

Lemieux's contribution is not, of course, restricted to this first stage of the Quiet Revolution, a necessary but not sufficient condition for the fulfillment of the higher goals set by the Quebec community. The painter has pushed his quest much further by carving out a profile of the Quebec identity with disarming simplicity, avoiding the needless complexities of programs and theories. No grandiose promises here of a future socialist paradise, which too often has a tendency to degenerate into the nightmare of dictatorship when ruthless elements manage to seize the reins of power. Lemieux's work is sufficiently elevated above the regional and anecdotal to allow him to sketch an understated profile of mankind in which freedom is still a viable option. The result of this is that the most Québécois of the province's painters becomes something much more than just Québécois, and is hailed as far away as Russia as an artist whose work has universal scope. This marks the transition, as it were, from being Québécois in name only to *being* Québécois. In the same way that Shakespeare is Elizabethan, Bach a *Kapellmeister* and Gauguin a Tahitian, Lemieux is Québécois. For an artist's first allegiance is to the land of his imagination, and this painter born in Quebec City has been cognizant of the pitfalls of regionalism for at least half a century, and his horizons are not defined by the constraints of political boundaries. It is thanks to artists such as Lemieux that the province of Quebec, rather than being tied down to narrow definitions or labels, offers opportunities for true self-realization with all its inherent problems of paradox and ambiguity. Such a process entails an opening up to the world and an end to brooding over old problems or smug contemplation of the navel: with feet well rooted in daily reality, the gaze is fixed on distant vistas, searching for a country still in the making, with the help of faces and landscapes. It is a process of discovery that each of us experiences first of all in our own hearts.

Pictorial Affinities

In an article published in November 1940, Lemieux stressed the crucial role of influences in the development of any artist's work, stating that "no one remains untouched by the great works of the past; nobody can claim to create something that is entirely unaffected by a previous vision or idea; there's nothing new under the sun, only transformations or metamorphoses of what has already been done." Critics are seldom presented with such a frank admission on the part of artists whose affinities and sources of inspiration they are interested in bringing to light. Lemieux has never had qualms about making such connections and revelations, unlike many artists who are often less than forthcoming on the subject of their affinities with previous artists and artistic styles.

At the Ile aux Coudres, on October 22, 1975, Lemieux noticed the author leafing through a book on the Italian Renaissance, which had a bookmark at the alleged portrait of Giovanna Degli Albizzi by Ghirlandajo; Lemieux commented simply: "I have always like this kind of Italian painting and still find it an inspiration." In 1963, Lemieux admitted that his style "had been softened by the Italian painters," in particular the stunning group that includes Giotto, Fra Angelico, Simone Martini, Piero della Francesca, Botticelli, Pontormo and, of course, Ghirlandajo.

Over the years, Lemieux has graciously taken advantage of the work of his predecessors. In the mid-forties, as we have already seen, a number of witty, anecdotal paintings were inspired by the Ashcan School and the American Scene. A few years later, the long processions winding their way out of half-open buildings, the depiction of several events

269

Pise (Pisa), 1965, 112 x 61 cm (Dr. & Mme. Marcel Carbotte)
(color p. 262)

in one painting and the use of a high-angle perspective recalled, to cite only Italian examples, certain works by Ambrogio Lorenzetti, Martini, Agostino Novello, Francesco del Cossa, Gentile da Fabriano, Paolo Uccello and Masolino. Lemieux, proud of these connections with the past, pointed to another most unusual affinity, given the context, namely, D.W. Griffith's use of dirigible balloons in 1916 for filming panoramic scenes from a high angle (see p. 76).

In 1965, a trip to Italy was preceded by several "Sienese" profiles and followed by pictures like *Pise* and *Hommage à la Toscane*. A number of other faces in profile painted by Lemieux recall such works as *Lionello d'Este* or the portrait by Pisanello of another princess from the same house; *Simonetta Vespucci*, which is sometimes attributed to Pollaiuolo and on other occasions to Piero di Cosimo; and *Battista Sforza* by Piero della Francesca. Lemieux still takes pleasure in recalling the serenity of the Romanesque and the enchanting air of the frescoes in Arezzo,[9] though in the next breath he may throw into the conversation Gainsborough and Bruegel, the fantasmagoric wonders of Hieronymus Bosch and the long series of *Water-lily* paintings by Monet (hints of their perfume drift through a number of Lemieux's landscapes, especially from 1964), not to mention Maxfield Parrish and Monsù Desiderio. The Norwegian artist Edvard Munch has exercised an unmistakable fascination on Lemieux for a very long time, while certain works of Francis Bacon, Delvaux, Balthus, Signac and Seurat have also managed to catch his attention. And Ensor would have felt at home in Lemieux's 1973 painting *Les masques* (p. 209).

---

[9] In a 1957 mural study depicting Quebec City, Lemieux alludes to the city of Jerusalem as painted in Arezzo by Piero della Francesca in his *Legend of the True Cross*. Lemieux's *Annonciation* of 1963 is also reminiscent of the Arezzo painting of the same name.

Hommage à la Toscane (Homage to Tuscany), 1965, 74 x 52 cm, RG

Portrait de femme (Portrait of Woman), 1972, 67 x 56 cm

Axel, 1964, 39 x 28 cm, OFQ

Petit garçon (Little Boy), 1964, 51 x 31 cm, OFQ

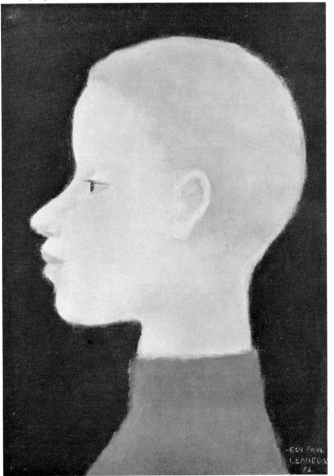

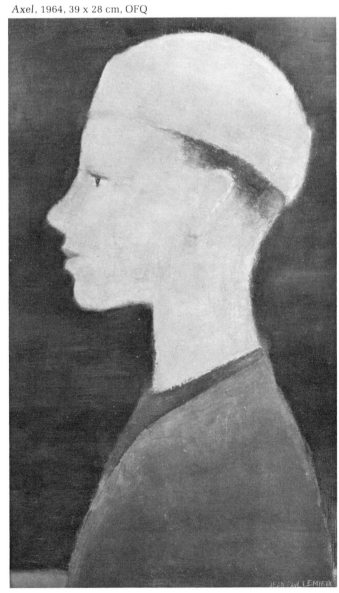

El Greco: Saint Ildefonse, 1605
(Monastère de l'Escurial)

Mgr de Laval, 60 x 30 cm

Lemieux undoubtedly takes more from Gauguin than just his pictorial reconstructions on canvas of a past mystified by dreams and nostalgia, and an aesthetic that achieves expression particularly through symbolic analogies. There are also resemblances in several of Lemieux's ideas on art, as well as in some elements of his pictorial technique: subdued tones, simplification of forms, reduced color range and the two-dimensional representation of figures.

We might also mention the vague relationship that exists between some of Lemieux's paintings and certain works of the "Metaphysical" school (in particular, *My Son*, by Carra, 1916; the melancholy pictures of Giogio de Chirico from his best period, i.e. 1912-15; and *Five Men in a Room*, by Oskar Schlemmer, 1928).

On home ground, Lemieux has found occasional inspiration in the traditional ex-voto religious motifs of the early eighteenth century, as well as in the style of tart observation characteristic of the old Quebec story tellers who would hold listeners spellbound during the long winter evenings with their penetrating humor. There was, quite naturally, a good deal of borrowing between Lemieux and his colleagues such as Goodridge Roberts, Stanley Cosgrove and Philip Surrey. John Lyman and A.Y. Jackson also made a few brief, discreet appearances in Lemieux's work during the 1930s; James Wilson Morrice made a deeper impression with his particular way of shading space into duration.

Elsewhere in Lemieux's work, we might point out a few fragmentary stylistic connections, such as those between the 1962 painting *Glaces au bord de la mer* (Ice by the Sea Shore) and the Lawren Harris painting *Iceberg*, painted in 1930. Several of Lemieux's paintings resound with the distant echo of *The Woolsey Family*, painted in 1809 by William von Moll Berczy, which throws a shroud of desperate isolation around each of its characters.

During the early fifties, Lemieux composed a portrait of Monseigneur de Laval (1623-1708), taking his inspiration from El Greco's *Saint Ildefonse*, painted three centuries earlier and now hanging in the Monastery of the Escorial. By Lemieux's own account, however, he has been more influenced by

Bruine (Drizzle), 1957, 38 x 94 cm, OFQ

Ville enneigée (Snow-Covered City), 1963, 89 x 142 cm, MQ

cinematic images and by television framing and close-ups than by any particular painter. A reference during an interview with the author to the washes of Victor Hugo failed to get much response.

Nicholas de Staël was born in Saint Petersburg in 1914, ten years after Lemieux was born in Quebec City. By the mid-1930s, it was possible to draw some striking comparisons between the Russian-born artist's drawings and watercolors and Lemieux's landscapes. Whether fortuitous or intuitive, the similarities between some of de Staël's landscapes painted in the 1951-55 period and certain paintings of Lemieux's completed between 1956 and 1964 are unmistakable. Here are a number of specific examples, using the *catalogue raisonné* of de Staël's work established by Jacques Dubourg and Françoise de Staël: #364 and *Bruine* (1957), #321 and *Métropole* (1960), #384 and *Gaspésie* (1962), #301 and *Ville enneigée* (1963). We could multiply such examples considerably, but there is no point in risking confusion. Whether these pictorial links are accidental or otherwise, they are nothing for Lemieux to be ashamed of in view of the quality of de Staël's work. It is a question of similarities, then, and not necessarily influences. The similarities are echoed in many aspects of Lemieux's style: the spare quality of his composition, the extremely low horizon, heavy skies, landscapes divided into large planes, the dynamic quality of his diagonals, the exaggerated vertical or horizontal format (cf. catalogue numbers 676, 692, 721, 777, 897-901, 962, 970, 971).

During the period under consideration, de Staël painted mostly with knife and spatula in thick layers which give a rugged texture to his paintings not shared by Lemieux's paintings. Lemieux works

273

his surfaces with careful brush strokes. Once de Staël returned to the brush (catalogue no. 871 ff.), the pictorial similarities become apparent again, particularly as regards internal tension and the artists' parallel efforts to suppress incidental elements from their pictures. Despite these similarities in the treatment of landscape, their human subjects have little in common: there is nothing, for example, in Lemieux's work that echoes the visual ethnicity of the soccer players painted by de Staël in 1952 and his nudes of 1953.

Did de Staël really influence Lemieux? It is difficult to say. There are clearly links between the two painters, not merely pictorial, as we have seen, but also aesthetic and intellectual. Could not Lemieux just as easily have signed the letter written by de Staël in January 1955, a few weeks before his suicide, from which the following extracts are taken: "Painting, real painting, always aspires to completeness, in other words to the impossible union of the present moment, the past and the future. . . . What is important is that it be true. . . . But the more this truth varies from one picture to another, the more absurd the road which leads there seems, the more I'm interested in following it." (*Nicolas de Staël*, 1968, p. 382)

Such artistic affinities are more or less the result of an intuitive choice on the part of the artist, rather than anything imposed on him. They are, as Goethe put it, elective affinities. They give the artist a sense of belonging which is often instrumental in allowing him to escape the bonds of solitude.

THE SEARCH FOR ORIGINS

Solitude offers no explanations; it is not cause, but consequence. Man is not born alone; he is born in the bosom of his family, a citizen of his country, a product of his culture, all of which he may later turn his back on in the search for another way of life. Gregarious by nature, man feels instinctively that his destiny is inextricably linked with his family, friends, neighbors and compatriots. Solitude represents a retreat, a flight from this sense of solidarity with "one's own." Renouncing one's milieu, or being rejected by it, may be the result of an unhappy past, an inability to adjust easily or some deep-seated incompatibility. A

a shortcut to t
this comment
of the world is
at its word. S
from the mear
wrote in an a
tures and not
that only a p
could ultima
new vision fil
ity tinged wi
work has bee
return, the so
travel back th
a child's gaz
which this s
representatio
realization of
described by
"The child at
kingdom wh
mind's eye, a
fantasy, peop
with a myste
unknown we
tion."

The Painting

In the
tirely given
dresses him
passés. Whe
and the littl
not want to
he immedia
the safety of

There
despite his
like is prom
industry too
travelling b
pleasures, a
cannot be c
voyages in
of his career
trips from C

Petite ville (Little Town), 1963

Montmorency Falls and dominating the Saint Lawrence and the Ile d'Orléans. His first drawings of any importance were executed during his sojourn in California at age twelve. The trip to France in 1929-30 had a profound effect on the young man of twenty-five, introducing him to European art from Impressionism onwards, prompting him to settle, however vaguely, on an artistic career, and convincing him to finish his studies at Montreal's Ecole des beaux-arts. At the end of 1930, another trip to California was extended to include the museums and galleries of Chicago, New York and Boston. This gave him a chance to see twentieth-century American art first-hand, an experience that left its mark in a number of his paintings over the next twenty-five years. These were years punctuated by regular vacation trips to Estrie and, in particular, Charlevoix County, first of all in the vicinity of Port-au-Persil, then in Les Eboulements and finally the Ile aux Coudres. But it was the trip to France in 1954-55 that became the most important turning-point of all in Lemieux's career; it led to the radically new style which later made his reputation at retrospectives in Canada, Western Europe and Russia. Since Lemieux's retirement from teaching in 1965, his year has been divided up into three periods, each connected with travel to a particular place: winter in Quebec City, the month of March in the friendlier climate of Florida and summer on the Ile aux Coudres. Two trips every year then: the one to Florida and the one to the island.

The notion of space is crucial to a painter like Lemieux. The dialectic of departure and return involved in the act of travelling has had an important effect on his visual dynamic, which is already imbued with an analogous sense of the pulsations of time. Duration and extension criss-cross in more or less continuous sequences, tied together in consciousness by the thread of memory, which is transformed by the alchemy of imagination into recollection. Everything takes place in life as if places and moments were so many islands grouped together into floating archipelagoes, into constellations whose permutations continue with the passing of the days and years. In relation to everything that is not, does not the here-and-now indeed have a profound and insular resonance? And does not each and every painting become an island in the eye of the beholder, a stopping-off point for his imagination?

Portrait de l'artiste (Portrait of the Artist), 1974 (p. 289)

Portrait de Claude (Portrait of Claude), 1953, 50 x 38 cm

As might be expected, the Ile aux Coudres holds great significance for Lemieux's life and outlook, as refuge, Eden and crucible. But it is also the immense archipelago of his work with a horizon that is continually murmuring his secrets. Here is what Pierre Machery says about the island in literary art (in *Pour une théorie de la production littéraire*, p. 225): "Ever since the eighteenth century, island life has been a model for fables and reveries: Defoe, Marivaux, Rousseau. In *Robinson Crusoe*, the fable and its setting (the island) form the basis of an object lesson: the story of man's development, or rather his re-development (since what is at stake here is a second life, which only develops against the distant backdrop of the first)." The painting becomes an island, as much for the painter as for us. It is an island in the sense of a place of generation and transformation, where the myth of the eternal return blossoms in the transfigured imagination.

The island is radically opposed to the idea of a no-man's land, for it is always inhabited. It comes alive not only by the play of reverie and story-telling but also because the island is an archetypal symbol: my mind is an island on the sea of meaning; the Earth is an island in our galaxy and in space; Greece is an island in the history of culture. The island is the origin of origins and the "nostalgia for one's origins" which Mircea Eliade speaks of in connection with the "myth of the eternal return," amounts to a nostalgia for the "original" island, the breast of the mother goddess. It is a nostalgia too for Childhood itself, which will learn to unite time and space in a single continuum. "What happens in our mind's eye when we think of the origins of something? From the moment it appears, the representation is given temporal and spatial form. . . . Space and Time become, by virtue of the mythic imagination, a creative and primordial milieu. . . . It is in Time and Space, by the grace of their figuration, that a living things relates to its being as it does to the principle of this relationship." (Gabrielle Dufour-Kowalska: *L'Origine*, pp. 61, 93, 103)

The island, the original encounter of duration and extension, where representation, which cannot invent what already exists, re-invents and re-presents, re-forms and trans-forms, trans-figures. This is the portrait.

The Portrait and the Double

Pascal was not mistaken in his manner of relating the portrait to the "thing represented": "A portrait portrays absence and presence." A transition point or a transit point, rather than a point of departure or arrival, the portrait draws from its ambiguity and its evanescence a power and fascination that Pascal cannot resist. And yet he attempts to dispel it with this acerbic remark: "What vanity there is in painting, which draws admiration for a resemblance to things whose originals are not admired at all!" (*Pensées*, Lafuma 260 & 40, Brunschweig 678 & 134)

Is it not precisely through its co-efficient of dissimilarity, in other words its freedom to invent, that painting (above all portraiture) transcends the vanity or triviality of the model, and the slavish subsurvience of the uninspired copyist? No portrait can avoid ellipses, short-cuts, implications; what is given may play a less important role than what is not. Absence and presence join forces and the dynamics of revealing are busily at work just below the thin veneer of appearance. The act of revelation, the inexhaustible dialectic of the visible and the invisible, is a perilous but fascinating encounter. Presence and absence are reconciled in the representation, presented according to the terms of the picture's new mode of being. The portrait delegates, mediates, and, by analogy, the work of art also becomes a path and journey moving in several directions. It becomes a place of action and an action of place; the duration of space and the extension of time; an active and open symbol whose manipulation is a privileged part of the imaginative process.

In *Metamorphosis of the Gods*, André Malraux poses the following question: "What portrait is solely the imitation of a face?"[10] To which Pierre Francastel replies: "The representation is not merely a double for some individual or scene," since it "explores the memory" and becomes a "conductive element of imagination" for both the artist and the person looking at the painting. (*La figure et le lieu*, p. 350) And

---

[10] André Malraux. *Metamorphosis of the Gods*. Trans. Stuart Gilbert (London: Secker & Warburg, 1960), p. 363.

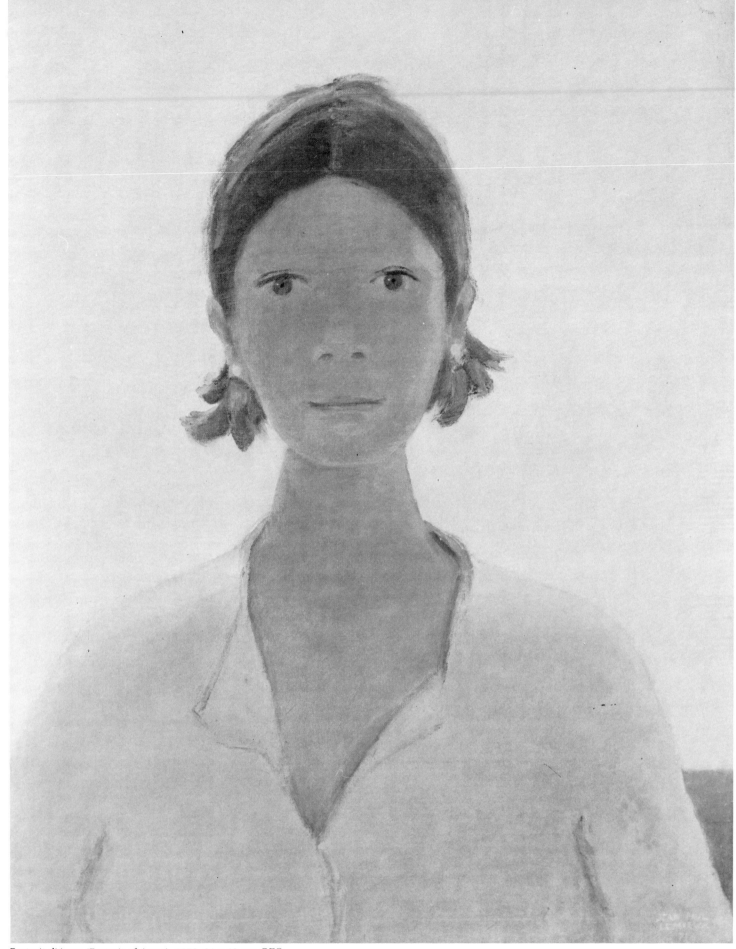

Portrait d'Anne (Portrait of Anne), 1972, 64 x 48 cm, OFQ

Gombrich reminds us for his part that the image, as re-presentation, serves a dual function as both substitute and double: a particular fetish, for example, may both symbolize and constitute fertility. Gombrich thus writes that "our attitude towards the image is inextricably bound up with our whole idea about the universe"[11] because all our ideas are part of the universal tapestry of images woven by all cultures.

In an article published in June 1938, Lemieux described painting as "the art of creating illusions on a surface" in a way that suggests the metaphor of the mirror, but with the difference that "the eye of the painter is a sentient mirror which reflects the changing image of the world and interprets it on canvas in terms of his sensibilities and personality." In November 1940, another article by Lemieux alluded to certain portraits in which the models "look upon existence with huge anguished eyes as though some unknown tragedy had wiped away their smile....To draw the human face, to bring out all its drama and feeling, the better to underline man's condition in an age where he is crushed by materialism."

A quarter of a century later, Lemieux himself would paint portraits like these in a series that brought together little *Françoise*, the poet *Nelligan* and various old people, all of whose faces encompass a wide range of stages within the cycle of life. Every work of art becomes a locus of change in several different senses: a change in the sensibility of the artist and in the alchemy of his imagination which the work reveals, and which in turn stimulates those who enter into communication with it; a change in the course of the artist's work as a whole, in which case the repercussions may be considerable, especially if stylistic influence can then be seen operating in the work of other artists; and a change in the visual universe, where an empty surface suddenly acquires figurative shape and the inevitable enigma it brings with it.

The notion of image raises the question of mimesis: but is this only a question of copying, of imitating? At one level the mime undoubtedly reproduces, but at another he also expresses; above all he produces more than he reproduces and presents more than he represents. An interplay occurs in the image

---

[11] E. H. Gombrich. *Symbolic Images* (London: Phaidon, 1972), p. 125.

Promenade, 1972, 41 x 34 cm

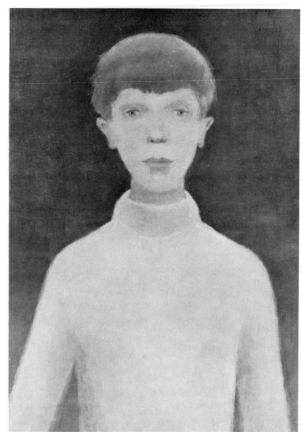

Jeune Anglais (English Boy), 1966, 61 x 46 cm, OFQ

François, 1964, 70 x 48 cm

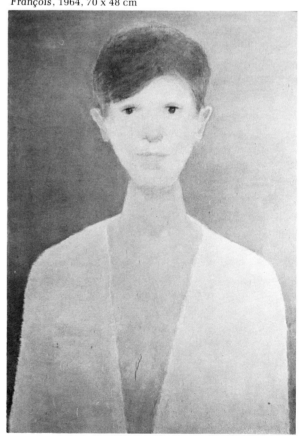

to the extent that it resembles a troubled reflection woven through both resemblance and divergence. The image acquires its own dynamic autonomy, to the point where it alone constitutes the stuff of imagination. Whether memory or "fantasy," the image informs memory as much as invention; it makes no attempt to segregate narrative and allegory and forms the basis for the architecture of analogy, that immense domain floating between the rigid poles of the equivocal and the unequivocal, constructed according to the rationale of reason. This domain constitutes the mobile field of what is vaguely termed "thought," where associations jostle one another within the continuing flood of images. With its considerable variations of rhythm and intensity, this flood can also be termed the field of consciousness, wherein images become doubles or signs for the furniture of the universe.

But let us not get lost in the labyrinth of signs and return instead, via the concept of the double, to the portrait. The ambiguity of portraiture evokes the ritual of the mask, of metamorphosis. Wearing a mask, the face becomes something else yet retains its identity under its new appearance. The portrait fixes a moment of the quest, and rescues from oblivion a proof of having existed. It was in funereal art that

Portrait du Cardinal Léger (Portrait of Cardinal Léger),
1962, 100 x 70 cm, OFQ

Nicolas, 1961, 81 x 46 cm, OFQ

portraiture first perfected its complex figuration, a process perhaps already completed in Paleolithic caves but certainly completed in Egyptian tombs of the era.

Roman art secularized the portrait, extending its scope to familial, social and political uses. It undertook to capture the fleeting passage of time and conjure up the ephemeral by adhering to a mimetic representation of physiognomy. Over the centuries, however, the portrait has remained a ceremonial locus wherein representation has attempted to bridge memory and conjuration. At once relic and fetish, the portrait joins past and future in one place while reflecting their strange present.

The numerous portraits painted by Lemieux illustrate this complex interplay of representation. One finds in his work portraits that are neither photographic likenesses nor flattering studies of their models. Lemieux has accepted a certain number of commissions for portraits, reserving for himself the privilege of being primarily concerned with painting a picture (in whatever stylistic register he sees fit), and only secondarily with a portrait as such. One is therefore not surprised to see that the most "representational" portraits painted by Lemieux are not his best, for example the 1962 *Portrait du cardinal Léger*.

The Self-Portrait

The notion of the double involved in portraiture becomes more fascinating still in the self-portrait, which is a long-standing tradition in the history of Western painting extending over an extremely wide affective range. At the beginning of the second chapter of his book *Della Pittura*, Alberti has painting develop from Narcissus' act of self-contemplation in the water of a fountain. This original self-portrait has, as it were, cast a disquieting shadow over a long and fruitful tradition, from the early reliefs of Saqqara to the present day.[12] More than twenty-five centuries ago, Theodore of Samos had no

---

[12] See Ludwig Goldscheider. *Five Hundred Self-Portraits* (Vienna: Phaidon, 1938).

Ti-Gus, 1962, 115 x 76 cm, OFQ

Marie-Gemma, 1958, 72 x 57 cm

Samuel, 1963, 81 x 56 cm, OFQ

Fillette (Little Girl), 1957, 40 x 35 cm

Eté 1914 (Summer 1914), 81 x 183 cm (see p. 18)

(see p. 18)

Intérieur (Interior), 1930, 25 x 28 cm

Self-portrait (Detail from *Fête-Dieu*, p. 77)

(Detail from *Fête-Dieu*, p. 77)

qualms about casting his own face in bronze, while two centuries later Phidias sculpted his own features onto the Parthenon. During the fifteenth century, painters like Lippi and Botticelli included themselves in their pictures. Dürer often exercised this narcissistic option over the course of his career, Rembrandt enriched his family albums with a hundred or more self-portraits, and Van Gogh left behind him some forty touching visual diagnoses of his mental well-being.

In the latter half of the fifteenth century, there circulated among the colleagues of Marsilio Ficino an adage attributed to Cosimo d'Medici: "Ogni dipintore dipinge se...." Every painter paints himself. To a greater or lesser degree, the artist leaves the mark of his own personality and his own genius on every piece of work, so that each painting becomes, in a sense, a fragmentary self-portrait. The actual self-portrait itself can never be more than a fragment, an aspect of its author, a mask, a double.

Lemieux has only rarely painted himself into his own pictures: he appears as a vague reflection in a mirror in *Intérieur* (1930); somewhat mischievously in the the guise of a tavern-keeper in *Fête-Dieu* (1944); and more nostalgically in several scenes from childhood, such as *1910 Remembered*, *Eté 1914*, *Les Temps passés* (and perhaps also in *Chacun sa nuit*, *Le Temps de Noël*, etc.). In 1974, when he was ill and

288

just about to turn seventy, Lemieux painted only a few pictures, but one of these was a good-sized composition which he considers his only real self-portrait.

First of all, *Portrait de l'artiste* rejects any narcissistic self-satisfaction, so common in this genre; its pictorial architecture has a distancing effect that cuts short any feeling of vanity. The painter sees himself as another person and paints the portrait of someone who turns out to be himself. Narcissus' mirror has no place here: the painter uses nothing but a sober optical tool instead of a model, a cold mirror which evokes both observer and observed without probing the personality.

The temporal and spatial co-ordinates of *Portrait de l'artiste* are related to two analytic modes, namely, the painter's biography and the pictorial context of his previous work. As regards the former, Lemieux has painted himself at three different stages of life: as a child of seven or eight, roughly contemporaneous with the child of *1910 Remembered*; as a young man of about eighteen; and finally as a man of seventy, as the artist saw himself while painting the picture. In this picture the painter reproduces two paintings from his previous work, *Le Visiteur du soir* (The Evening Visitor) (1956) and *Cavalier dans la neige* (Rider in the Snow) (1967). The self-portrait is thus marked off by a series of milestone years, "biographemes," ranging from the painter's early childhood to old age: 1904 (the year of his birth), 1910, c. 1920, 1956, 1967, 1974.

To what season does this self-portrait belong? To winter, because of the two landscapes "quoted" in the picture? To summer, because of the short-sleeved shirt worn by the young man? To some time in between, because of the little boy's outfit? To no season at all, because of the white, non-descript clothing worn by the painter in old age? Despite the numerous temporal "landmarks," time in this painting is frozen, neutralized, erased. The picture occupies the dimensions of duration and extension in a strange manner, eluding easy classification. Begun during the summer of 1974 and completed that fall, the picture cancels its moment of origin by expanding and blending into other moments of its own archeology. The duration of its scenography increases with the ambiguity of this very proliferation.

Portrait de l'artiste (Portrait of the Artist), 1974, 166 x 79 cm (color p. 279)

Space can be treated on several levels of analysis in *Portrait de l'artiste*. First of all, the private space of the artist's studio and home (for Lemieux, no barriers of protocol separate the domestic living space from his work area which, both on the Ile aux Coudres and in Quebec City, is a single room whose door is always open). The room in which the artist paints opens onto a doorless frame on the right. The high angle from which the spectator views the room (resulting from the position of the mirror used by the artist) gives him the uncomfortable feeling that he is intruding, looking down indiscreetly on a scene in which he does not belong. Public space slips surreptitiously into the picture in two main ways: through the presence of the two paintings hanging on the wall, paintings which are part of the history of the artist's work and have long since left the privacy of his studio; and through the depiction of the painter at three stages in his life, which makes the picture into an historical record.

The scenography of the self-portrait becomes a kind of exhibition place: the painter "exhibits" himself, surrounded by two sorts of figures from his past. There are two images from his youth and two (pictorial) images from later in life that have long since departed from his studio. This picture has a kind of hieratic quality about it which is emphasized by the frontal pose of the three "effigies" of the artist. We observe that the five figures in the picture are all truncated in various ways, and that the upper picture hanging on the wall has had about one-fifth of its surface cropped away. The five figures show only one hand among them all, the left hand of the little boy, which is itself partly hidden by his clothing.

The self-portrait awakens strange associations, and one is reminded of the following reflections: "I is another" (Rimbaud); "keyholes through which the 'I' keeps watch on others the better to keep watch on itself" (Jeanne Hersch, in the preface to *L'Origine*, by G. Dufour-Kowalska); " . . . putting to work a pulsating, libidinous and aggressive energy which allows one to detach the object from self and localize it in space, to establish an unstable equilibrium between two opposing movements: a distancing that will not lead to the ultimate disappearance of the object, and a reconciliation that carries with it the risk of annihilating self." (Sami-Ali, *L'Espace imaginaire*, pp. 195-6)

290

And since there can be no self-portrait without a mirror: "Does looking at oneself in a mirror not amount to thinking of death? In it immortal man recognizes his mortality. A mirror makes us climb out of our skin, our face. Nothing can resist its double." (Valéry: "Mélange-Avec soi seul," *Oeuvres*, I, p. 332)

In painting his *Portrait de l'artiste* Lemieux could have been illustrating an episode from the life of Buddha twenty-five centuries ago, when Gautama asked a Brahmin what he meant by "I": the infant he once was, the little boy, the adolescent, the young man, the mature man or the old man he then was. Kutadanta the Brahmin answered that he no longer recognized an "I" in this gallery of selves who were undergoing continual transformation....And the Quebec painter's tone of voice suddenly comes back to me, reciting, in the heartfelt manner he adopts when speaking English, the opening lines of Joyce's *A Portrait of the Artist as a Young Man*: "Once upon a time, and a very good time it was, there was...."

Once upon a time there was a painter who was happy to be painting his happy childhood....

The Never-Ending Task

An artist's work constitutes a corpus, some of whose elements will always elude explanation. There are projects that have been dropped, works lost or destroyed, altered or left incomplete: a whole other body of work presses against the margins of the publicly acknowledged paintings and forms an indispensable, if inaccessible part of its archeology. No *catalogue raisonné* can ever hope to be exhaustive and capable of accounting for all the work, both marginal and unclassifiable, eccentric and secret, some of which may actually have been forgotten by the artist himself.

Our task here is certainly not to provide a complete inventory of Lemieux's work but merely a study of it, in the sense that the mind constructs a certain set of principles upon which the sensibilities are then exercised. The theoretical dimensions of a work are not merely fabrication on the part of the aesthetician; on the contrary, they have their source in a familiarity with the whole world of art and in the proliferation of meaning encouraged by the works; by "meaning" is intended the conjunction of that which is tested in the alchemy of the sensibilities and that which is tested in the mind. In other words, the concern is with the semantic and thematic fertility which the work of art presents as essential to the over-all aesthetic. The work becomes a representation, and our multiple readings of this representation, reflecting its own multiplicity, have a claim to empirical validity.

According to this perspective, whereby a familiarity with the works replaces all theory, reflection is nevertheless not hindered. It is in fact given greater scope since the mind is more readily available. The driving force of the work of art, already mentioned in the preceding section "Sequences" in connection with the ritual of variants, is better understood in this way: the artistic power of the image (be it musical, literary, pictorial or whatever), is revealed at the level of figuration. This stimulates the functioning of the imagination, the artist's as much as that of the person who communicates with the work, and opens up inexhaustible fields of exploration. At the same time this expands the field of consciousness, first at the personal and later, the collective level. If we can speak of incompleteness in aesthetics, it is precisely because of this dynamic aspect whose essence is linked with the empirical impossibility of bringing to some definitive conclusion any lived experience, even by violent destruction or death: to kill the Sphinx is to reincarnate it as the Phoenix.

Let us reiterate a few of Lemieux's ideas on art: "Art is like a labyrinth. The artist is obliged to look long and hard before finding the light at the end of the tunnel. Witness Cézanne's early work, those anxious days when he was searching desperately for an architecture of form. Art constitutes a long, slow evolution, and each painting marks a stage in its forward progress." (1940) And as the subject of Cézanne has been raised, here is a comment by Galienne Francastel about the French artist which in turn clarifies Lemieux's own work:

"The fundamental problem for Cézanne, no longer consists, as it did, say, for Degas, of finding some way to reconcile traditional figurative forms and new sources of visual interest. All tangible matter awakens in him the desire to put the moving field of perceptions in order. A human figure constitutes a set of surfaces and lines situated in three dimensional space under a certain light, in the same way as a mountain or a basket of apples does. The objects of the external world which he apprehends through his senses are no longer of interest in themselves, but only to the extent that they invite an interpretation." (*Le Portrait*, p. 194)

Thus the phenomenology of perception releases a powerful desire in the artist, not a desire to possess but a desire to interpret, to "figure," to transfigure. The task of "putting the moving field of perceptions in order" depends once again on the dynamics of desire, the desire to translate, without misconstruing, "the perpetual movement of objects and life in the world," about which Lemieux wrote in 1940.

In the post-1956 period Lemieux's paintings have been divested of anecdotal, regional and picturesque elements so that they may more readily plunge into the vortex of the symbolic imagination. His pictorial representation has nothing esoteric or artificial about it although its extreme simplicity is a little surprising and disturbing, as though the artist had managed discreetly and without fanfare to reconcile the cosmic forces within the purview of his vision. This is of course only an apparent reconciliation since each picture questions itself at the same time as it turns itself into a question, rather than a sophisticated reply.

An uncompleted question — like a painting, Lemieux would say: "I sometimes stand a picture on its end or lay it on its side, and change the whole thing. It is really the painting that is the painter's master, and it's a slow business, all this. You can't do anything quickly, you have to do it all slowly, and reconsider the picture carefully, often. Of course, in an age where everything moves so fast, it seems a little ridiculous to take so much time, but it's necessary. Naturally there are painters who work in a fast, slapdash way, but those who are really looking for something take their time, time enough to get to the bottom of things. As long as one isn't satisfied, and one can never be satisfied, the painting remains unfinished...." (Interview of September 1972)

In 1940, Lemieux compared art to a labyrinth, or to a tunnel leading to the lift; George Kubler uses a similar metaphor in the following observation: "(The) history of art is like a vast mining enterprise, with innumerable shafts, most of them closed down long ago. Each artist works on in the dark, guided only by the tunnels and shafts of earlier work, following the vein and hoping for a bonanza, and fearing that the lode may play out tomorrow."[13]

Struck by this fear, the artist often hesitates in his work and asks uneasily if he can go on with it. He asks this not in order to finish it—which would mean shutting it down, sealing it off—but on the contrary, in order to open it up to something new, to expand it in the direction indicated by the artist's desire. In the best works, as Louis Marin remarks, "the painting is like a page from an old book, an ancient book of magic written in an unknown language and script." (*Etudes sémiologiques*, p. 97) It means plunging into hermetic archeology, into the archives of the past; it means opening the door to hermeneutical discoveries, which can only be empirical and intuitive—an idea that might not please ideologues and other mechanistic conceptualizers. In giving us his work throbbing with tangible delights, Jean Paul Lemieux has created images of his vision of man and the world that are at once complex and limpid. The ambiguity which pervades them is a measure of the difficult relationship (and how could it be otherwise?) between the tangible and the imaginary. The painting moves in and out of focus, taking its radiance from the miraculous light that shines through the nostalgic mists of childhood and inviting us to the endless spectacle of enduring variations on recollection.

The work, a figure of myth in its inexhaustible transfigurations, part of the continuous texture of all texts....

[13] George Kubler. *The Shape of Time* (New Haven: Yale University Press, 1962), p. 125.

BIBLIOGRAPHY

Written works by Jean Paul Lemieux

"A New Modern Setting in Montreal," *Technique* (Industrial Review), Montreal, November 1935, pp. 444-446.

"Aperçu sur la Peinture contemporaine," *Le Jour*, Montreal, June 18, 1938, p. 2.

Articles on exhibitions in the Quebec City area, in *Maritime Art*, Wolfville, October-November 1942, pp. 23-24; December 1942 and January 1943, pp. 57-58; February-March 1943, p. 88; April-May 1943, pp. 116-117; July-August 1943, pp. 159-160; subsequently in *Canadian Art*, Ottawa, October-November 1943, pp. 30-31; December 1943 and January 1944, pp. 75-76; February-March 1944, pp. 120-121; April-May 1944, p. 165; June-July 1944, pp. 214-215.

Causerie sur William Blake, March 30, 1939 (*L'Evénement-Journal*, Quebec City, March 31, 1939, p. 3).

Conférence sur Gauguin, 31 mars et 7 avril 1938, (*L'Evénement-Journal*, Quebec City, April 1, 1938, pp. 15-16; April 8, 1938, p. 16).

"Critique du professeur Jean Paul Lemieux sur l'Exposition de gravure," *Le Soleil*, Quebec City, January 18, 1941, p. 4.

"L'art au Canada français" ("Aperçu sur la Peinture contemporaine" published June 18, 1938; "suivi de quelques notes sur l'évolution de la peinture au Canada français"). *L'Evénement-Journal*, Quebec City, December 1, 1939, pp. 4 & 8.

"La camelote étrangère," *Arts et Pensée*, Montreal, January 1951, pp. 28-29.

"La Peinture chez les Canadiens français," *Le Jour*, Montreal, July 16, 1938, p. 3.

· "La Société des Arts plastiques" (in collaboration with Claude Picher), *Vie des Arts*, Montreal, January-February 1956, pp. 14-17.

"Notes sur l'art à Québec," *Regards*, Quebec City, November 1941, pp. 80-84.

"Notes sur le dessin," *Le Jour*, Montreal, October 1, 1938, p. 2 (reprinted in *Regards*, Quebec City, March 1942, pp. 276-278).

"Notes sur quelques toiles de Pellan," *Le Jour*, Montreal, May 14, 1938, p. 3.

"Pellan, peintre de l'abstraction, créateur de symboles," *Le Temps*, Quebec City, November 8, 1940, p. 5.

"Quebec City and the Arts," *Canadian Art*, Toronto, December 1947, p. 108-111.

"Réflexions sur l'art," *L'Evénement-Journal*, Quebec City, December 17, 1938 (Supplement, p. 18).

Talk on Art in French Canada, February 11, 1942 ("L'art a reculé au pays de Québec depuis 50 ans," *L'Evénement-Journal*, Quebec City, February 12, 1942, p. 4).

Books illustrated by Lemieux

Bruchési, Jean. *L'Epopée canadienne*. Montreal: Granger, 1934, 206 p. (illustrations by René Chicoine and Jean Paul Lemieux)

Choquette, Robert. *La pension Leblanc*. Montreal: Ed. Louis Carrier/Ed. du Mercure, 1927, 305 p., 5 illustrations.

Desrosiers, Emmanuel. *La Fin de la Terre*. Montreal: Librairie d'Action canadienne-française, 1931, 108 p., 5 illustrations.

Ernest-Beatrix. *Chez les Sauvages*. Montreal: Librairie d'Action canadienne-française, 1931, 172 p., 12 illustrations.

Maxine. *Le petit page de Frontenac*. Montreal: Librairie d'Action canadienne-française, 1930, 171 p., 12 illustrations.

Roy, Gabrielle. *La petite poule d'eau*. Montreal: Ed. Corbeil, 1971, 96 p., 20 illustrations.

Roy, Régis. *Le manoir hanté*. Montreal: Ed. Louis Carrier/Les Cahiers populaires, 1928, 227 p., 10 illustrations.

Monograph

Robert, Guy. *Jean Paul Lemieux* (ou la poétique de la souvenance). Quebec City: Ed. Garneau, 1968, 140 p., 95 illustrations, 7 in color.

Catalogues

Canadian Retrospective, organized by the Quebec Ministry of Cultural Affairs, 1974, 80 pp., 68 illustrations, 9 in color (text by Anne Hébert, pp. 10-11). The Musée d'art moderne de la Ville de Paris published a slightly different version, 58 pp., 40 illustrations (9 in color). The Russian version contained 40 pp., 23 illustrations (7 in color).

Clare Bice. "The Enchanted, Lonely World of Jean Paul Lemieux," introduction, *Retrospective Exhibition*, Art Gallery of London, Ontario, February 1966, 6 p., 4 illustrations.

Books in which Lemieux's work receives notice

Duval, Paul. *Four Decades* (1930-1970). Toronto: Clarke, Irwin & Co., 1972, 191 p. (p. 98-99).

Gagnon, Maurice. (Sur un état actuel de la) *Peinture canadienne*. Montreal: Ed. Pascal, 1945, 158 p. (p. 53 and 90).

Harper, J. Russel. *La Peinture au Canada*. Quebec City: Presses de l'Université Laval, 1966, 442 p. (p. 333 and 405).

Hubbard, R. H. *L'Evolution de l'art au Canada*. Ottawa: Galerie nationale du Canada, 1963, 137 p. (p. 115).

Lord, Barry. *The History of Painting in Canada*. Toronto:NC Press, 1974, 253 p. (p. 168-169).

Morisset, Gérard. *Coupe doeil sur les arts en Nouvelle-France*. s.é., Quebec City, 1941, 171 p. (p. 142).

Robert, Guy. *Ecole de Montreal*. Montreal: Ed. C.P.P., 1964, 151 p., (p. 29-30, 96-97).

Robert, Guy. *L'Art au Québec depuis 1940*. Montreal: Ed. La Presse, 1973, 501 p., (p. 56, 73, 83-86, 103-105, etc., see Index).

Viau, Guy. *La peinture moderne au Canada français*. Quebec City: ministère des Affaires culturelles, 1964, 93 p. (p. 32-34).

Articles on Lemieux and his work

Ayre, Robert. "All the lonely people," *The Montreal Star*, Montreal, September 23, 1967.

Corbeil, Gilles. "Jean Paul Lemieux, peintre intimiste," *Arts et pensée*, Montreal, November 1953, pp. 36-41.

Daigneault, Claude. "Guy Robert révèle Jean Paul Lemieux," *La Soleil*, Quebec City, October 5, 1968, p. 29.

Daigneault, Claude. "Lemieux au Musée du Québec," *Le Soleil*, Quebec City, October 21, 1967, p. 31.

de Repentigny, Rodolphe. "L'art expressif et ambigu de Lemieux," *La Presse*, Montreal, March 19, 1959.

Dickason, Olive. "Art that Sells," *Chatelaine*, Toronto, March 1968.

Dumas, Paul. "Rencontre avec Jean Paul Lemieux," *L'Information médicale et para-médicale*, Montreal, June 17, 1969, pp. 40-41.

Folch, Jacques. "Jean Paul Lemieux et le trouble de la majesté," *Liberté*, Montreal, March 1963, pp. 162-164.

Gagnon, Claire-P. "Le peintre Jean Paul Lemieux," *La Patrie*, Montreal, April 7, 1957, p. 28 (Magazine).

Gagnon, Jean-Louis. "La peinture à Québec," *Le Jour*, Montreal, December 3, 1938.

Girard, Henri. "Exposition des Anciens de l'Ecole des beaux-arts," *Le Canada*, Montreal, May 4, 1937, p. 2.

Jones, Richmond. "Lemieux Sees Bleak World," *The Gazette*, Montreal, September 23, 1967, p. 43.

Kritzwiser, Kay. "Touching Simplicity dominates Lemieux's Show," *Globe and Mail*, Toronto, December 9, 1967, p. 2.

L'Heureux, Gaston. "Jean Paul Lemieux . . . ," *Le Soleil*, Quebec City, November 28, 1964, p. 8.

Lamy, Laurent. "Jean Paul Lemieux," *Le Devoir*, Montreal, April 6, 1963, p. 41.

"La province de Québec et la peinture," *Le Soleil*, Quebec City, November 24, 1939, p. 9.

Lawson, Edward P. "Jean Paul Lemieux raconte sa jeunesse," *La Presse*, Montreal, September 15, 1967, p. 12.

"Les oeuvres de Jean Paul Lemieux," *L'Action catholique*, Quebec City, April 22, 1953, p. 11.

"Les récents travaux de deux peintres canadiens," *L'Action catholique*, Quebec City, November 12, 1938, p. 9.

Lévesque, Robert. "Jean Paul Lemieux et sa vision du pays," *Québec-Presse*, Montreal, June 23, 1974, p. 17.

Marteau, Robert. "De l'immobilité vivante de Lemieux," *Le Jour*, Montreal, February 1, 1975, p. 11.

Michel, Jacques. "À 70 ans, Lemieux reste solitaire . . . ," *Perspectives*, Montreal, March 1, 1975, pp. 20-22.

Morisset, Gerard. "En visitant l'exposition de M. et de Mme Jean Paul Lemieux," *Le Soleil*, Quebec City, November 14, 1938.

Morisset-Blackburn, Marthe. "Jean Paul Lemieux, peintre du temps muet," *Europe*, Paris, February 1969, pp. 256-260.

Nagle, Patrick. "Timeless Painter from Quebec," *Weekend Magazine*, Montreal, March 9, 1963, pp. 18-20.

Nantais, Lyse. "Recontre avec Jean Paul Lemieux," *Le Devoir*, Montreal, January 28, 1961.

O'Neil, Jean. "Ce qui me hante . . . ," *La Presse*, Montreal, April 13, 1963.

"Painter of solitude," *Time*, New York/Montreal, May 3, 1963.

Pfeiffer, Dorothy. "Jean Paul Lemieux," *The Gazette*, Montreal, April 6, 1963.

Picher, Claude. "La Côte d'Azur," *Vie des Arts*, Montreal, March 1956, p. 24-25.

Picher, Claude and Cadieux, Marcel. "Jean Paul Lemieux," *Canadian Art*, Toronto, September 1960, pp. 264-273.

R.B. "Exposition de Jean Paul Lemieux à L'Atelier," *L'Evénement-Journal*, Quebec City, March 2, 1956, p. 12.

Randall, L. V. preface to album entitled *Jean Paul Lemieux*, Galerie Agnès-Lefort, Montreal, 1967.

Reynald. "Jeunes anciens, pensers nouveaux," *La Presse*, Montreal, May 8, 1937, p. 46.

Reynald. "Quinze Anciens des Beaux-Arts," *La Presse*, Montreal, April 19, 1939, p. 10.

Roberge, Guy. "Visite à Madeleine Des Rosiers et Jean Paul Lemieux," *L'Evénement-Journal*, Quebec City, February 10, 1940, pp. 11 & 21.

Robert, Guy. "Le peintre du silence," *Le Maclean*, Montreal, July 1975, pp. 20-21 and 34-36.

Robillard, Y. "Un homme devant le mouvement des choses," *La Presse*, Montreal, September 16, 1967, p. 42.

Roy, Gabrielle. "Les Terres nouvelles," *Vie des Arts*, Montreal, Winter 1962, pp. 39-43.

Royer, Jean. "Ce matin-là ressemblait à un Lemieux," *Le Soleil*, Quebec City, April 12, 1974, p. 9.

Royer, Jean. "Jean Paul Lemieux au coeur du temps," *L'Action*, Quebec City, October 21, 1967.

Smith, Brydon. "Lemieux at Roberts Gallery," *Canadian Art*, Toronto, July 1963, p. 205.

Vézina, R. "Le Cycle de la vie humaine," *Vie des Arts*, Montreal, Winter 1974, pp. 20-25.

Books cited

Bachelard, Gaston. *La dialectique de la durée*. Paris: Presses Universitaires de France, 1950.

Barthes, Roland. *Roland Barthes by Roland Barthes*. Translated by Richard Howard. New York: Hill & Wang, 1977.

Bergson, Henri. *Matter and Memory*. Translated by Nancy Margaret Paul and W. Scott Palmer. London: George Allen & Unwin, 1911.

Bergson, Henri. *The Creative Mind*. Translated by Mabelle L. Ankison. New York: Philosophical Library, 1946.

Blake, William. *The Portable Blake*. New York: Viking Press, 1974.

Blanchot, Maurice. *L'entretien infini*. Paris: Gallimard, 1969.

d'Ors, Eugenio. *Du Baroque* (1935). Paris: Idées-Arts/Gallimard, 1968.

Doubrovsky, Serge. *Pourquoi la nouvelle critique*. Paris: Mercure de France, 1966.

Dufrenne, Mikel. *Le Poétique*. Paris: Presses Universitaires de France, 1963.

Duvignaud, Jean. *Fêtes et civilisations*. Geneva: Lib. Weber, 1973.

Foucault, Michel. *The Order of Things*. London: Tavistock, 1970.

Francastel, Galienne and Pierre. *Le Portrait*. Paris: Hachette, 1969.

Francastel, Pierre. *La figure et le lieu*. Paris: Gallimard, 1967.

Francastel, Pierre. *La réalité figurative*. Paris: Gonthier, 1965.

Gauguin, Paul. *Oviri*. Paris: Idées/Gallimard, 1974.

Goldscheider, Ludwig. *Five Hundred Self-Portraits*. Vienna: Phaidon, 1938.

Gombrich, E. H. *Symbolic Images*. London: Phaidon, 1972.

Guillerme, Jacques. *L'Atelier du temps*. Paris: Hermann, 1964.

Hill, Charles C. *Canadian Painting in the Thirties*. Ottawa: National Gallery of Canada, 1975.

Hytier, Jean. *André Gide*. Translated by Richard Howard. London: Constable, 1963.

Kandinsky, Wassily. *Concerning the Spiritual in Art*. New York: George Wittenborn Inc., 1947.

300

Klein, Robert. *La forme et l'intelligible*. Paris: Gallimard, 1970.

Kubler, George. *The Shape of Time*. New Haven: Yale University Press, 1962.

Lee, Rensselaer W. *Ut pictura poesis* (The Humanistic Theory of Painting). New York: W. W. Norton Inc., 1967.

Lord, Barry. *The History of Painting in Canada*. Toronto: NC Press, 1974.

Machery, Pierre. *Pour une théorie de la production littéraire*. Paris: Maspero, 1966.

Malraux, André. *Metamorphosis of the Gods*. Translated by Stuart Gilbert. London: Secker & Warburg, 1960.

Malraux, André. *La tête d'obsidienne*. Paris: Gallimard, 1974.

Marin, Louis. *Etudes sémiologiques*. Paris: Klincksieck, 1971.

Mauron, Charles. *Des métaphores obsédantes au mythe personnel*. Paris: Corti, 1962.

Merleau-Ponty, Maurice. *The Visible and the Invisible*. Translated by Alphonso Lingis. Evanston: Northwestern University Press, 1968.

Montaigne. *Oeuvres complètes*. Paris: L'Intégrale/Seuil, 1967.

Nicholas de Staël (Letters and descriptive catalogue). Paris: Ed. du Temps, 1968.

Proust, Marcel. *The Past Recaptured*. Book XII of *Remembrance of Times Past*. Translated by Andreas Mayor. New York: Vintage, 1971.

Rawson, Philip. *Tantra: the Indian Cult of Ecstasy*. London: Thames & Hudson, 1973.

Rawson, Philip and Legeza, Laszlo. *Tao: the Chinese Philosophy of Time and Change*. London: Thames & Hudson, 1973.

Richard, Jean-Pierre. *L'univers imaginaire de Mallarmé*. Paris: Seuil, 1961.

Robert, Guy. *Borduas*. Montreal: Presses de l'Université du Québec, 1972.

Robert, Guy. *Pellan*. Montreal: Ed. C.P.P., 1963.

Sami-Ali. *L'Espace imaginaire*. Paris: Gallimard, 1974.

Schefer, Jean-Louis. *Scénographie d'un tableau*. Paris: Seuil, 1969.

Valéry. *Oeuvres*. Paris: Pléiade/Gallimard. 2 volumes — I, 1957, II, 1960.

Interview between artist and author, March 26, 1975

TABLE OF CONTENTS

GUY ROBERT, who is a writer and professor and holds a doctorate in aesthetics, has published more than 500 articles and 30 books on art, literature and aesthetics since 1955. In 1964 he founded the Montreal Museum of Contemporary Art and subsequently administered the International Exhibition of Contemporary Sculpture at Expo 67. He contributes regularly to radio and television broadcasts and is actively involved in publishing. In addition to his earlier book and documentary film (1968 and 1973 respectively) on Jean Paul Lemieux, Guy Robert has written books on Riopelle, Borduas, Pellan, Jordi Bonet, Marc-Aurèle Fortin, Lardera, Dumouchel, contemporary sculpture, the Montreal School and art in Quebec since 1940. He has been a member of the International Association of Art Critics since 1963. The French edition of Guy Robert's book, *Lemieux*, was awarded the City of Montreal's Grand Prix for Literature in 1976.

Thirty-five hundred copies of this edition have been printed and bound by Hunter Rose Company, Toronto, in July of nineteen seventy-eight. This is a limited, numbered edition.

No. **2748**